THE HIDDEN VIRTUES OF DISCRETIONARY POWER IN EUROPEAN MIGRATION LAW

This book explores discretionary decision-making in migration systems in Europe. It investigates how European law influences the existence, exercise and effects of discretion.

Firstly, it argues that national lawmakers often regard discretionary decision-making as the most viable option to accommodate standards of European law in their national migration systems. Secondly, the book shows how the exercise of this power has changed from an area of free choice to an instance of legally instructed decision-making. Ultimately, it illustrates how both the proliferation and transformation of discretionary decision-making have improved the legal position of migrants in the European Union, providing a compelling interpretation of a key field of EU law.

Volume 142 in the Series Modern Studies in European Law

MODERN STUDIES IN EUROPEAN LAW

RECENT TITLES IN THIS SERIES

EU Diplomacy in Multilateral Fora
Edited by Christine Kaddous and Frank Hoffmeister

The Market Citizenship Illusion: Free Movement Rights for Atypical Workers
Alice Welsh

Actors and Roles in EU Disability Law
Edited by Delia Ferri and Eva S Krolla

The Impact of War (in Ukraine) on the EU
Edited by Inge Govaere, Sacha Garben and Eleanor Spaventa

The European Judiciary: A Community of Law and a Community of Judges
Edited by Alejandro Saiz Arnaiz and Joan Solanes Mullor

Dissensus over Liberal Democracy: Insights from European Judges
Edited by Ramona Coman, Viktor Kazai, Leonardo Puleo and Andrew Bradley

Structural Principles of EU Law
Marcus Klamert

Environmental NGOs and Access to Justice before the CJEU
Mario Pagano

Dealing with Rule of Law Crises in the European Union: Challenges from a Comparative Federalism Perspective
Niels F Kirst

EU Citizenship and Responsibility: The Evolving Roles of the Union, the Individual, and the Member States
Maria Haag

EU Cities Facilitating the Commons: Building Blocks of European Constitutional Law for Local Democracy
Chiara Salati

EU Competence and Power
Hannah Bogaert

Activating Human and Fundamental Rights Before the European Courts
Edited by Elise Muir, Sacha Garben and Inge Govaere

The Hidden Virtues of Discretionary Power in European Migration Law
Jonas Bornemann

For the complete list of titles in this series
see www.bloomsbury.com/uk/series/modern-studies-in-european-law/

The Hidden Virtues of Discretionary Power in European Migration Law

Jonas Bornemann

•HART•
OXFORD • LONDON • NEW YORK • NEW DELHI • SYDNEY

HART PUBLISHING
Bloomsbury Publishing Plc
Kemp House, Chawley Park, Cumnor Hill, Oxford, OX2 9PH, UK
1385 Broadway, New York, NY 10018, USA
Bloomsbury Publishing Ireland Limited, 29 Earlsfort Terrace, Dublin 2, D02 AY28, Ireland

HART PUBLISHING, the Hart/Stag logo, BLOOMSBURY and the Diana logo are trademarks of Bloomsbury Publishing Plc

First edition published by Hart Publishing in 2026
This edition first published 2026

1

A catalogue record for this book is available from the Library of Congress.

Library of Congress Control Number

ISBN: HB: 978-1-50998-417-6
ePDF: 978-1-50998-419-0
ePub: 978-1-50998-418-3

Typeset by Amnet

To my family.

ACKNOWLEDGEMENTS

This book is the product of a research journey that could have taken a different path at every turn and that – were it not for the serendipity of encountering the right people at the right moments – might never have materialised in its present form. It began as a rather undefined interest in the way migration authorities take decisions and gradually turned into the research that underpins the present book. At every turn, I benefitted from words of encouragement and guidance that supported me throughout the researching and writing process.

The most important guide over the years was Professor Dr Daniel Thym, who saw potential in my PhD project perhaps even before I did. I owe him much gratitude not only for his belief in my research, but also for creating a space for open and critical discussion at his chair at the University of Konstanz. I am grateful for the genuinely European and interdisciplinary academic environment that his chair offers, and I hope that these perspectives are reflected in this book. *Herzlichen Dank*!

I am particularly indebted to Professor Philippe De Bruycker, whose passion for European migration law has been a true source of inspiration and whose leaps of faith were vital in allowing me to pursue the research that culminated in this book. *Merci beaucoup*!

Much of the research for this book was carried out at the University of Konstanz – a campus, city and region that was entirely new to me before I moved there. I am deeply grateful to my colleagues who made me feel welcome and helped me navigate this new environment: among those I would like to mention are Sabine Gerber, whose tireless support helped me navigate university administration, and Dr Lukas Mitsch, whose hospitality, kindness and friendship helped me to settle into a new city and faculty and made my time in Konstanz both memorable and genuinely pleasant. Moreover, I am grateful to Professor Dr Marten Breuer, for words of encouragement, and for his quick evaluation of my thesis. I would also like to thank the Cluster of Excellence 'The Politics of Inequality', which hosted me during my PhD and awarded me a fellowship to finalise my research.

In finalising this book, I was able to benefit from the helpful and instructive comments provided by the two anonymous reviewers. I am also grateful to my research interns at the Rijksuniversiteit Groningen, Nina Klaić and Caroline Noack, who helped with the formatting of the manuscript.

I know that none of this would have been possible without the unwavering support of my family and friends. I am incredibly grateful to my parents, Ulrike and Christoph, for their genuine interest in my academic journey, and to my brother, Lennart, whose encouragement and support helped me push through even the worst writer's block. A special word of gratitude goes to Sylvi, for countless walks at the lakeside of Lake Constance and for being a wonderful travel companion – even on long Flixbus rides to Italy. *Danke für alles*!

Finalising the manuscript of this book gives me the chance to reflect on the many encounters and opportunities that have shaped my academic path over the years. From Maastricht to Brussels, Konstanz and Lausanne to Groningen – I was lucky enough to meet the right people at the right time, and I am extremely grateful for these encounters. None of this is taken for granted and I owe you all my deepest gratitude. Thank you!

Groningen, 27 September 2025

TABLE OF CONTENTS

LIST OF ABBREVIATIONS

AMMR	Asylum and Migration Management Regulation
Art	Article
BAMF	Bundesamt für Migration und Flüchtlinge (Federal Office for Migration and Refugees, Germany)
CEAS	Common European Asylum System
EASO	European Asylum Support Office
ECHR	European Convention on Human Rights
ECJ	Court of Justice of the EU
ECtHR	European Court of Human Rights
EU	European Union
EUAA	European Union Agency for Asylum
IND	Immigration and Naturalisation Service
TFEU	Treaty on the Functioning of the European Union

LIST OF PRIMARY SOURCES

EU Legislation

National Legislation, Statutes and Decrees

Other Materials

CASE LAW

European Court of Human Rights

Court of Justice of the EU

National Court Judgments

1

Discretion in European Migration Law: Misfit, Necessity, Virtue?

Discretionary power constitutes one of the defining traits of migration governance in Europe.[1] Public officials habitually exercise discretion, for instance, to assess whether a person poses a security risk to the potential host society or whether (s)he may be presumed to leave the national territory in due time.[2] The pervasiveness of discretionary decision-making in migration law, however, can be cause for criticism. Some of the most vital aspects of migrants' lives are thereby put on the line. Should an alien be allowed to enter state territory? Or should (s)he be expelled from it? Through the exercise of discretion in these situations, public officials are tasked to adopt decisions with far-reaching consequences for the individuals concerned, albeit in the absence of unequivocal instructions in law on how to decide in a specific case.

The subjectivity that discretionary decision-making implies may be said to tarnish the legal position of migrants. It sits uneasily with requirements flowing from the rule of law, including legal certainty, objectivity and vigorous judicial control.[3] Firm criticism may accordingly be levelled at the pervasiveness and prominence of discretionary decision-making in the field of migration governance. Discretionary practices have been singled out as a prominent source of arbitrariness in this regard.[4] Following this criticism, discretionary decision-making is often treated primarily as a problem – a misfit in the field

[1] See B Oomen et al, 'Strategies of Divergence: Local Authorities, Law, and Discretionary Spaces in Migration Governance' (2021) 34 *Journal of Refugee Studies* 3608. For the role of discretionary power in US migration law, see S Bibler Coutin et al, 'Deferred Action and the Discretionary State: Migration, Precarity and Resistance' (2017) 21 *Citizenship Studies* 951.

[2] See J Chlebny, 'Public Order, National Security and the Rights of Third-Country Nationals in Immigration Cases' (2018) 20 *European Journal of Migration and Law* 115; V Stehlík, 'Discretion of Member States Vis-à-Vis Public Security: Unveiling the Labyrinth' (2017) 17 *International and Comparative Law Review* 127.

[3] See C Dauvergne, 'Sovereignty, Migration and the Rule of Law in Global Times' (2004) 67 *The Modern Law Review* 588, 592.

[4] See insightfully TG Eule et al, *Migrants Before the Law. Contested Migration Control in Europe* (Palgrave Macmillan, 2019) 105. For a similar view in the context of migration detention, see F Asta, 'Arbitrary Decision-Making and the Rule of Law: The Role of the Jurisdiction in Migrants' Detention Proceedings – Between Discretion and Arbitrariness' (2020) 14 *Etikk i praksis Nordic Journal of Applied Ethics* 107.

of migration law whose existence should be reduced to a bare minimum if not repressed altogether.[5]

But does this view hold water? As a phenomenon, discretion is inherently linked to open-ended deliberations and the ramifications that it creates for individuals may not always be evident from the outset. Against this backdrop, the following investigation asks how the existence of discretion affects the situation of migrants. Does it expose them to arbitrariness and executive whim? Or could the exercise of discretion be assessed in a more positive light, engendering certain advantages for the individuals concerned?

As the following investigation suggests, discretion continues to play a prominent role in contemporary migration systems in Europe. It provides migration authorities with the flexibility needed to accommodate the diverse influences of European law while at the same time operating within safeguards that limit the risk of arbitrariness. Nowadays, the exercise of discretion is firmly delineated and instructed by standards of legality, and these safeguards often afford migrants a degree of protection rather than exposing them to unconstraint and unchecked decision-making freedom. In this sense, the following investigation concurs with the view that discretion constitutes a phenomenon 'with certain virtues . . . that has a useful role to play *within* a legal system', as Brand has suggested.[6] It is the main objective of the following investigation to draw out these hidden (or at least: less visible) virtues of discretionary power in relation to migration laws in Europe.

Discretion is routinely associated with the practices and conduct of street-level bureaucrats.[7] This focus notwithstanding, the existence, exercise and effects of discretionary power are determined at different *loci* in the policy process.[8] The question whether and why discretionary powers are afforded, for instance, may be best understood through the lenses of national lawmakers, whereas the effects that it creates for individuals will depend, amongst other, on the question whether they have options at their disposal to challenge discretionary decision-making.[9] To inquire into the merits of discretionary power, the following investigation will combine different perspectives to put forward three related claims.

First, from the perspective of national lawmakers, it will argue that discretion often presents itself as the only viable legal arrangement to duly accommodate

[5] See A Pratt and L Sossin, 'A Brief Introduction of the Puzzle of Discretion' (2009) 24 *Canadian Journal of Law and Society* 301, 302 ff, who insightfully argue that this negative connotation of discretion can be traced back to the influential works of AV Dicey, see AV Dicey, *Introduction to the Study of the Law of the Constitution*, 8th edn (Macmillan, 1908).

[6] M Brand, 'Discretion, Divergence, and Unity' in S Prechal and B van Roermund (eds), *The Coherence of EU Law: The Search for Unity in Divergent Concepts* (Oxford University Press, 2008) 218, italics in the original.

[7] See H Wagenaar, 'Discretion and Street-Level Practice' in T Evans and PL Hupe (eds), *Discretion and the Quest for Controlled Freedom* (Palgrave Macmillan, 2020).

[8] See PL Hupe and M Hill, 'Discretion in the Policy Process' in T Evans and PL Hupe (eds), *Discretion and the Quest for Controlled Freedom* (Palgrave Macmillan, 2020) 246 ff.

[9] For a similar argument, see K Hawkins, 'The Use of Legal Discretion: Perspectives from Law and Social Science' in K Hawkins (ed), *The Uses of Discretion* (Oxford University Press, 1992) 13 ff.

standards of European law in national legal systems. On several occasions, this can explain the persistence of discretionary decision-making in migration laws in Europe. Lawmakers tend to turn to discretion to allow for the processing of the variety of influences unfolding within this multi-levelled legal system.[10] In this vein, discretion has become the preferred tool for national lawmakers to ensure that national migration authorities are empowered to duly process the requirements of European law.

Where national migration authorities can be said to have a measure of discretion, second, it will be argued in the following investigation that the nature of its exercise has changed significantly in the fairway of European legal influences. Particularly, discretionary decision-making in the field of migration laws is nowadays firmly instructed by legal principles. From the perspective of administrators,[11] this establishes discretionary conduct as a rather challenging mode of decision-making. By virtue of such decision-making power, migration authorities are vested with a measure of deliberative freedom that does not, however, give them *carte blanche*. Instead, legal principles constitute standards of legality that instruct the conduct of migration authorities but do not predetermine the outcome of a specific case. The fact that the standards instructing and delineating the exercise of discretion often originate from various layers of a multi-levelled legal system complicates this task further.[12]

Third, this investigation will argue that the persistence and legally instructed nature of discretionary power create relative improvements for migrants. In contrast to some earlier efforts to regulate entry and stay in Europe, discretion no longer represents a mode of decision-making to which individuals are exposed with no option of redress whatsoever. While challenging discretionary decision-making may still be an uphill battle for individuals, it is no forlorn endeavour from the outset. The combination of standards of legality instructing the exercise of discretion and the availability of judicial review enables individuals to consider whether migration officials have exercised their discretion duly in the light of these standards. Moreover, instances of discretionary decision-making have come to replace legal arrangements that previously prescribed an unfavourable outcome by default. Such a proliferation of discretionary power marks a relative improvement for migrants and establishes discretion as a phenomenon that coincides with certain virtues from the perspective of individuals.

[10] For this phenomenon, see equally BG Mattarella, 'Law and Discretion. A Public Law Perspective on the EU' in J Mendes (ed), *EU Executive Discretion and the Limits of Law* (Oxford University Press, 2019) 33.

[11] While the phenomenon of administrative power is notoriously elusive, the present investigation allocates it in the application of law vis-á-vis individual persons, thus following an understanding proposed in C Möllers, *The Three Branches: A Comparative Model of Separation of Powers* (Oxford University Press, 2013) 97.

[12] See E Brouwer, 'Challenges to EU Legality in the Field of Asylum and Migration Law' in C Kilpatrick and J Scott (eds), *Contemporary Challenges to EU Legality* (Oxford University Press, 2021) 51 ff.

In each of the arguments outlined above, discretion is examined through the lens of what has been labelled (descriptively, not pejoratively) a 'legal paradigm'.[13] In contrast to investigations that explore the decision-making practices of street-level bureaucrats,[14] the following investigation focuses on the legal structures that govern discretionary conduct. In this sense, it does not capture the ways in which these powers are exercised in fact, but rather how they ought to be exercised in the light of applicable law. As a corollary, the following investigation will examine the effects that discretionary decision-making creates for migrants through an examination of their 'legal position'. As a workaround, this term avoids delving into the way in which individuals respond to discretionary decision-making in practice, focusing instead on the avenues that migrants have at their disposal to challenge discretionary decision-making in the abstract.

For the purposes of the following investigation, discretion will be understood as a phenomenon that relates to the decision-making power left to national executives by domestic lawmakers and courts. For that reason, its focus will principally lie on legal arrangements in national legal systems. This distinguishes this research from other research that focuses on the latitude afforded by one legal system to another. This latitude is often equally referred to as 'discretion'.[15] Analytically, however, it is important to bear in mind that the latter instance of latitude relates to the interaction between two formally distinct legal systems – EU law and Member States' legal systems – and does not, for that matter, constitute the object of investigation of this study. Throughout the chapters that follow, the terms 'discretion' or 'discretionary power' will be employed to refer to the object of investigation, that is, instances in which national migration officials exercise a degree of latitude that is afforded by law and not fully superseded by another executive or judicative actor.[16] By contrast, the latitude that is afforded to legal systems in their own right will be referred to as 'faculty'.[17]

This analytical distinction notwithstanding, the conduct of national migration authorities is strongly influenced by standards of international and supranational law.[18] These influences are of particular importance with a view to the exercise

[13] P Mascini, 'Discretion from a Legal Perspective' in T Evans and PL Hupe (eds), *Discretion and the Quest for Controlled Freedom* (Palgrave Macmillan, 2020) 123 ff.

[14] See particularly Eule et al (n 4) 84 ff.

[15] For this phenomenon and terminology, see for instance T van den Brink, 'Refining the Division of Competences in the EU: National Discretion in EU Legislation' in S Garben and I Govaere (eds), *The Division of Competences between the EU and the Member States: Reflections on the Past, the Present and the Future* (Hart, 2017).

[16] See in greater detail below at ch 2, s II.C.

[17] A famous example of such a form of faculty is the 'margin of appreciation' doctrine developed by the European Court on Human Rights, which is explicitly addressed not just to national executives, but likewise to legislatures and courts; *Handyside v The United Kingdom* Series A no 24 (1976) 1 EHRR 737, para 48.

[18] See C Costello, 'Administrative Governance and the Europeanisation of Asylum and Immigration Policy' in H Hofmann and A Türk (eds), *EU Administrative Governance* (Edward Elgar, 2006) 287 ff.

of discretion.[19] Unlike other modes of decision-making, discretionary conduct tasks national administrators to autonomously compile the legal standards that should govern the individual case at hand, including those that originate from outside their domestic legal orders. The following investigation will therefore draw particular attention to these multi-level legal influences on discretionary power in the field of migration law.

To account for the multi-levelled legal setting in which discretion operates, the following investigation employs the term 'European migration law'. Wording of that nature should not insinuate that the focus of analysis would be limited to European laws in the narrow sense, such as EU law or safeguards in the ECHR.[20] Instead, it ought to be understood as a shorthand for the versatile interactions that unfold between the layers of a multi-levelled legal regime, thus equally encompassing national legal frameworks. In this sense, the term 'European migration law' mirrors that of 'European administrative law' in that it treats national laws as an integral part thereof.[21] In substance, the term 'European migration law' will be used to refer to a rather broad range of aspects that govern migration, including instances of forced migration.[22] Specifically, it explores decision-making in relation to third-country nationals in the context of Dublin transfers, resettlement, visas, legal migration, asylum and return detention. The following investigation is primarily concerned with the evolution of discretionary power in the context of decision-making affecting third-country nationals and not, for that reason, mobile EU citizens (and, by extension, family members of the latter).

This investigation challenges the view that discretionary decision-making would constitute a pernicious feature of European migration systems. Unlike the pronounced criticism that is levelled at the prominence of discretion in European migration law (section I), this investigation will argue that, as a legal phenomenon, discretion coincides with certain virtues that may ultimately benefit the legal position of migrants. Empirically, discretion has formed a prominent element of migration laws in Europe from the outset and continues to do so to this day (section II). This persistence of instances of discretion in European migration law should not, however, paper over the significant transformation in the exercise of discretion that has followed from the applicability of legal principles, specifically by compelling migration authorities to consider the specificities of the individual case (section III). This proliferation and transformation of discretionary power

[19] See M Wendel, *Verwaltungsermessen Als Mehrebenenproblem: Zur Verbundstruktur Administrativer Entscheidungsspielräume Am Beispiel Des Migrations- Und Regulierungsrechts* (Mohr Siebeck, 2019) 85 ff.

[20] For a discussion of the term, see D Thym, *European Migration Law* (Oxford University Press, 2023) 4.

[21] For such an encompassing understanding, see for instance JB Auby, 'The Transformation of the Administrative State and Administrative Law' in S Cassese, A Bogdandy and P Huber (eds), *The Max Planck Handbooks in European Public Law: Volume I: The Administrative State* (Oxford University Press, 2017) 622.

[22] The appropriateness of including the phenomenon of flight and refuge into a definition of migration is contested, see in particular J Carling, 'The Phrase "Refugees and Migrants" Undermines Analysis, Policy and Protection' (2023) 61 *International Migration* 399.

coincides with an improved legal position of migrants, allowing them to effectively counter discretionary decision-making (section IV). To inquire into the merits of this legal phenomenon in the field of European migration law, the following investigation adopts a doctrinal research method that proceeds, in essence, deductively (section V).

I. Discretion and Its Critiques

The enduring presence of broad discretionary powers in modern legal systems has been met by firm scholarly opposition,[23] and migration law stands out as one of the fields where such critique is particularly pronounced. Vast (and occasionally even unfettered) discretionary powers continue to characterise this field of law. These instances of discretion have often been singled out as one of the principal sources of ambiguity and unpredictability to which migrants are subjected.[24] In this sense, discretion runs the risk of exposing individuals to arbitrariness and discriminatory practices,[25] thereby exacerbating the precarity they may already face.[26]

While scholars tend to agree that migration regimes assign a particularly prominent role to discretion, the degree to which this is viewed as problematic depends on the conceptual perspective one adopts regarding discretion. For instance, an influential view in the literature suggests that street-level bureaucrats will always have a degree of decision-making freedom, to the effect that discretion may be presented as an inevitable part of the exercise of public power.[27] From this perspective, the problematic nature of discretionary power lies not so much in its existence, but rather in the particularly far-reaching nature thereof.[28] Some scholars even suggest that, in the field of migration law, this power may include decisions that are prima facie unlawful but are not sanctioned by higher-ranking authorities.[29]

Much of the criticism levelled at discretion in the field of migration is articulated from this conceptual angle. Most visibly, this is the case for criticism voiced in relation to decision-making in the field of asylum law. In this regard, discretion frequently serves as the analytical category to explain how asylum authorities abuse the degree of decision-making freedom at their disposal to adopt restrictive

[23] See KC Davis, *Discretionary Justice: A Preliminary Inquiry* (Louisiana State University Press, 1969) 3; E Rubin, 'Discretion and Its Discontent' (1997) 72 *Chicago-Kent Law Review* 1299, 1300.

[24] See K Heyer, 'Keeping Migrants at the Margins. Governing through Ambiguity and the Politics of Discretion in the Post-2015 EUropean Migration and Border Regime' (2022) 97 *Political Geography* 1.

[25] See M Blake, 'Exclusion, Discretion, and Justice' in A Sager (ed), *The Ethics and Politics of Immigration. Core Issues and Emerging Trends* (Bloomsbury, 2016).

[26] See L Goldring, 'Precarious Legal Status Trajectories as Method, and the Work of Legal Status' (2022) 26 *Citizenship Studies* 460, 464.

[27] See M Lipsky, *Street-Level Bureaucracy: Dilemmas of the Individual in Public Services* (Russel Sage Foundation, 1980); Eule et al (n 4) 87.

[28] See Coutin et al (n 1) 952.

[29] For such an understanding of discretion, see particularly Oomen et al (n 1).

decision-making practices.[30] Short of unlawful administrative conduct, discretion serves as an analytical tool to account for divergences in asylum decision-making practice.[31] In this sense, it reverberates with the allegation of an 'asylum lottery',[32] which is meant to highlight the significant degree of uncertainty to which asylum applicants are subjected.[33] While structures of coherent decision-making may emerge from these discretionary practices,[34] the inherent risks associated with deliberative freedom in this field of law should not be ignored.

This criticism notwithstanding, other authors present the discretionary power of migration authorities in a more positive light.[35] Since discretionary powers are inherently linked to deliberative freedom, it allows for a measure of pragmatism and, possibly, compassion *vis-à-vis* the individual concerned.[36] Similarly, street-level bureaucrats may use the discretion vested in them to push back against restrictive migration policies.[37] While discretion may therefore occasionally benefit migrants, it is true that such a form of deliberative freedom 'serves as salvation in some observers' view, and a perdition in others', as Rubin notes.[38] On a more general level, it seems reasonable to acknowledge that the positive effects that discretion may create in some individual cases must be weighed against the risks of selectiveness and uncertainty that such freedom implies.[39]

II. European Migration Law: The Last Stronghold of Vast Discretionary Power?

In recent decades, the enduring prevalence of discretionary powers in legal systems has been the subject of pronounced criticism. As a consequence, such powers have been gradually curtailed, reined in by principles of legality and an expansion of judicial oversight in many areas of law. Migration law, however, appears to stand apart: it sometimes seems to constitute the last stronghold of vast – if not virtually

[30] See KA Rodriguez, 'Discretionary (In)Justice Continued: Discretion as a Tool to Deny Asylum' (2025) 31 *Washington and Lee Journal of Civil Rights and Social Justice* 1, 143 ff.

[31] See J Darling, 'The Politics of Discretion: Authority and Influence in Asylum Dispersal' (2022) 94 *Political Geography* 1, 3.

[32] Amongst others, J Spirig, *Like Cases Alike or Asylum Lottery: Inconsistency in Judicial Decision Making at the Swiss Federal Administrative Court* (Zurich Open Repository and Archive, 2018).

[33] See TM Liodden, 'Who Is a Refugee? Uncertainty and Discretion in Asylum Decisions' (2020) 32 *International Journal of Refugee Law* 645.

[34] See J Miaz, 'Asylum Adjudication and Street-Level Discretion: Negotiating Practice Rules' (2024) 26 *Journal of Comparative Policy Analysis* 25.

[35] For an overview, see LM Borrelli, L Johannesson and A Lindberg, 'Predictable Patterns of Unpredictability: A Literature Review of Discretion in Migration Control' (2025) 7 *Political Research Exchange* 1, 9, with further references.

[36] See B Jordan, B Stråth and A Triandafyllidou, 'Comparing Cultures of Discretion' (2003) 29 *Journal of Ethnic and Migration Studies* 373, 394; Eule et al (n 4) 87.

[37] See E Giacomelli, 'The Emergence of New Street-Level Bureaucracies in Italy's Asylum Reception System' (2021) 19 *Journal of Immigrant & Refugee Studies* 272, 281.

[38] Rubin (n 23) 1300.

[39] See similarly Jordan, Stråth and Triandafyllidou (n 36) 393.

unfettered – discretionary power. While the following investigation will trace and explain the enduring relevance and prominence of discretion in this field of law, it will argue that discretion should not be treated as a pervasive feature of migration decision-making, but rather as a phenomenon linked to specific instances of norm application (subsection A). The prominence of discretionary power in European migration law can be traced both to historical legacies as well as to more recent dynamics that suggest a contemporary revival of discretion (subsection B). The persistence of discretionary power can be further explained by structural characteristics of migration law and by theoretical considerations regarding the role of discretion (subsection C).

A. Defining Discretion as a Targeted Legal Phenomenon

As a phenomenon, discretion is known to most (if not all) national administrative systems in Europe. As such, it is home to some degree of conceptual and terminological diversity. In French administrative law, for instance, the term *pouvoir discrétionnaire* serves as a general reference to spheres of deliberative freedom.[40] In contrast, the German legal order distinguishes *Ermessen* (discretion proper) from a generic form of latitude inherent in the application of undetermined legal concepts – a distinction that may have equally influenced other administrative systems in Europe.[41] These terminological differences are not just semantic variations. Rather, different terms resonate with idiosyncratic conceptions of discretion that are reflective of specific national experiences.[42]

While national legal systems in Europe often put forward similar characteristics to substantiate the existence of discretion, it would be misleading to ignore the conceptual diversity that exists between them. The idiosyncratic understandings of the term discretion that exist in different national contexts have significant repercussions for the research design of the investigation that follows. An analysis of discretionary powers in different legal systems must stay abreast of the conceptual diversity that inheres within this process and needs to define the instances of administrative decision-making that it views as discretion and the reasons for doing so.

There are at least three conceivable ways of establishing which instances of decision-making should be viewed as discretion for the purposes of the following investigation. In the first place, an analysis may adopt the perspective on discretion prevalent within one national legal system and apply it to legal arrangements

[40] See C Grabenwarter, '§ 90 Ermessenslehren' in A Bogdandy, S Cassese and PM Huber (eds), *Handbuch Ius Publicum Europaeum.: Band V: Verwaltungsrecht in Europa: Grundzüge* (CF Müller, 2014) 1023.

[41] See J Mendes, 'Administrative Discretion in the EU: Comparative Perspectives' in S Rose-Ackerman and P Lindseth (eds), *Comparative Administrative Law* 2nd edn (Edward Elgar, 2017) 639.

[42] See R Caranta, 'On Discretion' in S Prechal and B van Roermund (eds), *The Coherence of EU Law: The Search for Unity in Divergent Concepts* (Oxford University Press, 2008) 186.

in another. This would, however, approach the phenomenon on false pretences. It would analytically superimpose a conception of discretion alien to the legal system at hand.[43] Such an approach would be akin to presuming that one conception of discretion prevailed over other understandings thereof – a view that does not hold water in European public law. Accordingly, such an analytical approach will be rejected.

In the second place, the phenomenon of discretionary power in European migration law could be treated from the perspective of each of its various national conceptual traditions. Such an approach would unreservedly accept the classifications of a respective legal system that a specific instance of decision-making should be viewed as discretionary or non-discretionary in nature. On the one hand, this would duly account for the diversity of conceptions that characterises discretionary power in European administrative law. It would take a legal system's word for it that a situation may involve discretion. On the other hand, such an approach invites a degree of analytical incoherence. It would tolerate that the scope of investigation varied significantly from one legal system to another. Where discretionary decision-making is conceptually viewed as the default mode of decision-making, for instance, the following investigation would adopt a much wider scope compared to a legal system in which discretion is conceptualised as a relatively specific mode of decision-making. Since the scope of investigation would accordingly be contingent on the respective conceptual specification in each legal system examined, this approach will not be used for the purposes of the investigation that follows.

Instead, the following examination adopts a third approach to exploring the phenomenon of discretionary decision-making in European migration law. It develops an abstract account of discretion – a framework definition – that will serve as an analytical point of reference to determine the legal arrangements viewed as discretion. Such an approach identifies elements that may be said to substantiate the existence of discretion in different legal systems, thereby delineating the scope of investigation. Nonetheless, this should not be viewed as a disguised attempt to analytically project a uniform understanding of discretion onto the diverse conceptions thereof that exist in European legal systems. Rather, by virtue of this framework definition, the phenomenon of discretion will be defined on the basis of properties that sufficiently reflect this conceptual diversity.

In this respect, the following investigation will presume that discretion exists in instances of legally warranted administrative self-programming powers that are not superseded in substance by courts. Paying heed to the conceptual diversity that marks the phenomenon of discretion in Europe, such a definition draws heavily from insights of legal theory as well as comparative analyses of legal traditions

[43] This resonates with the criticism in comparative law that researchers may often unknowingly project their own preconceptions onto legal arrangements within another legal system, see seminally G Frankenberg, 'Critical Comparisons: Re-Thinking Comparative Law' (1985) 26 *Harvard International Law Journal* 411, 413.

of discretion in European states.[44] For that reason, it can be presumed that it will routinely concur with national characterisations that a specific instance of decision-making power constitutes discretion. It is not inconceivable, however, that such classifications diverge. An abstract definition of this nature may, on some occasions, flag instances of decision-making as discretion that are not viewed as such in the respective legal system at hand. As a case in point, it may present the fleshing out of undetermined legal concepts as discretion, whereas the prevalent conception of discretion in German law would beg to differ. It should be noted, therefore, that the investigation that follows operates at a conceptual arms-length distance from national traditions of discretion.

B. Of Relics and Revivals: Discretionary Power in European Migration Law

The prominence of wide executive discretion is one of the defining characteristics of migration laws in Europe. In part, this prevalence can be traced back to the historical origins of migration control. In Europe, early efforts to regulate migration relied heavily on wide discretionary powers. In post-war France, for instance, the relevant legal framework on entry and stay of foreigners determined that the minister of interior may expel a foreigner if his or her 'presence in French territory . . . constitutes a severe threat to public order'.[45] Initially, the decision to expel a foreigner was therefore mostly a matter of ministerial preference, circumscribed only by the vague requirement that the person concerned was viewed as a 'severe threat to public order'. In 1975, the Conseil d'État ruled that such expulsion decisions should not be vitiated by a manifest error of assessment, which allowed judges to exert some degree of control over the minister's decision.[46] While this arrangement was later circumscribed by more detailed standards of legality,[47] it exemplifies the evolution of discretionary power in French migration law, from vast discretionary decision-making to some form of controlled deliberative freedom.

A similar trend may be discernible in other (Western) European legal systems. Wide discretionary powers equally featured in early legal arrangements on migration in the Federal Republic of Germany. While the constitutional order established by the Basic Law principally envisages a relatively high intensity of judicial control, the Ausländergesetz of 1965 included blanket clauses on several occasions. In this vein, the competent migration authorities had discretion inter alia to authorise

[44] See below at ch 2, s III.

[45] Ordonnance n° 45-2658 du 2 novembre 1945, relative aux conditions d'entrée et de séjour des étrangers en France, JO n° 259, 4 novembre 1945, p 7225, art 23, para 1; the author's translation of 'l'expulsion peut être prononcée par arrêté du ministre de l'intérieur si la présence sur le territoire français d'un étranger constitue une menace grave pour l'ordre public'.

[46] Conseil d'État, 3 February 1975, *Pardov*, 94108.

[47] See PL Frier and J Petit, *Droit Administratif* 9th edn (Librairie générale de droit et de jurisprudence, 2014) 542 ff.

a foreigner's stay and work.[48] Whereas it may be questioned whether discretion therefore constituted a 'general property' of early migration law in Germany,[49] it is certainly correct to suggest that discretion assumed a central role in the relevant legal framework during the first decades after the war.

The same conclusions may be drawn with a view to the legal framework on migration in the Netherlands, which included discretionary decision-making in several central aspects. The Vreemdelingenwet of 1965 determined that the stay of foreigners may be authorised 'in so far and as long as . . . they do not pose a threat to public peace, public order or national security'.[50] Such an authorisation could, moreover, be withdrawn on the same grounds.[51] However, it would be inapt to characterise Dutch migration law at that time in terms of unfettered discretionary power. Rather, the Vreemdelingenwet of 1965 already included legislative specifications to limit the competent migration authorities' assessments, and allowed for appeals to a court.[52]

Notwithstanding some differences, this cursory overview suggests that initial attempts to govern migration relied heavily on discretionary power. Some of the instances of discretionary decision-making in contemporary migration laws in Europe can be viewed as relics of these earlier phases of the evolution of national laws.[53] Besides such continuities, however, legal systems have introduced additional instances of discretionary decision-making in the field of migration law in recent years. Accordingly, it may not be unreasonable to observe that European migration law has seen the revival of discretionary power as a contemporary phenomenon of migration control.

On several occasions, this revival of discretionary decision-making is rooted in influences of European origin.[54] European law may impel national legal systems to vest individual decision-makers with a degree of discretion. In the context of migration law, this phenomenon features in particularly pronounced terms in relation to the requirement to carry out an individualised assessment. Following notably from the jurisprudence of the European Court of Human Rights, decisions restricting the entry or stay of migrants may interfere with the human right of migrants to respect for their family and private life.[55] While such restrictions of this right may be justified, the European Court of Human Rights (ECtHR) insists

[48] See C Gusy, 'Ermessen Und Ermessensbindung Im Ausländerrecht' (1984) 5 *Verwaltungsblätter für Baden-Württemberg* 393, 393.

[49] For this conclusion, Wendel (n 19) 106, the author's approximated translation of 'Grundinstrumentarium'.

[50] Vreemdelingenwet 1965, art 8; the author's translation of 'indien en zolang zij . . . geen gevaar opleveren voor de openbare rust [literally: calm, here translated as public peace], de openbare orde of de nationale veiligheid'.

[51] Vreemdelingenwet 1965, art 12.

[52] ibid, art 40 ff.

[53] In the context of German law, see T Gross, 'Das Ausländerrecht Zwischen Obrigkeitsstaatlicher Tradition Und Menschenrechtlicher Herausforderung' (2014) 139 *Archiv des öffentlichen Rechts* 420, 427 ff.

[54] For this phenomenon more generally, see insightfully Wendel (n 19) 77.

[55] Seminally, ECtHR, *Abdulaziz, Cabales and Balkandali v The United Kingdom*, Series A no 94 (1985) 7 EHRR 471.

that any measure restricting migrants' private or family life must duly consider the specific characteristics of the individual case.[56]

Such a requirement to consider the specificities of the individual case presupposes that migration officials can carry out an open-ended deliberation in the first place. An automatic refusal or restriction of entry and stay in the territory would defy the notion of an individualised assessment. From the perspective of national lawmakers, this precludes legal arrangements that prescribe a negative outcome by default. National legal systems must allow migration officials some degree of flexibility to duly consider each individual case on its merits. In this vein, a requirement to provide for an individualised assessment can be viewed as a European safeguard of national administrative autonomy. As the following investigation sets out to illustrate, national legal systems frequently accommodate this autonomy through legal arrangements that qualify, from the purposes of this investigation, as discretion.[57]

While the emergence of instances of discretionary decision-making that follows European safeguards of administrative autonomy occurs in a somewhat incidental fashion, European law occasionally compels national legal systems to provide for discretion in more explicit terms. Notably, the Court of Justice explicitly employs the term 'discretion' to command that Member State lawmakers redesign national legal systems to the effect that migration authorities have a measure of deliberative freedom. In the context of visa law, for instance, the Court ruled that the competent national authorities must have 'wide discretion' to refuse a visa.[58] A similar line of jurisprudence later transpired in areas closely linked to visa policy, in particular the authorisation of stay of students and researchers, and the termination of short-term legal stay.[59]

To be sure, a supranational label of 'discretion' does not premeditate the intensity of judicial control,[60] and therefore may not necessarily give rise to national legal arrangements that would qualify as discretion for the purposes of this investigation. However, it is worth noticing that the Court of Justice's case law in the field of migration law has expressly ruled that 'since the competent national authorities have a wide discretion in assessing the facts, judicial review is limited . . . to the absence of manifest error'.[61] In such a situation, the jurisprudence of the Court compels national legal systems to spell out a legal framework that qualifies as discretion for the purposes of the present investigation.

[56] See D Thym, 'Residence as de Facto Citizenship? Protection of Long-Term Residence under Article 8 ECHR' in R Rubio-Marín (ed), *Human Rights and Immigration* (Oxford University Press, 2014).

[57] See below at ch 3, s I.

[58] Case C-84/12 *Koushkaki v Bundesrepublik Deutschland* ECLI:EU:C:2013:862, [2013], para 60.

[59] Case C-544/15 *Fahimian v Bundesrepublik Deutschland* ECLI:EU:C:2017:255, [2017], para 41; Case C-380/18 *Staatssecretaris van Justitie en Veiligheid v E.P.* ECLI:EU:C:2019:1071, [2019], para 37.

[60] Rather, the intensity and method of judicial review is routinely left to Member States' procedural autonomy. Explicitly on this point, Case C-84/12 *Koushkaki v Bundesrepublik Deutschland* ECLI:EU:C:2013:232, [2013], Opinion of AG Mengozzi, para 27.

[61] *Fahimian* n (59) para 46.

On an intermediate level of analysis, this suggests that the re-emergence of discretion in the field of European migration law does not just follow incidentally, but that European law may have a vested interest in the existence of discretion in national legal systems. Instances of explicitly ordained discretionary powers complement those that follow European law's more incidental impulses, such as those emerging from a requirement to provide for an individualised assessment, and existing traditional avenues of migration authorities' discretion. As a contemporary phenomenon, discretion therefore presents itself not as a misfit but rather as a purposefully deployed, expedient tool to accommodate standards of European law in national legal systems.

C. Beyond Sovereign Choice: Explaining the Prominence of Migration Discretion

While the pronounced criticism levelled at discretion has led to a gradual repression of vast and uncontrolled discretionary powers in other fields of law, discretion appears to linger as a prominent trait of decision-making in European migration law. Several theoretical arguments have been advanced in the literature to account for this. On a rather abstract level, a recurrent line of reasoning emphasises the close link that is often presumed to exist between migration control and sovereign power. On this view, the concentration of extensive discretionary powers in the hands of national executives serves to ensure that migration decision-making remains aligned with the expression of sovereign will.[62] However, it should be noted that the existence and scope of discretionary decision-making tends to be reflective of the authority attributed to the decision-making institution in relation to other actors within a legal system.[63] Accordingly, it cannot be a foregone conclusion that other actors within a legal system – such as legislatures or courts – would readily accept that migration decision-making would be the exclusive domain of the executive branch, to the effect that executive discretion may be significantly limited and subject to forms of judicial control.

In European legal systems, the enduring relevance and prominence of discretionary powers in migration control may therefore be linked to other, more functional, considerations. As Mattarella suggests, there are several theoretical arguments that would rally in favour of wide discretionary powers in practice.[64] There seems to be a commonly shared understanding – a pan-European gut feeling, as it were – that certain characteristics of decision-making should routinely coincide with the existence of discretionary power. In the field of migration

[62] See Dauvergne (n 3) 592.

[63] For this phenomenon, see J Mendes and I Venzke, 'Introducing the Idea of Relative Authority' in J Mendes and I Venzke (eds), *Allocating Authority: Who Should Do What in European and International Law?* (Hart, 2018) 3 ff.

[64] See Mattarella (n 10) 32 ff.

governance, several characteristics may be viewed as reasons why some measure of discretion should be awarded to executive decision-makers.

When discussing the reasons underpinning the enduring relevance of migration discretion, one reason that often springs to mind is the complexity that decision-making in this field of law entails. Complexity, in this sense, results from imponderables regarding factual situations abroad or from assessments regarding the prospective conduct of the person concerned. In such situations, the authority of the decision-maker will result from the expertise needed to master this complexity.[65] Moreover, decision-makers may frequently have discretion where extraordinary situations put significant public interests on the line. Accordingly, crisis or risk situations may activate broad discretionary powers, which can relate to the assessment of problems, the identification of possible solutions, or both.[66] Against this backdrop, it should be noted that decision-making in the field of migration law is often intimately linked to efforts of safeguarding public security and public order. While such a security paradigm in migration decision-making may be criticised, it is true that states tend to allocate foreigners wishing to enter their territory on 'a continuum of insecurity',[67] to the effect that migration authorities may frequently have discretionary power to take steps to safeguard public security (and possibly, by extension, public order).

While these considerations may explain the prominence of discretion in migration decision-making, it would be inapt to presume that the case for discretion would be equally compelling in all sub-areas of migration law alike. Rather, the prevalence of discretionary decision-making may vary significantly from one sub-area of migration law to another. The reasons to accept wide discretion, for instance, may be particularly cogent in the context of visas where, as a rule, decision-making takes place at consulates abroad and frequently involves a degree of complexity.[68] Decisions whether to grant a visa are moreover intrinsically linked to an assessment of the prospective behaviour of individuals. Would the person return to her or his native State in due time? Or does (s)he pose a threat to public security to the host country? Since human behaviour is fickle, it is impossible to anticipate with certainty the future conduct of the person concerned. Accordingly, assessments of such nature may require a high level of expertise or, at the very least, experience, and may therefore give rise to wide discretionary power.

On the flipside, weighty legal arguments militate against the existence of wide discretionary powers in other areas of migration law. Especially, this applies to

[65] For philosophical discussion of the link between discretion and expertise, see M Luntley, 'Expertise and the Space for Discretion' in T Evans and PL Hupe (eds), *Discretion and the Quest for Controlled Freedom* (Palgrave Macmillan, 2020) 341 ff.

[66] See Mattarella (n 10) 37.

[67] Cited from E Guild, *Security and Migration in the 21st Century* (Polity Press, 2009) 2, with reference to D Bigo, 'Security and Immigration: Toward a Critique of the Governmentality of Unease' (2002) 27 *Alternatives* 63.

[68] See, for example, International Organization for Migration (ed), *Laws for Legal Immigration in the 27 EU Member States*, vol 16 (2009) 38.

situations in which the rights of migrants are at stake. While non-citizens are not habitually empowered, by virtue of individual rights, to access the territory of another State, they may benefit from certain rights and safeguards, nonetheless. By imposing limits on public authorities, such standards may rally against the existence of wide discretion.[69] This may explain the marginal role that discretion usually assumes in other sub-areas of European migration law, such as asylum decision-making, which is underpinned by significant human rights safeguards.

III. Discretion and Tempered Executive Dominance: The Transformation of Discretionary Power

The exercise of discretion is sometimes presented as an instance of free choice – a power to opt, within certain legal limits, for one of several equivalent options.[70] This view suggests that administrative decision-makers could, within the limits of their discretion, act as they please. A contemporary conception of discretion in European migration law, however, challenges such an understanding. Specifically, it is called into question by the growing importance that legal principles assume in instructing the exercise of discretion.[71] These principles can be described as 'inconclusive standards, which nonetheless lend justificatory support to courses of action'.[72] Although standards of that nature do not prescribe a certain outcome and therefore do not bound or nullify the discretion that administrators have, they serve as benchmarks of legality against which the exercise of discretion can be measured. Conceptually, this implies that it would be inapt to present the exercise of discretion in European migration law as a form of uninstructed choice among several, legally equivalent options.

While this conceptual transformation may sound like a technicality, it creates significant repercussions for administrative practice. For administrators, the exercise of discretion emerges as a particularly demanding mode of decision-making. In contrast to bounded decision-making, it requires them to autonomously compile and apply the standards relevant for the case before them. At the same time, they must respect legal principles instructing their deliberation, and disregard for any of these standards may render administrative conduct unlawful.

The legal design through which the exercise of discretion may be instructed varies. One of the most pertinent ways in which this is done, however, is through the principle of proportionality. While the rigour and workings of this principle differ,[73] proportionality compels administrators to appraise the interests of

[69] In this sense, see Mattarella (n 10) 24 ff.
[70] See particularly Hawkins (n 9) 11.
[71] See Brouwer (n 12) 51 ff.
[72] Mascini (n 13) 124.
[73] See for instance S Ranchordás and B Waard, 'Concluding Remarks' in S Ranchordás and B Waard (eds), *The Judge and the Proportionate Use of Discretion: A Comparative Study* (Routledge, 2016) 193.

the individual concerned and weigh them against those pursued by its actions. Besides, legal systems may subject the exercise of discretionary power to procedural safeguards, such as a duty to state reasons, or indicate the objectives to be achieved through the exercise of discretion.[74] What these standards of legality have in common is that they do not ultimately forego an autonomous assessment by the administrator. Instead, they place significant responsibility in the hands of administrators to exercise discretion in a diligent fashion, respecting both the limits of their legality and the guidance that can be derived from legal principles.

In Europe, the intricacy that the exercise of discretion implies is exacerbated by the fact that the standards of legality instructing and delineating the exercise of discretion often originate from different levels of a multi-levelled legal system. While, formally, standards of international and supranational law are external to the domestic legal system in which administrations operate, they serve as limits and guiding standards for national administrative conduct. Where national administrations are afforded discretionary power, they are tasked to acknowledge and apply these standards in a relatively autonomous fashion.[75] In the context of EU migration law, empirical research has shown that street-level decision-makers often struggle with this task.[76]

On a higher level of abstraction, this transformation of the exercise of discretion reflects the change in executive power in European migration law. On the one hand, a conventional understanding of discretionary practices as uninstructed, free choice may suggest that street-level bureaucrats could 'deny entry, reject visa applicants, and detain people with little accountability, opportunity for redress, or even explanation to people harmed'.[77] On the other hand, it may be noted that the exercise of discretion in European migration law increasingly departs from such an understanding, instead establishing discretionary conduct as a form of legally instructed decision-making freedom.

IV. Discretionary Power and the Legal Position of Migrants

The question when and how discretionary power is afforded and exercised is usually addressed through the lens of public officials. This is sensible, given that it is administrators who exercise such powers. However, discretion equally affects

[74] Teleological determinations of that nature have gained traction in the fairway of EU secondary law instruments, see A Vincze, *Unionsrecht Und Verwaltungsrecht: Eine Rechtsvergleichende Untersuchung Zur Rezeption Des Unionsrechts* (Nomos, 2016) 112 ff.

[75] On this point, see Wendel (n 19) 104 ff.

[76] See N Dörrenbächer, 'Frontline Uses of European Union (EU) Law: A Parallel Legal Order? How Structural Discretion Conditions Uses of EU Law in Dutch and German Migration Offices' (2018) 38 *Journal of Public Policy* 455, 473.

[77] A Sager, 'Immigration Enforcement and Domination: An Indirect Argument for Much More Open Borders' (2017) 70 *Political Research Quarterly* 42, 43.

individuals. The existence and exercise of discretionary power is reflective of the legal position that individuals hold vis-á-vis administrative authorities. In relation to citizens, this legal position has gradually been strengthened.[78] Democratic systems across Europe have developed mechanisms that allow citizens to engage with public authorities, enabling them to benefit from a range of rights that safeguard their legitimate interests vis-á-vis public authorities.[79] This marks a partial departure from the conventional characterisation of executive action, which conceives the relationship between public authorities and private persons solely in terms of a 'command to which obedience was due'.[80]

While this change in the nature of executive power has catered to the invigoration of the legal position of citizens vis-á-vis the respective State authorities, the same conclusion may not be drawn without qualification in relation to non-national migrants. Migrants often do not benefit from safeguards comparable to those of nationals. To be sure, this is not to say that the legal situation of migrants would be hopeless entirely. On several occasions, they may benefit from safeguards, including those guaranteeing equal treatment.[81] However, distinctions based on nationality continue to form a constitutive element of migration regimes in Europe.[82] In relation to decision-making on entry, stay and return of migrants, legal systems tend to stick to legal constellations characterised by a sharp hierarchical asymmetry between public officials and the individual concerned (*in casu*: a migrant).

Against this backdrop, the argument can be put forward that a rather conventional understanding of administrative power has lingered in relation to migration matters. Accordingly, the following investigation starts from the premise that the change in the nature of administrative power in European migration law may have occurred with some delay compared to other fields of European administrative law. It will argue that this arrear, however, has been significantly reduced in recent years. Developments in European migration law have successively caught up with a general trend in European administrative law, namely the readjustment of the interrelationship of public officials and individuals.

The transformation of discretionary power reflects this change in the nature of administrative power. The comparatively weak legal position of migrants may have been one of the main rationales for legal systems to accept wide discretionary powers in migration matters in the first place.[83] The readjustment of the relation-

[78] On a similar note, see F Bignami, 'Comparative Administrative Law' in M Bussani and U Mattei (eds), *The Cambridge Companion to Comparative Law* (Cambridge University Press, 2012) 16 ff.

[79] See Auby (n 21) 614.

[80] E Chiti, 'Is EU Administrative Law Failing in Some of Its Crucial Tasks?' (2016) 22 *European Law Journal* 576, 584.

[81] See D Thym, 'Legal Framework for EU Immigration Policy' in Daniel Thym and Kay Hailbronner (eds), *EU Immigration and Asylum Law: Article-by-Article Commentary* 3rd edn (Beck; Hart; Nomos, 2022) 410 ff.

[82] On this point, see for instance JB Farcy, 'Equality in Immigration Law: An Impossible Quest?' (2020) 20 *Human Rights Law Review* 725, 728 ff.

[83] For this argument, albeit not in the context of migration law, see Mattarella (n 10) 21 ff.

ship of migration authorities and the individual concerned therefore equally affects the exercise and scope of discretionary power. While, for migrants, challenging discretionary decision-making may still be an uphill battle, it is no forlorn endeavour from the start. Rather, the transformation of discretionary power coincides with a relative invigoration of the interest of migrants vis-á-vis public interests (subsection A). This creates practical improvements for migrants. It precludes decisions that would adversely affect migrants by default and instead promotes decision-making that duly considers the specificities of the individual case at hand (subsection B).

A. Legitimate Interests of Migrants

Discretion is sometimes presented as a choice among several lawful options from which the public official is authorised to pick and choose as (s)he deems fit.[84] As such, it is reflective of the highly asymmetrical power relationship characteristic of conventional conceptions of administrative power. By exercising discretion, public officials may themselves determine how the public interest and individual interests could best be reconciled. In European migration law, such a conventional view on discretion, however, is challenged by the growing relevance of legal principles for the exercise of discretionary power.[85] While the power asymmetry at play is not levelled entirely in this vein, the legally instructed nature of discretionary conduct incentivises a more balanced assessment.

Most prominently, this readjustment can be linked to the principle of proportionality, which compels public authorities to draw attention to the legitimate interests of the person concerned.[86] Where discretion has previously been viewed as a sphere of choice between several feasible options, this influence necessitates a conceptual readjustment. In this situation, the exercise of discretion may not just be viewed as a pick-and-choose from several equivalent options but rather needs to be conceptualised as a legally structured deliberative process, requiring decision-makers inter alia to weigh and reconcile opposing interests.

In European migration law, this phenomenon has been notably incentivised by influences of European provenance. Owing particularly to the jurisprudence of the ECtHR, the legal position of migrants has been significantly strengthened. Where a migrant's private or family life is at stake, the Strasbourg Court insists that a 'fair balance' must be struck between competing interests of the individual and the community as a whole.[87] In this vein, national decision-makers are compelled

[84] In this sense, for instance, Hawkins (n 9) 11.

[85] On this point, see above at s III.

[86] For a comparative analysis of this principle, see J Mathews, 'Proportionality Review in Administrative Law' in S Rose-Ackerman, P Lindseth and B Emerson (eds), *Comparative Administrative Law* 2nd edn (Edgar Elgar, 2019) 409 ff.

[87] This follows from the Strasbourg Court's interpretation of Article 8 ECHR, inter alia in *Gül v Switzerland* (1996) 22 EHRR 93, para 38.

to consider, in one way or another, the individual situation of migrants, assessing the impact of their decision on the person's private or family life.

At first sight, such a safeguard appears to be of minor significance. Neither does it ensure a positive outcome for the individual concerned, nor would it necessarily fix the elements that should be viewed as relevant in this regard. In the context of European migration law, however, the obligation to draw close attention to the specificities of the individual migrants' situation may constitute a significant paradigm change regarding the relationship of public authorities and the individual concerned. Several national migration laws originally presumed that the public interests in adopting a negative migration decision would automatically prevail over any interest of the individual concerned. While the following investigation will highlight that such a view has not lost traction entirely, it will illustrate that the influences of European law in this field challenge such a conventional conception of administrative power.

B. Relative Improvements for Migrants

The invigorated legal position of migrants may be at the heart of a proliferation of discretionary decision-making in some areas of European migration law. As this investigation suggests, national legal systems resort to discretion to equip decision-makers with the authority to duly consider the individual case before them and to adjust their decision accordingly. To be sure, these instances of discretionary power need not necessarily produce positive outcomes for migrants. The exercise of discretion is inherently open-ended, to the effect that it may turn out one way or another. Yet, the existence and proliferation of discretionary decision-making may create improvements for the legal position of migrants in at least two respects:

First, previous legal arrangements in European migration law often prescribed a negative outcome for migrants by default. In this vein, the proliferation of discretionary decision-making marks a relative improvement in contrast to earlier arrangements. Discretion has come to replace instances of decision-making that would otherwise automatically affect migrants unfavourably. The relative improvements that this change engenders may be aptly encapsulated by the notion that 'hope-filled uncertainty is [preferable] to hopeless certainty'.[88] From a migrant's perspective, the proliferation of discretion implies that certain preconditions may swing the outcome of a decision in favour of the migrant in the first place.

A second relative improvement for the legal position of migrants follows from the existence of legal principles that instruct the exercise of discretion. These

[88] This wording is borrowed from M Hernández-Carretero, 'Hope and Uncertainty in Senegalese Migration to Spain: Taking Chances on Emigration but Not upon Return' in N Kleist and D Thorsten (eds), *Hope and Uncertainty in Contemporary African Migration* (Routledge, 2017), cited from A Triandafyllidou, 'The Migration Archipelago: Social Navigation and Migrant Agency' (2018) 57 *International Migration* 5, 8.

standards serve as benchmarks against which the legality of discretionary decisions can be assessed. Unlike instances of discretion that would essentially afford migration authorities a measure of free choice, legal principles instructing the exercise of discretion equip migrants with legal arguments to challenge discretionary decision-making. In combination with the availability of judicial review, the subjugation of discretionary conduct to standards of legality thus enables migrants to challenge decisions that would previously have defied any substantive (judicial) control.

V. Methodology and Research Design

The following investigation employs a doctrinal research method. Such a method requires, as a preliminary step, the sources of law relevant to the investigation to be located and the reasons for their inclusion to be spelled out.[89] With respect to the present investigation, this specifically concerns the question which legal arrangements should be viewed as discretion. Since the phenomenon of discretionary power is characterised by theoretical and empirical divergence, no uniform understanding of discretionary power can be singled out from an analysis of legal systems in Europe.[90] Against this background, the following investigation will revisit discussions in legal theory and national administrative laws to highlight several characteristics that will be viewed as formative for the phenomenon of discretion.

In this vein, the following investigation will rely on a framework definition of discretionary power. This framework definition incorporates properties that are habitually attributed to discretionary power in legal systems in Europe.[91] Discretion, in this regard, is defined as an instance of administrative self-programming power that is legally warranted and not, in substance, superseded by another actor.[92] Such a definition avoids turning a blind eye to the conceptual divergences that exist between legal systems in Europe. It does not, for instance, specify whether discretionary power should be found exclusively in explicit authorisations or whether its existence may equally follow from more implicit awards of administrative self-programming power. Instead, the framework definition adopted here merely insists that discretion exists as a 'legally warranted' phenomenon, without specifying how it may be rooted in law. Similarly, such a definition accepts different modes and intensities of judicial review as hallmarks of discretionary power, insofar as they are not tantamount to a form of review that effectively enables judges to supersede the initial decision of administrators in substance.

[89] For this understanding of the doctrinal method, see T Hutchinson and N Duncan, 'Defining and Describing What We Do: Doctrinal Legal Research' (2012) 17 *Deaking Law Review* 83, 110 ff.

[90] See Brand (n 6) 218 ff.

[91] For such an approach, see O Bukve, *Designing Social Science Research* (Palgrave Macmillan, 2019) 41 ff, with further references.

[92] See above at s II.A.

Based on this framework definition, the phenomenon of discretionary power in European migration law can be charted. As a corollary of this approach, the different properties through which discretion is defined will determine the focus of the investigation that follows. Specific attention will be drawn, accordingly, to instances in which legal arrangements vest migration officials with self-programming power or preclude the award thereof. Moreover, an emphasis will be put on the standards of legality that instruct and govern the exercise of this power. Last, the investigation will explore the mode and intensity of judicial control that is exercised in relation to these instances of administrative autonomy. In this vein, the framework definition premeditates the focus of the following investigation. It directs the analysis to aspects that condition the existence and exercise of discretionary power in European migration law.

A. Deductive Reasoning

The research design of the investigation that follows is deductive in nature. It relies on insights from European administrative law to define discretion as a legal phenomenon and to explore the mechanisms that condition its existence, exercise and effects for the individuals concerned. In this regard, it can fall back on a rich body of literature. Elaborate research has been carried out, for instance, with respect to the nature of judicial control,[93] and the Europeanisation of administrative discretion.[94] This research may explain some of the processes that condition the existence and exercise of discretionary power in European migration law and the effects that it creates for migrants. Where developments in European migration law diverge from those in European administrative law more generally, the following investigation will punctually depart from a deductive reasoning, exploring these instances inductively instead.

Moreover, the following investigation is premised on the axiomatic view that the relative improvements that the existence of discretionary power creates for migrants follow notably from influences of European law. To be sure, such improvements may likewise materialise in the absence of European influences.[95] In relation to European migration law, however, the view will be put forward that the transformation of discretionary decision-making, and the improvements that it engenders for the legal position of migrants, coincide with the emergence of standards that originate from European law.[96] In the chapters that follow, particular attention will be drawn to these interactions.

[93] See the contributions in J Poorter, E Hirsch Ballin and S Lavrijssen (eds), *Judicial Review of Administrative Discretion in the Administrative State* (Asser; Springer, 2019).

[94] See Vincze (n 74) 78 ff.

[95] Accordingly, instances in which the existence or exercise of discretionary power has changed in the absence of European influences will only be considered punctually in the following investigation.

[96] See likewise Wendel (n 19) 185 ff.

The following investigation will explore the way in which European standards of law influence the ability of national migration authorities to self-programme their conduct, how legal principles derived from European law condition the exercise of discretionary powers, and the standards that affect the availability and intensity of judicial review in this regard. To some extent, it can rely on previous research in this regard. Analytical attention has been devoted, for instance, to aspects of judicial control, especially in the field of asylum law.[97] In addition, Wendel has instructively examined how influences of European law affect the existence and exercise of discretion in German migration law, focusing particularly on the ramifications that this creates for the relatively specific conception of discretion prevalent in German law.[98] While the following investigation builds on this research, it will consider how standards of European law play out in different national contexts and with respect to each of the properties through which the phenomenon of discretion is defined.

B. Course of Investigation

After this introductory chapter, the following investigation proceeds in five steps. In line with the doctrinal research method that it employs, it will first establish the legal arrangements that will be viewed as discretion for the purposes of the present investigation (chapter two). To this end, it revisits discussions in legal theory and European administrative law to advance a framework definition of discretion. As an analytical tool, such a definition will serve as a point of reference for pinning down the scope of investigation. While a framework definition of that nature operates at a conceptual arms-length from understandings of discretion in real life, it incorporates properties that are routinely considered hallmarks of discretion in conceptions of discretionary power in administrative systems in Europe. Specifically, discretion will be defined as a phenomenon implying a legally warranted self-programming power that is not, in substance, superseded by other actors, specifically courts.

Based on this definition, it will be possible to chart the ways in which standards of European law affect the existence, exercise and effects of discretionary power in European migration law. Each of these aspects will be explored consecutively, in the three chapters that follow.

The first of these chapter will argue that, from the perspective of national lawmakers, discretion often presents itself as the only feasible option to accommodate standards of European law in national migration systems (chapter three). To be sure, this finding is not imperative from the conceptual angle of the framework

[97] See D Baldinger, *Rigorous Scrutiny versus Marginal Review: Standards on Judicial Scrutiny and Evidence in International and European Asylum Law* (Wolf Legal Publishers, 2013); M Reneman, *EU Asylum Procedures and the Right to an Effective Remedy* (Hart, 2014).

[98] See Wendel (n 19).

definition of discretion adopted here. On many occasions, European law warrants a measure of national administrative self-programming power but refrains from spelling out the repercussions that this creates for the intensity of judicial review. Accordingly, it cannot be a foregone conclusion that such an influence would materialise in a legal arrangement that qualifies as discretion for the purposes of the present investigation. While, in such constellations, the existence of discretionary power follows rather incidentally from influences of European law, the following investigation will highlight that the latter may occasionally prescribe the existence of discretion in more explicit terms. This phenomenon features pronouncedly in European migration law on several occasions. This chapter will highlight these instances of influence, arguing that this may speak to a vested European interest in the existence of national administrative discretion.

With a view to those instances in which discretionary power can be said to exist, the second empirical section focuses on the way in which it is exercised (chapter four). In this vein, it adopts the perspective of administrators, arguing that, in European migration law, the nature of discretionary conduct has been transformed in the fairway of European influences. In contemporary migration law, legal principles instruct and delineate the conduct of migration authorities, without prescribing a specific course of action. For migration officials, this establishes a particularly challenging mode of decision-making. In their exercise of discretionary power, they are tasked to autonomously compile and apply standards of law that emanate from different layers of a multi-levelled system. Unlike previous instances in which the exercise of discretion has essentially been constructed as an exercise of free choice, the exercise of discretion emerges as a mode of deliberative freedom that is firmly pervaded and delineated by standards of legality. This chapter will present this transformation in the exercise of discretionary power.

Based on the argument that standards of European provenance have influenced the existence and exercise of discretionary power in European migration law, the third empirical chapter assesses the implications that this creates for migrants (chapter five). It suggests that the targeted consolidation and transformation of discretionary power coincides with improvements of their legal position. Notably, these improvements materialise in two respects. First, instances of discretionary decision-making have often come to replace legal arrangements that previously prescribed an unfavourable outcome by default. While, in such a situation, the existence of discretion need not necessarily manifest in a positive outcome for migrants, it renders such an outcome legally feasible in the first place. A second improvement results from the legally instructed nature of discretionary conduct. Unlike instances of administrative choice, legal principles serve as benchmarks against which the lawfulness of the exercise of discretion can be measured. Coupled with an option to challenge such decision-making before a court, this equips migrants with tools to go against discretionary decisions affecting them unfavourably. The investigation concludes by summarising and discussing its key findings (chapter six).

2

Discretion: A Conceptual Approximation

Discretion has attracted vast analytical attention as an object of comparison.[1] Most legal systems in Europe are familiar with discretion as a legal phenomenon. Despite its widespread occurrence, however, there can be various overt and subtle differences in the way discretion is conceptualised. Accordingly, it is true, as Galligan notes, that discretion 'is not a precise term of the art, with a settled meaning, nor is it a concept which, when found to be present, leads to fixed consequences'.[2] Rather, various autochthonous legal conceptions of discretion, as well as the manifold demotic uses of the term, smudge its analytical contours.[3]

This conceptual elusiveness is further exacerbated by the fact that discretion may equally be said to figure in the interactions of formally distinct but functionally intertwined legal systems.[4] Discretion, in this sense, denotes the degree of flexibility that one legal system affords another in the context of a multi-levelled system of European law. This adds another set of phenomena to the list of instances that may reasonably be viewed as embodiments of discretion. Against this backdrop, it may be questioned which legal arrangements may qualify as discretion and for what reason so. How can discretion – as a versatile and elusive legal phenomenon – be pinned down in analytical terms?

The following section intends to unravel some of the perplexities surrounding discretion and, by exploring its conceptual contours, it sets out to delineate the scope of investigation of discretion in European migration law. To this end, it first revisits discussions on discretion in legal theory, thereby drawing up some of the elements routinely associated with the phenomenon in theoretical accounts

[1] See R Caranta, 'On Discretion' in S Prechal and B van Roermund (eds), *The Coherence of EU Law: The Search for Unity in Divergent Concepts* (Oxford University Press, 2008) 187; C Grabenwarter, '§ 90 Ermessenslehren' in A Bogdandy, S Cassese and PM Huber (eds), *Handbuch Ius Publicum Europaeum.: Band V: Verwaltungsrecht in Europa: Grundzüge* (CF Müller, 2014). For pioneering works in this regard, see J Schwarze, *European Administrative Law* (Sweet & Maxwell, 1992) 261 ff.; C Starck, 'Rechtsvergleichender Generalbericht' in M Bullinger (ed), *Verwaltungsermessen im modernen Staat* (Nomos, 1986).

[2] D Galligan, *Discretionary Powers: A Legal Study of Official Discretion* (Oxford University Press, 1986) 54.

[3] On the many uses of the term discretion, see the insightful overview provided by G Fletscher, 'Some Unwise Reflections About Discretion' (1984) 47 *Law and Contemporary Problems* 269.

[4] See, on this point, BG Mattarella, 'Law and Discretion. A Public Law Perspective on the EU' in J Mendes (ed), *EU Executive Discretion and the Limits of Law* (Oxford University Press, 2019) 30.

(Section I). Despite significant divergencies in conceptions of discretion in administrative systems in Europe (Section II), this may allow for the development of an abstract definition of discretionary power which can be used to delineate the scope of the present investigation (Section III).

I. Legal Theory on Discretion

A great deal of scholarly attention is devoted to the study of discretion from the perspective of legal theory. In this context, attempts have been made on several occasions to define the phenomenon in abstract terms. While prominent scholars have put their mind to the matter, no universally shared understanding of discretion appears to emerge from these accounts in legal theory. Rather, different schools of thought advance specific understandings of discretion, which may be one of the causes for the 'conceptual confusion' surrounding discussions on discretion.[5] The following section revisits attempts to define discretion as a legal phenomenon and situates them within the legal theory discourse on discretion.

Multiple authors have attempted to distil the essence of what characterises discretion. In this regard, Van Roermund presumes that at 'a rather high level of abstraction', the contours of discretion may be brought to light.[6] This view has it that, from afar, various idiosyncratic understandings of discretion merge into one, exposing elements of similarity that link them all. In line with this impression, authors tend to agree that discretion resonates with a degree of deliberative freedom in a system of public authority.[7] However, most – if not all – attempts to define discretion in such abstract terms are contested on one or multiple accounts. Inquiries probing into the essence of discretion tend to downplay that pugnacity and threaten to underestimate the differences that exist between various conceptions of discretion.

Against this background, this section identifies four aspects that differentiate these abstract accounts of discretion. Discretion may firstly be considered either an avenue of unfettered autonomy, a *carte blanche* so to speak, or an instance of choice that is subjected to various limitations (subsection A). Second, conceptions of discretion may either be indifferent to the institutional context in which discretion arises or, conversely, consider the relative authority of institutions and decision-makers and the repercussions this may have on discretionary power (subsection B). Third, there are divergent views on the interaction of discretion and law, as well as the role that the judicial control plays as a formative element of

[5] B van Roermund, 'Law at Cross-Purposes: Conceptual Confusion and Political Divergence' in S Prechal and B van Roermund (eds), *The Coherence of EU Law: The Search for Unity in Divergent Concepts* (Oxford University Press, 2008) 316 ff.

[6] ibid 320.

[7] See Galligan (n 2) 21; M Brand, 'Discretion, Divergence, and Unity' in S Prechal and B van Roermund (eds), *The Coherence of EU Law: The Search for Unity in Divergent Concepts* (Oxford University Press, 2008) 219; Caranta (n 1) 185.

discretion (subsection C). Fourth, it may be possible to discern various attempts to attribute and locate discretion in specific logical moments of the decision-making process (subsection D).

A. Discretion as (Un)fettered Choice

In legal theory, views differ as to the question of whether discretion should be conceptualised as a sphere of deliberative autonomy or, conversely, as a form of legally instructed decision-making freedom. While most authors agree that discretion constitutes a phenomenon rooted in law, their views differ as to the way in which the interaction between discretion and law should be understood. A prominent view in legal theory suggests that discretion forms a category residual to law (subsection i), whereas an alternative view argues that discretion is rooted in structures of law and should therefore best be viewed as an inherent part of its application (subsection ii). Both views will be briefly presented in the following.

i. The Residual Thesis

One of the most influential definitions of discretion views it as a choice among several equally lawful options. Famously resembling the whole in the doughnut, as Dworkin had argued,[8] discretion should best be described as 'the space . . . between legal rules in which legal actors may exercise choice'.[9] This view premises on a clear-cut distinction between a sphere of legal norms, on the one hand, and one of decision-making autonomy, that is, discretion, on the other.[10] Whenever a decision-making process is not determined by standards of law, the decision-maker is said to exercise discretion. Accordingly, this theoretical account of discretion – which may be termed the residual thesis[11] – continues to be influential, both in theoretical and empirical accounts of discretion, including in the field of migration law.[12] In these contexts, discretion is often singled out as a source of unstructured deliberation whose existence should, as far as possible, be repressed.[13] This attitude is prominently borne out by Davis, who grudgingly acknowledges that '[w]here

[8] See R Dworkin, *Taking Rights Seriously* (Harvard University Press, 1977) 31. This line of argument has later been followed, amongst others, by JH Grey, 'Discretion in Administrative Law' (1979) 17 *Osgoode Hall Law Journal* 107, 107.

[9] K Hawkins, 'The Use of Legal Discretion: Perspectives from Law and Social Science' in K Hawkins (ed), *The Uses of Discretion* (Oxford University Press, 1992) 11.

[10] See P Mascini, 'Discretion from a Legal Perspective' in T Evans and PL Hupe (eds), *Discretion and the Quest for Controlled Freedom* (Palgrave Macmillan, 2020) 123.

[11] See similarly P Hupe and T Evans, 'Controlled Freedom: Dealing with Discretion' in T Evans and PL Hupe (eds), *Discretion and the Quest for Controlled Freedom* (Palgrave Macmillan, 2020) 411.

[12] For instance, see D Kantstroom, 'Surrounding the Hole in the Doughnut: Discretion and Deference in U.S. Immigration Law' (1997) 71 *Tulane Law Review* 703, 722.

[13] Cf. Mascini (n 10) 123.

law ends, discretion begins, and the exercise of discretion may mean either beneficence or tyranny, either justice or injustice, either reasonableness or arbitrariness'.[14]

Defining discretion residually, that is, as a shorthand for the absence of legal determination in decision-making processes, is subject to two analytical blind spots. Such a view first ignores the rich patterns of administrative conduct in practice; unless decision-makers act unlawfully, legal analyses would accordingly turn a blind eye to the process and outcome of decision-making.[15] Furthermore, second, the categorical distinction between spheres of law and decision-making autonomy broadly overlooks the existence of legal principles, which may not determine the outcome of a decision-making process entirely, but guide it, nonetheless. Legal principles guiding discretionary conduct may be characterised as 'thinner legality',[16] thus blurring any categorical distinction between spheres of law and decision-making autonomy. Against this backdrop, empirically, it may be argued that the relevance of legal principles exposes the 'false discretion/law binary', as Pratt argues.[17]

If the existence of legal principles is taken for an empirical fact, there are essentially two possibilities of defining discretion by virtue of its residuality to law. Discretion may be said to exist once a legal norm provides a priori for decision-making autonomy, which may be limited or even nullified by legal principles. In such a situation, one would speak of reduced or 'nullified discretion' – but discretion, nonetheless. In contrast, another account of discretion defines it as the margin of decision-making autonomy that is left a posteriori, that is, after all pertinent legal standards guiding the exercise of discretion have been applied to a specific situation.[18] This view still premises on discretion's residuality to law. However, it presumes that the existence of discretion can be determined only after the law, including legal principles guiding decision-making, has been thoroughly explored. If that exploration discloses the existence of a margin of decision-making autonomy, one could speak of discretion.

ii. The Original Thesis

Unlike the 'residual thesis', an opposing (and in European administrative law, prevailing) view has it that discretion should be considered not beside but within

[14] KC Davis, *Discretionary Justice: A Preliminary Inquiry* (Louisiana State University Press, 1969) 3. For a critical acclaim of Davis' (incongruent) use of the term discretion, see N Lacey, 'The Jurisprudence of Discretion: Escaping the Legal Paradigm' in K Hawkins (ed), *The Uses of Discretion* (Oxford University Press, 1992) 361 ff.

[15] See Mascini (n 10) 123.

[16] This terminology is borrowed from J Mendes, 'Administrative Discretion in the EU: Comparative Perspectives' in S Rose-Ackerman and P Lindseth (eds), *Comparative Administrative Law* 2nd edn (Edward Elgar, 2017) 643.

[17] A Pratt, 'Dunking the Doughnut: Discretionary Power, Law and the Administration of the Canadian Immigration Act' (1999) 8 *Social & Legal Studies* 199, 217.

[18] For instance, see E Nickels, 'A Note on the Status of Discretion in Police Research' (2007) 35 *Journal of Criminal Justice* 570, 571.

the fabric of law. Discretion exists by virtue of legal rules, and may be directed by objective standards, retrieved through the application, interpretation or creation of legal rules.[19] As such, discretion originates from law and may only be detected therein. Whether to pick a Martini or a Sherry, as Hart aptly put it, is a matter of personal preference and whim rather than an exercise of discretion based on fixed standards of decision-making.[20] Galligan argues along similar lines, holding that discretion should not merely resemble a choice between options, but a choice 'for good reasons'.[21] Discretion is thus understood as a degree of deliberative freedom, but one that exists by virtue and under the instruction of law.

This view, which may be termed the 'original thesis', raises two questions. Which norms give rise to discretion? And when may standards guiding discretion qualify as 'objective'? With a view to the first question, it is commonly agreed in the literature that, if discretion may be said to exist by virtue of legal rules, it arises in the application thereof.[22] There are, however, different perceptions as to when such application of norms provides for discretion. On the one hand, it has been argued that discretion arises in the interpretation of decision-making standards to put them into practice in a specific situation. In Dworkin's influential work, this qualifies as a 'weaker sense' of discretion,[23] which is contrasted, on the other hand, with a 'strong sense' of discretion, whereby a decision-maker is to develop standards of deliberation for her- or himself.[24]

With a view to the question of which standards may be considered as 'objective' in guiding discretionary decision-making, a prominent response focuses on legal principles guiding discretion.[25] As legal standards, they may outline to what ends discretion should be exercised or indicate the interests to be considered in the pursuit of the public interest.[26] Galligan equally accepts extra-legal standards as 'objective' guidance to the exercise of discretion, such as moral outlooks of decision-makers.[27] Routinely, however, it is flatly rejected that such moral standards may form standards guiding the exercise of discretion, insofar as they have not made their way into codified law. In this context, it must be borne in mind that the perception of standards as legal or non-legal does not easily lend itself to universally shared conclusions. Some authors rally for the pertinence of rationality in discretionary decision-making, others focus on precedents as binding authority

[19] See Brand (n 7) 219. Hart and Dworkin seem to agree on that point; see HLA Hart, 'Discretion' (1956) 127 *Harvard Law Review* 652, 657; Dworkin (n 8) 68 ff.

[20] The illustrative example is originally given by Hart (n 19) 657.

[21] Galligan (n 2) 7.

[22] See Hawkins, *The Uses of Discretion* (n 9) 11 ff.

[23] Dworkin (n 8) 31 ff.

[24] ibid; Galligan (n 2) 21.

[25] Prominently, for instance, see J Raz, 'Legal Principles and the Limits of Law' (1972) 81 *The Yale Law Journal* 823, 841.

[26] See MS Giannini, *Il Potere Discrezionale Della Pubblica Amministrazione: Concetto e Problemi* (Giuffrè, 1939) 74 ff. as referenced in J Mendes, 'Administrative Discretion in the EU: Comparative Perspectives' in S Rose-Ackerman, P Lindseth and B Emerson (eds), *Comparative Administrative Law* 2nd edn (Edgar Elgar, 2019).

[27] See Galligan (n 2) 31 ff.

in this context.[28] Whether the thus derived standards are perceived as law, however, will reflect the respective presumption of the authors and legal systems in question.

B. Discretion, Delegation and the Relative Authority of Executives

Discretion is occasionally said to exist irrespective of institutional context. Empirically, however, it is most frequently linked to the decision-making powers of *executive* actors.[29] In this vein, much of the analytical focus in theoretical discussions has been put on the form of delegation or empowerment through which discretion is afforded. For instance, Galligan notes that a central sense of discretion refers to powers 'delegated within a system of authority to an official or set of officials'.[30] This emphasis on the delegated nature of discretionary power highlights the significance of the institutional context in which discretion occurs. The existence and scope of discretion is largely influenced by the interaction of different branches of power. In this sense, it may be correct to note that attentional should be paid to the 'network of relationships' in which discretion occurs.[31]

The scope of discretionary power will routinely reflect the executive's authority in relation to other institutional actors. Discretionary powers are, in this vein, contingent on the decision-makers' 'relative authority'.[32] In this respect, discretion has most prominently been discussed through the bilateral relationship of administrative bodies and courts. This is perhaps most aptly articulated by Caranta who stipulates that 'discretion is what is left outside judicial control'.[33] Whereas historical developments in Europe may reasonably explain the inclination to honour the absence of judicial control as a *raison d'être* of discretion,[34] it appears to be analytically outmoded. As Mendes convincingly argues, a 'judicial paradigm' invites a degree of formalism that fails to do justice to the riches of phenomena relating to discretion.[35] In this respect, the act empowering an executive actor to exercise a measure of discretion is just as formative for the existence and scope of discretion

[28] For a discussion, see for instance, R Shiner, 'Precedent, Discretion and Fairness' in MA Stewart (ed), *Law, Morality and Rights* (Springer Science, 1983).

[29] For instance, see C Coglianese and CS Yoo, 'Introduction: The Bounds of Executive Discretion in the Regulatory State' (2016) 164 *University of Pennsylvania Law Review* 1587.

[30] Galligan (n 2) 21.

[31] T Evans and PL Hupe, 'Conceptualizing Discretion' in T Evans and PL Hupe (eds), *Discretion and the Quest for Controlled Freedom* (Palgrave Macmillan, 2020) 8.

[32] N Roughan, 'Polities and Relative Authorities' (2018) 16 *International Journal of Constitutional Law* 1215; J Mendes and I Venzke, 'Introducing the Idea of Relative Authority' in J Mendes and I Venzke (eds), *Allocating Authority: Who Should Do What in European and International Law?* (Hart, 2018).

[33] Caranta (n 1) 185.

[34] See, amongst others, D Ritleng, 'Judicial Review of EU Administrative Discretion: How Far Does the Separation of Powers Matter?' in J Mendes and I Venzke (eds), *Allocating Authority: Who Should Do What in European and International Law?* (Hart, 2018) 184, with further references, particularly relating to French law.

[35] Mendes, 'Administrative Discretion in the EU: Comparative Perspectives' (n 26) 641.

as the way in which judges control it. Accordingly, it seems correct to note that the institutional context in which discretion arises should be considered as tri- rather than bilateral, involving all three branches of public power.[36]

Against this backdrop, one may reflect on the argumentative resources that may support the delegation of discretionary powers to executive actors. Democratic systems generally accept direct responsiveness to the electorate as a justification for wide margins of discretion. In a presidential system, for instance, a directly elected president may be entrusted with wide decision-making powers.[37] However, a similar conclusion may not be drawn with respect to executive bodies that are relatively detached from expressions of democratic will. Instead, in such a constellation, the delegation of discretionary powers to executive actors may be justified by more functional considerations. Frequently, this include the degree of expertise that is presumed to be available exclusively in specialised institutional bodies.[38] Likewise, awards of discretionary powers may be justified by the need to adapt the exercise of public power to the specificities of the individual case.[39]

This suggests that the existence and scope of discretionary power vested in executive actors correlates with the authority that the latter hold vis-á-vis lawmakers and courts. Although it may not be inconceivable to conceptually present discretion as a uniform phenomenon that affects all branches of public power alike, it is more commonly considered in relation to the authority vested in executive actors by other branches of power.

C. Discretion, Legality and Judicial Review

In the formation of discretion as a contemporary phenomenon, the role of courts cannot be overestimated.[40] Judicial interventions have been formative in establishing discretion as a form of 'controlled freedom'.[41] Courts have gradually subjugated discretion to standards of review, thereby giving effect to the limits of legality that circumscribe executive decision-making power. Conceptually, however, this has occasionally given rise to accounts that present discretion primarily as a phenomenon shaped by judicial control.[42] As rightly highlighted by Mendes, such a judicial paradigm may not accurately encapsulate the interaction of discretion, legality and judicial control.[43] This argument centres on the assertion that the application of

[36] See M Wendel, *Verwaltungsermessen Als Mehrebenenproblem: Zur Verbundstruktur Administrativer Entscheidungsspielräume Am Beispiel Des Migrations- Und Regulierungsrechts* (Mohr Siebeck, 2019) 27.

[37] This example is given in PL Hupe and M Hill, 'Discretion in the Policy Process' in T Evans and PL Hupe (eds), *Discretion and the Quest for Controlled Freedom* (Palgrave Macmillan, 2020) 248.

[38] See M Luntley, 'Expertise and the Space for Discretion' in T Evans and PL Hupe (eds), *Discretion and the Quest for Controlled Freedom* (Palgrave Macmillan, 2020).

[39] See PL Hupe and T Evans, 'Discretion in Governance: An Introduction' in T Evans and PL Hupe (eds), *Discretion and the Quest for Controlled Freedom* (Palgrave Macmillan, 2020) 214.

[40] See Mascini (n 10) 123.

[41] See Hupe and Evans (n 11) 410.

[42] See Caranta (n 1) 185.

[43] See above s II.A.ii.

a norm by the decision-maker, and control thereof, are two distinct processes. Accordingly, the decision-maker is obliged, in the first place, to interpret legal standards to apply them to a specific situation and, in doing so, exercise discretion. Judicial control may then follow as a second step.[44]

If discretion is to be perceived as free choice among legally equivalent options, it can be presumed that judicial control is to merely verify the lawfulness of the decision taken. No more no less. In such a situation, judges will explore the limits of lawful discretionary conduct and withhold from articulating themselves on the probity of the decision. In this sense, their role resembles that of a soccer referee: they intervene whenever rules are violated but do not instruct players on how to play.[45] On the contrary, if standards of law outline a specific purpose for which discretion has been awarded or legal principles indicate the way it is to be exercised, judges may verify whether these standards of legality have been respected.

While legality thus guides the control of discretion as a ground for review, it may not necessarily determine the intensity of judicial control. When faced with discretionary decision-making, judges often devise strategies of limited review, to the effect that they may merely sanction 'manifest' or 'unreasonable' decisions.[46] Whether judges opt for a strategy of limited or rather intensive control may be determined by positive legal specifications to that end. In the absence thereof, however, strategies of judicial control are routinely reflective of the relative authority attributed to the initial decision-maker and the controlling court, respectively.

In line with the assumption that discretion operates against the backdrop of institutions' relative authority, the intensity of judicial control may thus be dependent on the institutional context. Courts tend to exercise limited review if they consider another authority to be better placed to take a decision in substance. For instance, courts may adopt strategies of limited review if a decision entails a high degree of complexity, and the executive decision-maker may be best placed, by virtue of her or his expertise, to master that complexity.

D. Conceptual Allocation of Discretion in the Decision-Making Process

In legal theory, accounts of discretion tend to link discretion to specific stages of decision-making. For example, decision-makers may be said to exercise a degree of cognitive autonomy in the finding and appraising of facts, or in casting those facts

[44] See Mendes, 'Administrative Discretion in the EU: Comparative Perspectives' (n 26) 642. For pioneering work in relation to the German legal system, see K Stern, *Ermessen Und Unzulässige Ermessensausübung: Eine Analyse Der Subjektiven Und Objektiven Elemente* (Duncker & Humblot, 1964) 11.

[45] For this illustrative characterisation, see J Parchomiuk, 'Abuse of Discretionary Powers in Administrative Law. Evolution of the Judicial Review Models: From "Administrative Morality" to the Principle of Proportionality' (2018) 26 *Časopis pro právní vědu a praxi* 453, 476.

[46] For an overview of forms of limited judicial review, see Caranta (n 1) 187 ff.

in terms of categories of law.[47] As Galligan notes, however, it is rather uncommon to speak of discretion in this regard. Instead, he posits the view that a 'central sense' of discretion relates to a degree of autonomy in settling the standards for a decision to be taken.[48] In this vein, public officials may be authorised to choose among various courses of action or decide how a legal category may be understood.

This points to an important distinction. Decision-makers may have a measure of deliberative freedom on various accounts, including in settling facts or attributing them to categories of law. It would be unusual, however, to speak of discretion in this regard. Rather, discretion is analytically allocated at specific stages of decision-making. Theoretical accounts presume that discretion occurs exclusively in the context of choices between lawful courses of action, or more comprehensively, at any of the component stages of administrative decision-making. Analytical precision demands attention to this allocation of discretion. Does the term relate to a specific effort in the decision-making process, or is it used rather indifferently, comprising decision-making in its entirety?

Against this background, it should be borne in mind that such distinctions are analytical in nature. Decision-making processes, however, are not synthetic. For this reason, it should be questioned whether, in practice, the thought-processes underpinning decision-making could be surgically dissected in such a way. Facts may be selected and framed in such a way that a public official may exercise deliberative freedom in laying down the standards that guide the deliberation.[49] Yet, this leeway may often not be viewed as discretion. Rather, discretion is often conceptually attributed to specific moments of deliberative freedom other than the finding of facts.

E. Interim Conclusion

The preceding section illustrates that the significant 'conceptual confusion'[50] surrounding the term discretion may be reduced but not ultimately resolved from the angle of legal theory. Efforts that seek to create a universally shared definition of discretion are thus of no avail. Different schools of thought treat discretion on their own terms, to the effect that no uniform understanding may emerge from these considerations. However, the conceptual contours of discretion are not obscured in their entirety. From the perspective of legal theory, at least three aspects may be said to be frequently associated with discretion as a legal phenomenon. For the purposes of the following investigation, this allows for a first conceptual approximation to discretion as a legal phenomenon.

[47] See Galligan (n 2) 33 ff.

[48] See ibid 21 ff.

[49] This effect may be witnessed in relation to EU asylum law, which affords migration authorities significant decision-making freedom which is not, however, analytically be viewed as discretion, see below at ch 3, s IV.A.

[50] van Roermund (n 5) 316.

In the first place, theoretical conceptions of discretion largely agree that discretion resonates with some form of deliberative autonomy. Perceptions, however, differ regarding the type of judgement said to underly this autonomy. While some theoretical accounts of discretion view with indifference the exact processes that give rise thereto, discretion is frequently associated either with choosing a course of action, interpreting indefinite legal terms or appraising various interests for the purpose of putting them into relation in a specific situation. In addition, it is conceivable (although uncommon) to presume discretion to feature in the appraisal of facts. While discretion may therefore be inherently linked to deliberative autonomy, this suggests that, in legal theory, there is no unambiguous indications as to whether the exercise of discretion should imply an act of volition, such as choosing among courses of action, a cognitive effort in appraising certain facts or feasible interpretations of law, or both, volitive and cognitive efforts combined.[51]

In the second place, it is worth noticing that the theoretical accounts explored above view discretion as a *legal* phenomenon. As such, it is linked, in one way or another, to manifestations in law. The precise relationship of discretion and law, however, is strongly contested in legal theory. Whereas discretion may occasionally be defined as a category residual to the latter, most theoretical conceptions thereof depict discretion as a phenomenon arising in the application of norms. Accordingly, it may be safely presumed that discretion – as a sphere of deliberative autonomy – materialises in relation to certain standards of legality, even though it may not be evident, at least from a theoretical angle, whether this may relate to authorisations, limitations or instructions in law.

In the third place, discretion may characteristically imply that a deliberation is not superseded in substance by another institution. Most tangibly, this is reflected in the fact that accounts in legal theory tend to agree that the exercise of discretion creates repercussions for judicial control. There seems to be agreement that the role of courts is effectively limited in this regard. This has heartened the argument that 'discretion is what is left outside judicial control'.[52] Although such a view sketches a lopsided portray, it is true that strategies of limited judicial control may furnish proof of the existence of discretion.[53]

II. Traditions of Discretion in European Administrative Law

Discretion may be said to bring to the fore some of the most fundamental characteristics of a legal system. Where should the limits to executive power lie? Which entity may be expected to legitimately wield decision-making power? And how

[51] On this effect, see J Mendes, 'Bounded Discretion in EU Law: A Limited Judicial Paradigm in a Changing EU' (2017) 80 *The Modern Law Review* 443, 458.

[52] Caranta (n 1) 185.

[53] Similarly also Galligan (n 2) 13 ff.

should it be controlled by courts? Like a burning lens, conceptions of administrative discretion focalise a legal system's emblematic responses to these questions. It is thus not surprising that discretion has been a key object of comparative inquiries into administrative systems in Europe.[54]

These comparative accounts suggest that conceptions of discretionary power trend similar legal designs, although the specific understandings thereof remain tethered to the legal system in which they arise. As a corollary, conceptions of discretion remain relatively impervious to influences of alien legal systems, and thus, to convergence. Early on, Schwarze highlighted that administrative legal arrangements 'prove resistant to change and will hamper efforts to achieve convergence among the various administrative rules' in Europe.[55] This finding does not categorically rule out convergence between legal arrangements of administrative law, but fleshes out a presumption that comparative administrative law operates against the background of similar, but not identical, conceptions of discretion.[56] Even where legal arrangements reify a high degree of formal similarity, divergent legal effects may result from context – that is, the syntax into which a norm is embedded and from which it cannot be unlaced.[57] Scholarly negligence of, or insensitivity to the persistence and vitality of distinct conceptions of discretionary power would run the risk of advancing universalism where there is none.[58]

This conceptual diversity has analytical bearings for the investigation that follows. With a view to an investigation focusing on discretionary powers in multiple European administrative systems, it may be questioned which instances of administrative power should be viewed as such, and for which reasons so. The following section therefore sets out to respond to this question by exploring and contrasting different conceptions of discretion in administrative systems in Europe. By doing so, it carries out a 'complex interconnection task',[59] linking conceptions to discretionary power in national legal systems to discretion as a broader legal phenomenon. Unlike mere descriptive portrays, it explores multiple conceptions

[54] Among the rich body of comparative literature concerning administrative discretion, pioneering works include Schwarze (n 1) 294 ff.; R Brinktrine, *Verwaltungsermessen in Deutschland Und England: Eine Rechtsvergleichende Untersuchung von Entscheidungsspielräumen Der Verwaltung Im Deutschen Und Englischen Verwaltungsrecht* (CF Müller, 1998).

[55] Schwarze (n 1) 294 ff.

[56] See M Ruffert, 'Europäisierung Des Verwaltungsrechts' in A Bogdandy, S Cassese and PM Huber (eds), *Handbuch Ius Publicum Europaeum.: Band V: Verwaltungsrecht in Europa: Grundzüge* (CF Müller, 2014) 1237.

[57] A phenomenon that is well-known in comparative law, see P Müller-Graff, 'Modern Comparative Law: The Forces behind and the Challenges Ahead in the Age of Transnational Harmonisation' in A Bakardjieva Engelbrekt and J Nergelius (eds), *New Directions in Comparative Law* (Edward Elgar, 2009) 262; J Husa, 'The Truth Is Out There? Legal Pluralism and the Language-Game' in SP Donlan and L Heckendorn Urscheler (eds), *Concepts of Law. Comparative, Jurisprudential, and Social Science Perspectives* (Routledge, 2014) 76.

[58] See similarly C Schönberger, 'Verwaltungsrechtsvergleichung: Eigenheiten, Methoden Und Geschichte' in A Bogdandy, S Cassese and PM Huber (eds), *Handbuch Ius Publicum Europaeum: Band IV: Verwaltungsrecht in Europa: Wissenschaft* (CF Müller, 2014) 538.

[59] M Fehling, 'Rechtsvergleichende Methode Und Europäisches Verwaltungsrecht' (2016) 1 *Europarecht* 59, 77 (translated from the original: 'komplexe … Vernetzungsaufgabe').

of discretionary power deductively, that is, through the lens of a theoretical account of this abstract phenomenon developed in the preceding subsection.[60]

The following analysis will treat 'traditions of administrative discretion' as units of analysis. As such, it does not limit itself to comparing specific statutory provisions of various legal systems. Instead, it acknowledges that perceptions of discretion may equally be the result of scholarly work[61] or ongoing public debates. Reference to tradition, in this regard, serves as an analytical workaround. It permits the comparison of prevalent perceptions of administrative discretion in various legal systems, without insinuating that those perceptions need necessarily figure in legal provisions. In this respect, it should be acknowledged that conceptions of discretion are by no means static, perfectly insular perceptions during a time immemorial. Rather, a tradition of discretion is subject to continuous debate and therefore may not permeate a legal system monolithically or in an uncontested fashion. Perceptions of discretion may moreover differ from one substantive field of law to another or undergo reform.[62] Reference to traditions of discretion is neither intended to provide a historical account, nor carry out a discourse analysis on diverging conceptions of discretion but merely utilises the term 'tradition' as an analytical tool.

The analysis that follows will essentially premise on the elements that are routinely associated with discretion in theoretical discussions. In this respect, European administrative legal systems tend to agree that discretion coincides with a degree of deliberative autonomy (subsection A) that materialise in one way or another in structures of law (subsection B) and that is not, in substance, superseded by other actors, especially, courts (subsection C).

A. Deliberative Autonomy

In theoretical discussions, discretion is usually associated with a degree of deliberative autonomy. Empirically, however, the proclivity of legal systems to afford such deliberative freedom varies greatly. Some traditions of discretionary power conceptualise discretionary decision-making as a relatively exceptional and rare encounter, while others endorse it as the default mode of administrative decision-making (subsection i). In administrative systems in Europe, conceptions of discretion moreover differ in relation to the thought-processes that are said to underly deliberative autonomy. The considerations that are at the core of this autonomy may be allocated in different context of decision-making (subsection ii).

[60] See above at s I.E.

[61] This is particularly the case for the French term *pouvoir discrétionnaire*; see Grabenwarter (n 1) 1023.

[62] See JB Auby, 'The Transformation of the Administrative State and Administrative Law' in S Cassese, A Bogdandy and P Huber (eds), *The Max Planck Handbooks in European Public Law: Volume I: The Administrative State* (Oxford University Press, 2017) 611 ff.

i. Discretiophobia or Discretiophoria?

In administrative systems in Europe, conceptions of discretion coincide with the degree of trust vested in administrative authorities in the respective society in which it is to take effect. As such, it is reflective of the decision-maker's relative authority.[63] A society that views bureaucratic institutions rather favourably is more likely to accept extensive discretionary powers than one in which administrative deliberation is generally met with distrust. Accordingly, national traditions tend to reflect that legitimacy assets that administrations have in their respective societies.[64]

This effect can be aptly exemplified by way of contrasting the German tradition of discretionary power which is marked by normative suspicion vis-á-vis administrative freedom with other traditions that view discretion more favourably. The German tradition of discretionary power is largely reflective of historical experiences of totalitarianism and misuse of administrative power. This has catered to a sentiment of general mistrust in relation to administrative autonomy generally, and administrative discretion particularly.[65] The German constitution, the Basic Law, normatively mirrors this suspicion. Under Article 20 paragraph 3 Basic Law, both the executive and the judiciary are tied to 'law and justice' (in German: Gesetz und Recht), effectively confirming superiority of law over any administrative conduct and instituting a caveat to act only by virtue of law.[66] Additionally, Article 19 paragraph 4 Basic Law warrants effective legal protection for any person whose rights be violated by public authority, thus enshrining a predisposition in favour of judicial control of administrative decision-making.[67] Against this backdrop, Sachs had argued that the German legal order is indeed marked by 'discretiophobia' – a sense of general discomfort regarding deliberative administrative freedom.[68]

Unlike the German tradition of discretion, other traditions of administrative discretion are much more willing to acknowledge the functional benefits of discretionary power. Above all, this holds true for the French tradition of discretion, which rests on the premise that public authorities should principally be equipped with the flexibility necessary to pursue the *intérêt général*.[69] Accordingly, the

[63] For this notion, see above at s I.B and Mendes and Venzke (n 32) 3 ff.

[64] On this point, see N Garoupa and J Mathews, 'Strategic Delegation, Discretion, and Deference: Explaining the Comparative Law of Administrative Review' (2014) 62 *The American Journal of Comparative Law* 1.

[65] See M Bullinger, 'Das Ermessen Der Öffentlichen Verwaltung: Entwicklung, Funktionen, Gerichtskontrolle' (1984) 39 *JuristenZeitung* 1001, 1001 ff.

[66] See M Jestaedt, 'Maßstäbe Des Verwaltungshandelns' in D Ehlers and H Pünder (eds), *Allgemeines Verwaltungsrecht* 15th edn (De Gruyter, 2016) paras 5 ff.

[67] See E Schmidt-Aßmann, 'GG Art. 19 Abs. 4' in R Herzog et al (eds), *Grundgesetz: Kommentar*, vol 88 (CH Beck, 2019) para 180.

[68] Aptly, M Sachs, '§ 40 Ermessen' in P Stelkens, H Joachim Bonk and M Sachs (eds), *VwVfG Verwaltungsverfahrensgesetz: Kommentar* 8th edn (CH Beck, 2014) para 17.

[69] As stipulated by the Code des relations entre le public et l'administration, art L. 100-2 (2015): 'L'administration agit dans l'intérêt general et respecte le principe de légalité. …'; see D Truchet, *Les Fonctions de La Notion d'intérêt Général Dans La Jurisprudence Du Conseil d'état* (Pichon et Durand-Auzias, 1977) 87 ff.

French tradition of discretion makes a virtue of necessity. Administrative authorities must have the power to flexibly adapt their decisions to the specificities of each individual case at hand.[70] Legal provisions should afford the degree of discretion that is needed to that end.[71]

A similar stance may be detected in the English legal system. In this context, discretionary power is considered the principal normative feature to allow for deliberative freedom in administrative action. It must be authorised either by statutory law or, occasionally, by common law.[72] Whereas the former owes its legitimacy to parliamentary authorisation, the latter is a 'royal prerogative' and thus lends its authority from the crown.[73] Besides, the exercise of administrative discretion is subject to the rule of law. The relegation to either parliamentary or royal sources of legitimacy strengthens the legitimacy of administrative authority in the English legal system, underlining the idea of government as trust.[74] Whereas 'unfettered governmental discretion is a contradiction in terms',[75] administrations may be afforded relatively wide margins of discretionary power without compromising the legitimacy of their actions.

This suggests that a general sentiment of discretiophobia is not shared among European traditions of discretionary power beyond the German example. On the flipside, however, this need not mean that other legal systems would indulge in 'discretiophoria' to the effect that broad discretionary powers would be welcomed on any occasion and at any price. The English tradition of discretion, for instance, adopts a rather sedate approach. The administrative flexibility that discretion embodies is viewed a necessity to put into practice parliamentary determinations to individual circumstances.[76] Accordingly, administrative autonomy is perceived of as a characteristic of legitimate individual decision-making. For that reason, it can be presumed that the legislature will routinely acknowledge the necessity of affording administrative discretion, drafting reticent standards guiding administrative power to that end.

ii. Types of Deliberations and Normative Allocations of Discretion

Theoretical conceptions largely agree that discretion resonates with some form of deliberative autonomy. However, traditions of discretion in administrative systems in Europe differ with respect to the type of judgement that is said to underly this

[70] See R Grote, 'Ermessenslehre Und Ermessenspraxis in Frankreich' (1986) *Neue Zeitschrift für Verwaltungsrecht* 269, 270.

[71] See R Chapus, *Droit Administratif Général* 15th edn (Montchrestien, 2001) 1056.

[72] See Brinktrine (n 54) 182 ff; 258 ff.

[73] Influentially, Dicey defined the prerogative as 'the remaining portion of the Crown's original authority' and therefore as 'the residue of discretionary power left at any moment in the hands of the Crown', cited in House of Lords, UKHL 9 (22 November 1984), *Council of Civil Service Unions v Minister for the Civil Service*.

[74] See T von Danwitz, *Europäisches Verwaltungsrecht* (Springer, 2008) 48.

[75] Grey (n 8) 121.

[76] See von Danwitz (n 74) 35 ff.

autonomy. While some theoretical accounts of discretion view with indifference the exact processes that give rise thereto, discretion is frequently associated either with choosing a course of action, interpreting indefinite legal terms or appraising various interests for the purpose of putting them into relation in a specific situation. In addition, it is conceivable (although uncommon) to presume that discretion occurs in the appraisal of facts.

The French tradition of discretion, for example, rejects the idea that discretion could relate to the establishing of facts, respect for procedural rules or correctness in the reading of the law. Although all these instances may indeed engender a degree of cognitive freedom, they conceptually do not correspond with discretion in the French tradition thereof. Conversely, *pouvoir discrétionnaire* occurs in instances where an administrator is tasked to put into relation certain preliminary conditions for a decision to be taken with the substance of that decision.[77]

The question of allocating discretion in the decision-making process has been a prominent topos in some administrative systems in Europe. The German tradition, for instance, maintains that a distinction should be made between discretion proper, that is, *Ermessen*, and *Beurteilungsspielräume*. *Ermessen*, on the one hand, is a type of discretion that awards the decision-maker a choice among various courses of action once certain conditions are met (which is referred to as *Rechtsfolge*).[78] *Beurteilungsspielräume*, on the other hand, may result from undetermined legal terms that feature in the context of preconditions for administrative action, the so-called *Tatbestandsseite*. A similar distinction exists in Polish administrative law, which allocates discretionary power in a specific logical moment of decision-making, namely in the choice of legal consequences authorised by higher law.[79]

Other traditions of discretionary power may have difficulties to conceptually allocate discretion in the decision-making process. In relation to the concept of discretion in English law, academic contributions merely describe discretion as 'choice', without specifying whether this relates to the appraisal of certain facts, interpretation of vaguely-termed norms or choice of courses of action.[80] Galligan endorses this definition, adding that such choice must be a rational one, namely one that is based on 'good reasons'.[81] In his view, it is irrelevant whether discretionary power results from cognitive freedom in factual appraisals, in the interpretation of laws, in correlating one to another or in choosing a course of action. All these deliberative moments may engender choice, and hence, discretion. However, the fact remains that discretion, in its English tradition, 'is not a precise term of the

[77] See P Chrétien, N Chifflot and M Tourbe, *Droit Administratif* (Dalloz, 2018) 800; Y Gaudemet, *Droit Administratif* 21st edn (Librairie générale de droit et de jurisprudence, 2015) 123 ff.

[78] § 40 Verwaltungsverfahrensgesetz (VwVfg), BGBI I 1976, § 40. See for a comprehensive analysis of *Ermessen*, L Rode, *§ 40 VwVfG Und Die Deutsche Ermessenslehre* (Peter Lang, 2003).

[79] This characterisation essentially rests on a perception proposed by Mincer in 1983, which continues to exert influence on the Polish tradition of administrative discretion to the present day, and which in return reproduces the conception prevalent in German law, see M Mincer, *Uznanie Administracyjne* (1983) 63 ff.

[80] See Brinktrine (n 54) 272, with further references.

[81] Galligan (n 2) 7.

art', as Galligan emphasises.[82] Conversely, another view stipulates that, principally, discretion neither exists in questions of law nor in questions of fact, but rather in the merits of a decision,[83] an understanding that bears a strong resemblance with the conceptual allocation of discretion in its French tradition.

All this suggests that discretion is inherently linked to deliberative autonomy, but that, in administrative systems in Europe, there are different views as to whether the exercise of discretion should imply an act of volition, such as choosing among courses of action, a cognitive effort in appraising certain facts or feasible interpretations of law, or both, volitive and cognitive efforts combined.[84] This difference is aptly illustrated in the Italian tradition of discretion. In this context, discretion – *discrezionalità* – is perceived as a measure of choice in conciliating public and private interests in a specific situation.[85] The balance struck with individual interests will vary according to the circumstances of each individual situation, since the interplay of interests may not be generally determined in advance. The choice left to the decision-maker in this instance constitutes a value judgement.[86]

Discretionary power in considering conflicting interests is to be distinguished from technical evaluations (which are routinely and misleadingly termed technical discretion).[87] In this view, factual complexity does not give rise to discretion, whereas conflicting interests do. Technical evaluations concern the establishment and qualification of facts by virtue of scientific assessments.[88] Although these assessments allow for a degree of cognitive freedom, they differ conceptually from discretionary power, as they do not imply acts of volition. Mendes highlights that, in the influential works of Giannini, the exercise of discretion requires both cognition and volition.[89] It rests on cognition in so far as the decision-maker must understand and establish the interplay of various conflicting interests. Volition characterises the process of attributing certain weight to each of those interests to reconcile them with a view to an individual case.[90]

B. Manifestations in Law

The prevalence of discretion in administrative systems in Europe is largely conditioned by the degree of trust vested in administrative authority. This trust,

[82] ibid 54.
[83] See Brinktrine (n 54) 211, 276.
[84] On this effect, see Mendes, 'Bounded Discretion in EU Law: A Limited Judicial Paradigm in a Changing EU' (n 51) 458.
[85] See Giannini (n 26) 74 ff; Caranta (n 1) 191 ff.
[86] See Mendes, 'Bounded Discretion in EU Law: A Limited Judicial Paradigm in a Changing EU' (n 51) 457, with further references.
[87] See Caranta (n 1) 191.
[88] See Giannini (n 26) 42 ff.
[89] See Mendes, 'Bounded Discretion in EU Law: A Limited Judicial Paradigm in a Changing EU' (n 51) 458.
[90] See ibid.

however, does not result from starry-eyed naivety. Rather, it is preconditioned by mechanisms that correct, constrain and remedy practices viewed as imprudent. In Europe, one of the principal rationales for accepting discretion as a legitimate means of wielding power stems from the superiority of law and its capacity to constrain administrative action.[91] Accordingly, manifestations of discretionary power in law may be viewed as the second property that is routinely associated with discretionary power on a theoretical level.

The way that discretionary power and law interact, however, is strongly disputed in theoretical discussions and, correspondingly, administrative systems in Europe adopt different positions on this point. A first matter of contestation concerns the question in how far discretion needs to be explicitly or implicitly authorised by law. It is a prominent trait of German administrative law that discretion must always be linked to some form of normative authorisation.[92] Other legal systems adopt a similar position, presuming that discretion should be authorised or delegated, in one way or another, by structures of law. Still, disagreement exists on the question whether such authorisations may equally transpire implicitly in statutory norms. While Polish administrative law would reject the notion of implicit authorisations altogether,[93] other traditions would routinely accept that certain formulations in statutory norms speak to an authorisation of discretion. Terms such as 'can', 'may' or 'is authorised to' can be viewed as indications that lawmakers wanted to afford a measure of discretion to administrators. This view tallies with the argument raised by Galligan, who suggests that discretion can be identified where the structure of a norm is marked by 'a relative absence of guiding standards, accompanied by the inference, whether express or implied, that it is for the authority to establish its own'.[94]

Moreover, administrative systems in Europe commonly agree that discretionary conduct must respect the pertinent standards of legality that constrain administrative conduct. These standards broadly include constitutional and parliamentary law, by-laws, international agreements, supra- and international laws[95] as well as general principles of law, essentially all exigencies that lawful administrative conduct entails.[96] While '[p]rocedural and substantive policies and guidelines, bureaucratic culture, and "unwritten rules" may tangibly influence the exercise of

[91] For this effect, see L Azoulai and L Clément-Wilz, 'Le Principe de Légalité' in JB Auby and J Dutheil de la Rochère (eds), *Traité de Droit Administratif Européen* 2nd edn (Bruylant, 2014) 546.

[92] An approach most aptly termed 'Normative Ermächtigungslehre'; see particularly E Schmidt-Aßmann, *Das Allgemeine Verwaltungsrecht Als Ordnungsidee: Grundlagen Und Aufgaben Der Verwaltu ngsrechtlichen Systembildung* 2nd edn (Springer, 2006) 207 ff; E Pache, *Tatbestandliche Abwägung Und Beurteilungsspielräume* (Mohr Siebeck, 2001) 72 ff.

[93] See von Danwitz (n 74) 101.

[94] Galligan (n 2) 23.

[95] See generally on this point Jestaedt (n 66); M Verhoeven and R Widdershoven, 'National Legality and European Obligations' in L Besselink, F Pennings and S Prechal (eds), *The Eclipse of the Legality Principle in the European Union* (Wolters Kluwer, 2011) 56 ff.

[96] See Grabenwarter (n 1) 1022.

discretion', as Pottie and Sossin rightly acknowledge,[97] influences of such nature will be excluded from the investigation that follows, at least insofar as they do not feature in positive terms.

It is therefore commonplace among *legal* conceptions of discretion that the exercise thereof must be lawful. This is reflected in administrative systems throughout Europe. In Polish law, for example, the administration is obliged to act 'on the basis of, and within the limits of, the law'.[98] Similar constitutional arrangements exist in Germany and Italy.[99] Although the United Kingdom has no written constitution of that sort, limits of legality are firmly embedded in the rule of law. It is one of the core guarantees in this respect that administrative bodies are to respect the law. Accordingly, Lord Diplock, who influenced the English tradition of discretion in significant ways, included in his observations that discretion should denote a degree of choice among several *lawful* courses of action.[100]

Another aspect of conceptual importance relates to the role that legal principles play in the exercise of discretion. Legal theory suggests that discretion may be approached in one of two ways; either a priori, whereby discretion may be limited or nullified by legal principles, or a posteriori, whereby discretion is said to exist once all pertinent standards of law, including legal principles, have been applied to the specific situation at hand and leave a measure of autonomy to the decision-maker.[101] In the former view, discretion constitutes a variable feature, which may be limited or nullified by standards of law. In the latter view, to the contrary, discretion is said to be a static object of examination.[102] Both these perceptions, however, highlight the significant repercussions that standards of legality exert on the exercise of discretionary power. Most, if not all, traditions of discretion examined accept that standards of legality may instruct the exercise of discretion.

Among the standards instructing the exercise of discretionary power, the principle of proportionality stands out. Although the rigour with which the principle of proportionality is applied varies significantly, administrative traditions in Europe frequently view it as one of the pivotal standards instructing the exercise of discretion.[103] In this vein, it approximates traditions of discretion in Europe.[104] Conceptually, however, the way that the principle of proportionality is deemed to

[97] L Pottie and L Sossin, 'Demystifying the Boundaries of Public Law: Policy, Discretion, and Social Welfare' (2005) 28 *University of Columbia Law Review* 147, 162.

[98] Non-official translation of Article 7 Konstytucja Rzeczypospolitej Polskiej z dnia 2 kwietnia 1997 r. [Constitution] art. 7 (Poland), available via www.sejm.gov.pl/prawo/konst/angielski/kon1.htm. This premise is reiterated by Kodeks postępowania administracyjnego [Code of Administrative Procedures] 14 June, 1960, art. 6 (Poland).

[99] For the former, see above at s II.A.i and for the latter, see the unofficial English translation of Art 23 of the Italian Constitution, which stipulates that '[n]o obligation of a personal or financial nature may be imposed on any person except by law'. Constituzione della Repubblica Italiana (1948) art 23 (IT).

[100] *Council of Civil Service Unions v Minister for the Civil Service* [1984] UKHL 9 (HL).

[101] See above at s I.A.i.

[102] For that distinction, see Mascini (n 10) 123.

[103] See S Ranchordás and B Waard, 'Concluding Remarks' in S Ranchordás and B Waard (eds), *The Judge and the Proportionate Use of Discretion: A Comparative Study* (Routledge, 2016) 193.

[104] See insightfully on this point, Wendel (n 36) 44.

instruct the exercise of discretion may differ, depending on the respective tradition thereof.

In the German legal system, the principle of proportionality instructs administrative decision-making comprehensively and is thus not limited to situations involving discretion. Along the lines of a four-pronged test, the principle ordains that a measure pursues a legitimate objective, is capable of pursuing said objective, that there are no less onerous means of equally achieving that objective and proportionality *sensu stricto*, meaning that an overall assessment of purpose of action and its repercussions reasonably relate to each other.[105] With a view to the exercise of administrative discretion, the principle of proportionality in German law corroborates that the purpose for which an administrative decision was adopted indeed corresponded to the objective of authorisation.[106] In addition, proportionality *sensu stricto* may implicate on administrative decision-makers a requirement to appraise and balance various interests.[107] In this vein, the principle of proportionality can render several courses of action unlawful or even nullify discretion altogether.[108]

Proportionality, as coined in German law, has moreover inspired the emergence of similarly structured normative standards in other legal systems in Europe. In Polish law, for instance, the principle of proportionality duplicates the test prevalent in German law and accordingly affects administrative decision-making in a similar vein.[109] In French law, the *principe de proportionnalité* plays an equally important role in constraining administrative discretion. It renders administrative decisions unlawful if these decisions are inadequate in light of the individual situation and the objective pursued, or – in other words – where cost-benefits are vastly out of proportion.[110]

In contrast to the legal systems in Germany, Poland and France, proportionality constitutes a less prominent (or at least less visible) standard of guidance in other traditions of discretion in Europe. Although proportionality did not figure explicitly in Italian administrative law until rather recently,[111] it may be argued that the principle was implicitly acknowledged all along. Conceptually, Italian administrative law centres on the balancing of conflicting interests, which may be viewed as a standard of proportionality in the strict sense of the term.[112] Accordingly,

[105] For an overview, see amongst others N Marsch and V Tünsmeyer, 'The Principle of Proportionality in German Administrative Law' in S Ranchordás and B Waard (eds), *The Judge and the Proportionate Use of Discretion: A Comparative Study* (Routledge, 2016) 30 ff.

[106] See M Aschke, '§ 40 VwVfG' in J Bader and M Ronellenfitsch (eds), *BeckOK VwVfG* (CH Beck, 2019) para 55.

[107] With a reference to balancing deficits ('Abwägungsdefizite'), see R Alexy, 'Ermessensfehler' (1986) 41 *JuristenZeitung* 701, 711.

[108] See Marsch and Tünsmeyer (n 105) 22, with further references.

[109] See already Wyrok [judgment] TK [Tribunał Konstytucyjny] z [of] January 26, 1993, U 10/92 OTK 1993 (1 p 32).

[110] See Chrétien, Chifflot and Tourbe (n 77) 800.

[111] See DU Galetta, 'Le Principe de Proportionnalité' in JB Auby and J Dutheil de la Rochère (eds), *Traité de Droit Administratif Européen* 2nd edn (Bruylant, 2014) 517.

[112] For this view, see already D Pretis, 'Grundzüge Des Verwaltungsrechts in Gemeineuropäischer Perspektive: Italien' in A Bogdandy, S Cassese and PM Huber (eds), *Handbuch Ius Publicum Europaeum.: Band V: Verwaltungsrecht in Europa: Grundzüge* (CF Müller, 2014) 426.

proportionality affects the very process of balancing conflicting interests, which constitutes the type of judgement conceptually underpinning the exercise of discretionary power in Italian law.

Moreover, the principle of proportionality has famously remained an outlier in the English tradition of discretion. Ever since it 'knocked on the door' of common law countries, mainly in the guise of European law, proportionality caused intense debates about appropriate administrative decision-making.[113] Accordingly, different perceptions persist as to whether the principle of proportionality should be viewed as a standard delimiting the exercise of discretionary powers. These views range from denial of the proportionality principle's existence as a ground of review to its implicit inherence in standards of rationality or the stipulation that it has been transplanted into the English legal system, at least within the field of applicability of the general principles of Union law,[114] prior to the UK's withdrawal from the EU.

C. Limited Judicial Review

Probably the most tangible and thoroughly explored element associated with discretionary power concerns the intensity of judicial review.[115] On the one hand, this has catered to a lopsided portray of discretion as a phenomenon fleshed out primarily by judicial control, or rather, a lack thereof. As the preceding explorations indicate, such a judicial paradigm does not appear to aptly reflect administrative reality. From the perspective of a diligent administrator, discretion is not simply a means to sidestep judicial control.[116] Rather, it imposes on the administrative decision-maker an intricate deliberation of the purpose of authorisation, on the legitimacy of its own actions, on standards of legality. On the other hand, however, there is no denying that strategies of judicial control have largely influenced traditions of discretion. Judicial attempts to extend control into the realms of previously unfettered executive powers have shaped the latter in significant ways.

Unlike methods of 'full' review, courts routinely employ 'limited' judicial control, to the effect that judges do not supersede the assessment of the initial decision-maker in substance. Such forms of limited control are said to furnish proof of the existence of discretion.[117] It precludes judges from superseding a discretionary assessment in substance. The intensity and nature of that control,

[113] A Barak, *Proportionality: Constitutional Rights and Their Limitations* (Cambridge University Press, 2012) 371 ff.

[114] See G de Búrca, 'Proportionality and Wednesbury Unreasonableness: The Influence of European Legal Concepts on UK Law' (1997) 3 *European Public Law* 561, 561; Brinktrine (n 54) 528 ff.

[115] See amongst others J Bell, 'Judicial Review in the Administrative State' in J de Poorter, E Hirsch Ballin and S Lavrijssen (eds), *Judicial Review of Administrative Discretion in the Administrative State* (TMC Asser Press, 2019) 15; Caranta (n 1).

[116] See Mendes, 'Administrative Discretion in the EU: Comparative Perspectives' (n 26) 641.

[117] See amongst others Galligan (n 2) 13 who stipulates that attitudes of those tasked to exercise control over administrative decision-making constitutes an elementary variable of discretion.

however, varies from one legal system to another. Specifically, administrative systems in Europe differ with respect to the rigour of 'limited' control (subsection i) and various legal mechanisms have been developed that preclude courts from deciding the substance of a discretionary assessment (subsection ii). Against this backdrop, it may be concluded that 'limited' review of discretion, unlike the notion of 'full' review, is subject to significant conceptual divergence among the traditions of discretion in Europe (subsection iii).

i. Varying Degrees of Reduced Intensity Review

Administrative systems in Europe routinely agree that discretionary power should coincide with a form of limited judicial review. Frequently, this assigns a rather marginal role to the reviewing court. In French administrative law, for instance, courts review discretionary decision-making by way of restraint control (*contrôle restreint*), requiring judges to merely verify the absence of manifest errors of appreciations (*erreurs manifestes d'appréciation*) when reviewing discretionary conduct.[118] Restraint control therefore embodies an avenue for marginal review, aimed generally at inflicting a minimum level of rationality on administrative decision-makers in the exercise of *pouvoir discrétionnaire*.[119]

In the English tradition of discretion, judicial review is restrained following to the so-called Wednesbury test.[120] This test aims at safeguarding the reasonability of discretionary decision-making. It was first coined by Lord Greene MR, who argued that a decision could be considered unreasonable if it was 'so absurd that no sensible person could ever dream that it lay within the powers of the authority'.[121] The test was equally put into practice with a view to the royal prerogative, with Lord Diplock coining the standard formula of Wednesbury unreasonableness test, stating that it 'applies to a decision which is so outrageous in its defiance of logic or of accepted moral standards that no sensible person who had applied his mind to the question to be decided could have arrived at it'.[122] Accordingly, Wednesbury unreasonableness fleshes out an abstentionist judicial attitude, tasking courts to merely intervene in administrative discretionary power in most extreme cases of administrative turpitude.[123]

Notwithstanding these traditions of restraint judicial control, it may be a jump to conclusions to presume that limited judicial control would always imply a marginal role for reviewing courts. Indeed, in several legal systems, courts have undertaken significant efforts to intensify their review of discretionary

[118] See D Lagasse, *L'Erreur Manifeste d'Appreciation en Droit Administratif: Essai sur les Limites du Pouvoir Discrétionnaire de l'Administration* (Bruylant, 1986).

[119] See Chrétien, Chifflot and Tourbe (n 77) 800 although without further indications what would make for reasonable decision-making in this regard.

[120] See Caranta (n 1) 194.

[121] *Associated Provincial Picture House Ltd v Wednesbury Corporation* [1948] 1 KB 223 (CA).

[122] *Council of Civil Service Unions v Minister for the Civil Service* [1984] UKHL 9 (HL).

[123] See Caranta (n 1) 193.

decision-making.[124] In German administrative law, for instance, judicial review of discretion is centred on the concept of *Ermessensfehler*, which approximately translates as error in discretion. Although the contours of the term are subject to debate,[125] this form of limited review constitutes a relatively rigorous form of control. It includes, among other aspects, the verification that administrators have not transgressed the limits of their discretion and that the exercise of discretion is not based on considerations alien or extraneous to the purpose of authorisation.[126] This does not just include arbitrariness in the exercise of discretion, but equally the pursuit of objectives other than those foreseen in its authorisation.[127] It enables courts to review, at least to some extent, the substance of a discretionary decision, by ascertaining which motives underpinned this decision and to very that this aligns with the objective for which administrative authorities have been authorised to exercise discretion.

A similarly rigorous method of limited review can be identified in Italian administrative law. Since the exercise of administrative power is conceptualised as a balancing of legitimate interests, this enables the reviewing court to ascertain whether the initial decision-maker correctly and comprehensively appraised these interests.[128] In addition, national courts control the legality and factual acuity of administrative decisions. Where the reconciliation of legitimate reasons warrants several legally equivalent solutions, the decision-maker is said to exercise discretion. In such a situation, judicial control has been operationalised through the ground of *eccesso di potere*, which gives rise to a method of limited review.[129]

In the literature, judicial review based on *eccesso di potere* has been criticised for being casuistic and, occasionally, contradictory.[130] As a corollary, the initial approach has been reformed. Whereas Italian courts traditionally refrained from explicit references to the principle of proportionality,[131] it resulted from 'mechanisms of progressive osmosis among national systems' that proportionality nowadays forms a firmly established ground of review.[132] Accordingly, to some extent, Italian courts may review the substance (*merito*) of discretionary decision-making on this basis. This may not amount to full review, allowing courts to substitute their own assessment for that of the initial decision-maker, but it enables them to assess aspects of the substance of discretionary decision-making, nonetheless.

[124] See E Hirsch Ballin, 'Constitutional Genealogy of Judicial Review in the Administrative State' in J Poorter, E Hirsch Ballin and S Lavrijssen (eds), *Judicial Review of Administrative Discretion in the Administrative State* (Asser; Springer, 2019) 32 ff.

[125] See Alexy (n 107); Brinktrine (n 54) 101 ff.

[126] See A Decker, '§ 114' in H Posser, HA Wolff and A Decker (eds), *BeckOK VwGO* (CH Beck, 2025) paras 24 ff; K Rennert, '§ 114' in E Eyermann (ed), *VwGO* (CH Beck, 2019) para 20.

[127] See Rennert (n 126) para 20.

[128] See Pretis (n 112) 425.

[129] See Caranta (n 1) 191.

[130] See ibid.

[131] See Galetta (n 111) 517.

[132] Cited from ibid, in the original: 'mécanisme d'osmose progressive dans les systèmes nationaux'.

ii. Other Mechanisms Precluding Full Judicial Review

While most administrative systems in Europe give effect to forms of limited judicial review through substantive grounds of review, it is not unreasonable to argue that limited judicial review may likewise result from procedural mechanisms. Polish law, for instance, advances a so-called cassation model of review.[133] Following this model, national courts establish the legality of administrative actions, albeit without adopting a decision *en lieu* of the administrative authority.[134] Under the current legislative framework, courts may set aside administrative decisions violating substantive or procedural law or declare it invalid.[135] If they do, administrative courts remit the decision to the administrative authority, either obliging the latter to decide within a specified time limit or by determining the manner in which the case should be handled.[136] Yet, judges may not vary the decision themselves. Article 145a of the Law on proceedings before administrative courts stipulates that courts may not determine the way discretionary decisions should be taken.[137] The task of judges is therefore to verify whether an administrative decision is adopted with due respect for the law, not to assume the role of the decision-maker themselves.

iii. Limited Review: What Is In a Name?

The preceding analysis suggests that courts have developed and consolidated strategies of judicial control over discretion in administrative systems throughout Europe. Although these strategies do not, in principle, enable judges to supersede the initial decision-makers' assessment (and hence, to carry out 'full' review), forms of 'limited' review are used to subjugate discretionary decision-making to a mode of judicial control that does not, however, unduly impinge upon administrative deliberation. Still, as the preceding section illustrates, the rigour of this review may vary. Some traditions in European administrative laws have developed relatively rigorous modes of control, whereas other traditions stick to marginal standards of review.

To some extent, standards of legality, such as the principle of proportionality, enable courts to consider the substance of discretionary decision-making. In extreme cases, this may amount to full review, whereby a national court establishes that merely one solution may have been warranted in the light of standards of legality.[138] Where they do, judges walk a tightrope. Depending on the trust vested in administrations and courts respectively, judicial interferences with administrative

[133] See von Danwitz (n 74) 99.

[134] See for a discussion of the introduction of that model into Polish administrative law, Z Kmieciak, 'The Efficiency of Administrative Courts (in the Light of European and Polish Experiences)' (2013) 15 *Comparative Law Review* 135, 148 ff.

[135] Prawo o postępowaniu przed sądami administracyjnymi 2002 [Law on Proceedings before Administrative Courts] (Dz. U. 2002, no 153, item 1270) art 145 § 1.

[136] ibid, art 145a § 1.

[137] ibid.

[138] For such a nullification of discretion, see above at s II.B.

discretion may be considered an illegitimate 'occupation of administrative leeway'[139] or 'an unacceptable transfer of exclusive rights and competences of the administrative organ to the judicial power'.[140]

Strategies of limited review may equally cling to more marginal standards of review. Control of 'manifest errors' by French courts or Wednesbury unreasonableness in English law illustrate this attitude. Although these tests allow for a degree of judicial fine-tuning,[141] they are by and large reflective of a more restrained manner of judicial control vis-á-vis administrative decision-making. Judicial interventions, in this view, may only sanction blatant administrative malpractice and are designed to safeguard a minimum degree of rationality in administrative decision-making.

III. A Framework Definition of Discretionary Power

The preceding section suggests that, despite the rich conceptual variety characterising discretionary power in administrative laws in Europe, it is possible to analytically link certain instances of administrative decision-making to a general phenomenon of discretion. In the present investigation, this will be done through an abstract framework definition of discretion. This definition will be informed by theoretical discussions and empirical developments in administrative systems in Europe as previously explored. Discretion, defined in such a way, can be said to exist where three characteristics coincide.

First, such a framework definition should acknowledge that discretion constitutes a form of administrative autonomy. This autonomy may, in principle, relate to instances of volition, cognition or the two combined. An administrative authority may have such deliberative autonomy on multiple accounts, for instance, in determining its course of action, in recognising certain preconditions for its actions, or in the balancing of various interests. For the purposes of the following investigation, however, not all instances of deliberative autonomy will be viewed as hallmark of discretion. Rather, the abstract definition of discretionary power applied here will merely consider those instances of administrative autonomy as discretion that entail a measure of self-programming power. Discretionary decision-making is thus, by definition, viewed as a mode of deliberation whereby the administrator may determine her- or himself the standards guiding the decision.

Against this backdrop, some instances of mere cognition may not be viewed as formative properties of discretion. From a comparative angle, for instance, it would be unusual to assume the existence of discretion in the establishment of facts or

[139] Sachs (n 68) para 30.

[140] Cited from Z Kmieciak and J Wegner, 'Deference to the Public Administration in Judicial Review: A Polish Perspective' in G Zhu (ed), *Deference to the Administration in Judicial Review: Comparative Perspectives* (Springer, 2019) 375.

[141] See amongst others P Craig, *UK, EU and Global Administrative Law: Foundations and Challenges* (Cambridge University Press, 2015) 22.

the correct interpretation of the law.[142] In these situations, administrators may be incapable of setting their own decision-making standards but rather apply those established in advance. While this need not factor out administrative latitude, as will be illustrated in the context of asylum decision-making,[143] such instances of cognition will be excluded from the abstract definition of discretionary power. Likewise, intricate 'technical evaluations'– as they are termed in the Italian tradition of discretion – will not be viewed as discretionary power unless they equally entail a measure of volition, for instance in the balancing of equivalent interests.[144]

A second element of a framework definition of discretion relates to the fact that discretion, as understood in this study, is nested and observable in structures of law. Unlike theoretical conceptualisations of discretion that view it as an inevitable by-product of norm application, the framework definition applied here insists that discretion emerges from specific indications in law that an administrative authority should have a degree of self-programming power. This need not be limited to explicit acknowledgements. Rather, an abstract definition of discretionary power will likewise include instances of deliberative autonomy that follow from vague legal terminology. The notion of *Beurteilungsspielraum* in the German tradition of discretionary power may, for instance, be viewed as such an implicit manifestation of administrative self-programming power.

Admittedly, it is difficult if not impossible to draw a categorical line between vague legal terminology that gives rise to discretion for the purposes of the present investigation, on the one hand, and the degree of deliberative autonomy inherent in the application of any legal norm, on the other hand. Both differ in degree, not in nature. Accordingly, there is no clear-cut yardstick as to which instances of legal ambiguity may be viewed as discretionary power in this regard. In relation to European migration law, however, this analytical imprecision may be reduced empirically. For the purposes of the following investigation, for instance, the former category will recurrently relate to legal concepts that tend to be associated with the existence of wide discretionary power, such as the application of public order grounds enabling administrative authorities to adopt measures to thwart security risks.

A third element of the framework definition of discretion concerns the intensity of control performed by reviewing courts. The present investigation will be based on an understanding that discretion coincides with forms of judicial review that do not allow judges to replace the initial decision with their own assessment. In this regard, it should be borne in mind that legal systems may have different options at their disposal to preclude the replacement of an administrative assessment in substances. Most traditions of discretion utilise modes of 'limited' control in this

[142] Arguably, with the exception of traditions of discretionary power that view the latter rather indifferently as 'choice', and thus, not conceptually distinguishing between instances of cognition and volition, see above s I.D.

[143] See below at ch 3, s IV.A.

[144] On this point, see above at s II.A.ii.

regard. The rigour of this mode of review may vary from one tradition to another. While some traditions of discretionary power allow for a relatively rigorous review of the initial decision, others cling to a rather deferential approach. It should moreover be noted that some national traditions of discretion do not formally endorse a standard of limited judicial review but preclude courts from superseding the substance of discretionary deliberation by other means, for instance, through the obligation for courts to remit a case to the initial decision-maker.

3

Discretion in European Migration Law: Persistence and Targeted Consolidation

Discretionary power is a prominent trait of migration laws in Europe. In part, this prominence can be traced back to the historical evolution of regulatory approaches to migration in Western European countries.[1] However, as the following section argues, discretion equally surfaces as an expedient feature of contemporary migration laws in Europe, allowing national legal systems to process the versatile influences that occur within a multi-levelled system of law. In this sense, the prominence of discretionary power in contemporary migration laws can be explained by the influences that European law exert on national regulatory approaches to migration. For national lawmakers, discretion may often present itself as the only regulatory tool that allows national legal systems to duly process these influences of European law.

Four forms of influence can be discerned that condition the existence of discretion in European migration law. First, standards of European law may prompt national lawmakers to provide for an individualised assessment in certain instances – a requirement that is routinely accommodated by national legal systems through legal designs that qualify as discretion for the purposes of this investigation (Section I). Other forms of influence command national lawmakers to provide for discretion in more explicit terms, requiring national legal systems to vest migration authorities with 'wide discretion' (Section II). Moreover, discretion has served as a compensation valve for some of the dysfunctionalities of transnational administrative systems, especially the Dublin system (Section III). Fourth and last, in some instances, influences of European law explicitly preclude national legal systems from affording discretion to administrative authorities (Section IV). All of this supports the impression that discretion, as a contemporary phenomenon, represents a targeted and purposefully employed tool to accommodate influences of European law in national migration systems (Section V).

[1] See above at ch 1, s II.A.

I. Discretion to Accommodate European Individualisation Requirements

European law often requires national legal systems to provide for an individualised assessment. This form of influence is well-known in EU free movement law,[2] and it likewise shapes European interactions with national migration laws. By virtue of such a requirement, administrators are obliged to duly consider the specificities of the individual case before them. While such a requirement is first and foremostly addressed to the administrative authority deciding the individual case, it presupposes that the national legal framework enables the administrative decision-maker to adjust the decision to the specificities of the individual situation before her or him. In this vein, European individualisation requirements safeguard a measure of administrative autonomy, precluding national lawmakers from fully programming administrative conduct.[3]

The following section argues that the prominence of such individualisation requirements in European migration law can be singled out as one of the reasons underpinning the enduring prominence, and indeed, the proliferation of discretionary decision-making in European migration law. While such a form of influence may not, in and of itself, premeditate the existence of discretion as defined for the purposes of this analysis,[4] the following section sets out to highlight that, empirically, national lawmakers routinely opt for discretion as a means to accommodate such individualisation requirements.

This argument will be substantiated by way of reference to European influences in two sub-fields of European law, namely, decision-making in relation to family reunification and long-term residence. In both contexts, European individualisation requirements can be traced back to fundamental rights safeguards (subsection A). These safeguards require national legal systems to provide for a degree of administrative autonomy (subsection B), which is frequently fleshed out through legal arrangements that qualify as discretion for the purposes of this investigation (subsection C).

A. Fundamental Rights-based Origin of Individualisation Requirements

The obligation to carry out an individualisation requirement can be traced back to influences that follow from fundamental rights safeguards. In the field of legal migration, this relates particularly to the right to respect for private and family

[2] See amongst others M Blauberger and SK Schmidt, 'Free Movement, the Welfare State, and the European Union's over-Constitutionalization: Administrating Contradictions' (2017) 95 *Public Administration* 437, 440 ff. and leading case law, including Case C-165/14 *Rendón Marín* ECLI:EU:C:2016:675, [2016], para 85.

[3] Insightfully on this point, see M Wendel, *Verwaltungsermessen Als Mehrebenenproblem: Zur Verbundstruktur Administrativer Entscheidungsspielräume Am Beispiel Des Migrations- Und Regulierungsrechts* (Mohr Siebeck, 2019) 205.

[4] Specifically, it does not premeditate the existence of a limited form of judicial review, which constitutes one of the elements of the definition of discretion employed here, see above at ch 2, s III.

life as interpreted by the European Court of Human Rights (ECtHR).[5] On the one hand, this fundamental rights safeguard is traditionally limited to light touch interventions. The ECtHR's jurisprudence starts from premise that States have the right to control the entry of non-nationals into their respective territories and that, accordingly, migrants cannot principally infer a human right to enter the territory of a State from States' obligations under the European Convention on Human Rights (ECHR).[6] On the other hand, the influence that this fundamental rights safeguard creates for national legal systems should not be underestimated. By prompting legal systems to allow for a 'fair balance' between competing interests of the individual and the community as a whole,[7] it compels national lawmakers to design legal frameworks capable of providing for such assessment.

Although the requirement to provide for a 'fair balance' may be given effect through a variety of different legal arrangements,[8] EU legislative instruments in the field of legal migration largely tend to implement this fundamental-right induced requirement through legal arrangements that provide for an individualised assessment. Accordingly, both the Family Reunification Directive and the Long-Term Residence Directive require Member States to allow for an individualised assessment in decisions that interfere with the right to respect for family and private life.

Early on, the European Court of Justice (ECJ) made Member States' implementation of the Family Reunification Directive subject to a general fundamental rights caveat. This caveat resulted from the European Parliament's challenge to the legality of the Directive, premised on the argument that the Directive would violate fundamental rights, particularly the right to respect for family life and the right to non-discrimination, as they result from the ECHR and constitutional traditions common to the Member States.[9] The challenge was unsuccessful, as the ECJ 'saved' the legality of Directive by passing responsibility for safeguarding fundamental rights to the sphere of Member States' implementation.[10] While the Directive itself would therefore not violate fundamental rights, restrictive provisions therein may not be used by Member States in a way that would fail to respect fundamental rights of migrants. In effect, this subjects Member States' implementation of the Directive to a general fundamental rights caveat.

[5] See A Desmond, 'The Private Life of Family Matters: Curtailing Human Rights Protection for Migrants under Article 8 of the ECHR?' (2018) 29 *The European Journal of International Law* 261, 273 ff.

[6] The ECtHR routinely takes this view as a starting point of its reasoning, originally in the seminal judgment in *Abdulaziz, Cabales and Balkandali v UK* Series A no 94 (1985), para 67, and routinely repeated, inter alia in *I.A.A. and others v UK* App no 25960/13 (ECtHR, 8 March 2016), para 39.

[7] *I.A.A. and others v UK* App no 25960/13 (ECtHR, 8 March 2016), paras 38 ff.

[8] For a discussion on this point, see D Thym, '"Public Policy" as a Chameleonlike Concept: The Quest for Coherence in the CJEU Case Law On Migration and Union Citizenship' (2024) 9 *European Papers* 1366, 1381 ff.

[9] Case C-540/03 *Parliament v Council* ECLI:EU:C:2006:429, [2006] ECR I-05769; note that the litigation arose before the Charter of Fundamental Rights gained binding legal force.

[10] See P Dąbrowska-Kłosińska, 'The Right to Family Reunion vs Integration Conditions for Third-Country Nationals: The CJEU's Approach and the Road Not Taken' (2018) 20 *European Journal of Migration and Law* 251, 265.

This interpretation of the Family Reunification Directive highlighted the importance of individualised decision-making in line with Article 17 of the Directive.[11] The provision stipulates that Member States must base their assessments on several considerations concerning the individual position of the person concerned. In its subsequent jurisprudence in *Chakroun*, the Court has interpreted that provision as requiring Member States to carry out an assessment centred on an 'actual examination of the situation of each applicant' and hence, an 'individual examination'.[12] This illustrates that the Court's reference to Article 17 of the Family Reunification Directive initially served as a confirmation of the instrument's compatibility with fundamental rights, specifically spelling out a requirement to base restrictive measures on an individualised assessment to that end.

The Strasbourg court had moreover highlighted the fact that the situation of 'settled aliens' may likewise fall within the scope of the right to respect for the persons' family and private life in Article 8 ECHR.[13] Unlike the interpretation of the Family Reunification Directive, however, the ECJ neither recognised a generalised fundamental rights caveat in the Long-Term Residence Directive from the outset, nor engaged in a practice of referencing the ECtHR's jurisprudence. Instead, the requirement to carry out an individualised assessment has made its way into the interpretation of restrictive provisions in the Long-Term Residence Directive via references to other fields of Union law. This detour is illustrated, for instance, by the ECJ's reasoning in *X*, where it highlighted that Member States must provide for an 'actual examination of the situation of each applicant' by way of reference to its judgment in *Chakroun* and hence, the Family Reunification Directive.[14] In *López Pastuzano*, in contrast, it referred to its jurisprudence concerning Turkish citizens under Decision No 1/80 of the Association Council to impose on Member States the requirement to carry out a 'case-by-case assessment' based on various elements mentioned in the respective provision in the Long-Term Residence Directive.[15] Despite these differences in the practice of the Court's self-citation, its interpretation of the Long-Term Residence Directive has successively put in place a general requirement to provide for an individualised assessment when implementing restrictive provisions. In comparison to other instruments of legal migration, this assertion featured with some delay but is nowadays firmly established in several contexts.[16]

[11] *Parliament v Council* (n 9), para 64.

[12] Case C-578/08 *Chakroun* ECLI:EU:C:2010:117, [2006], *para 48*; Case C-153/14 *Minister van Buitenlandse Zaken v K and A* ECLI:EU:C:2015:453, [2015], para 60.

[13] For a discussion of this case law, see D Thym, 'Respect for Private and Family Life under Article 8 ECHR in Immigration Cases: A Human Right to Regularize Illegal Stay?' (2008) 57 *International and Comparative Law Quarterly* 87, 96 ff.

[14] Case C-302/18 *X v Belgische Staat* ECLI:EU:C:2019:830, [2019], para 39.

[15] Case C-636/16 *Wilber López Pastuzano v Delegación del Gobierno en Navarra* ECLI:EU:C:2017:949, [2017], para 27.

[16] The instances in which the ECJ has spelled out such an individualisation requirement in this regard will be discussed in detail in the following sections.

B. Individualised Decision-Making and Administrative Autonomy

The precise nature and implications of the requirement to carry out an individualised assessment may be disputed. It is not unreasonable, for instance, to adopt a rather formalistic understanding according to which the individualised nature of decision-making should merely refer to the fact that a decision is adopted vis-á-vis a person. The Court of Justice, however, attributes substantive meaning to the individualised nature of decision-making, to the effect that such a deliberation must premise on several factors and that no single factor may automatically outweigh all other considerations. A requirement to provide for individualised decision-making, thus understood, may be viewed as a safeguard of a degree of administrative self-programming power (subsection i). While national lawmakers may finetune this decision-making power, a European requirement to carry out an individualised assessment bars them from replacing this administrative autonomy in its entirety (subsection ii).

i. A Safeguard of Administrative Autonomy

Owing to the origin in fundamental rights protection, individualisation requirements feature most prominently in instances where decisions affect migrants unfavourably.[17] In relation to family reunification or long-term residence, for instance, such restrictions may be adopted on the ground that a third country national does not have stable and regular resources sufficient to maintain her- or himself and, if applicable, her or his family members. In these contexts, the ECJ has ruled that decision-making must rest on an individualised assessment. The Court has adopted a coherent interpretation of both the Family Reunification Directive as well as the Long-Term Residence Directive in this regard, even though the former makes it optional for Member States to introduce such a requirement and the latter is mandatory in this respect. In its interpretation of both instruments, the Court highlights that Member States must provide for an 'actual examination'[18] of the situation of the applicant concerned, which essentially embodies a requirement to carry out an individualised assessment.

This line of jurisprudence first featured in *Chakroun*.[19] The case concerned the interpretation of a provision allowing Member States to require the sponsor to provide evidence that (s)he has stable and regular resources sufficient to maintain herself or himself as well as the family members, without recourse to the social

[17] For an overview of such situations, see K Groenendijk and T Strik, 'Directive 2003/86 on the Right to Family Reunification: A Surprising Anchor in a Sensitive Field' in E Tsourdi and P De Bruycker (eds), *Research Handbook on EU Migration and Asylum Law* (Edward Elgar, 2022) 313 ff.

[18] *Chakroun (n 12), para 48.*

[19] ibid, para 43.

assistance system.[20] In this case, the Netherlands had put into place a legislative arrangement that would have automatically precluded family reunification if the sponsor's resources would fall below a certain amount of income. The Court acknowledged that the costs of living and needs may vary greatly from one region and family to another, and therefore rejected the notion that applicants whose resources would be below a certain threshold could automatically be rejected. Instead, it insisted that Member States carry out an 'actual examination of the situation of each applicant'.[21] Accordingly, a certain sum may serve as a reference point but cannot forego an individualised examination altogether. In the case of the Chakrouns, the Court rather overtly advocated for their reunification, highlighting that they had been married for 37 years and were still not authorised to reunite.[22]

This line of interpretation was followed in later jurisprudence, including in the context of the administrative assessment whether a third country national may be considered as having stable and regular resources sufficient to maintain himself as well as the family members. In *Khachab*, the Court reiterated that Member States must base their decision on a 'case-by-case basis', which must allow for a 'balanced and reasonable assessment of all the interests in play'.[23] This may include assessments of prospective future resources, thereby allowing national migration authorities to carry out a prognosis regarding the likelihood of resources being retained in the years following the application's submission. In this case, however, the Court sticks to the idea that such a decision must be based on an individualised assessment.

In the context of the Long-Term Residence Directive, Member States are obliged to ascertain whether third country nationals have sufficient resources to acquire such a status. In *X*, the ECJ accordingly conferred its jurisprudence regarding the Family Reunification to the Long-Term Residence Directive. In the case, the Belgian migration authority had rejected an application for long-term residence status on the ground that the applicant did not have sufficient resources for himself but relied on his brother for subsistence instead.[24]

In this regard, the Court stressed that the resources requirement's specific objective is to preserve the social assistance systems of the Member States, which must render the conditions of 'resources' narrower than in comparison to those in the Free Movement Directive.[25] In the context of third country nationals, the Long-Term Residents Directive, just as the Family Reunification Directive, provides that these resources must be 'stable' and 'regular' and therefore presume a certain degree of permanence and continuity.[26] Even though it may be question-

[20] Council Directive 2003/86/EC of 22 September 2003 on the right to family reunification (Family Reunification Directive) [2003] OJ L251/12, art 7(1)(c).

[21] *Chakroun (n 12), para 48.*

[22] As explicitly acknowledged by the Court, ibid, para 65.

[23] Case C-558/14 *Mimoun Khachab v Subdelegación del Gobierno en Álava* ECLI:EU:C:2016:285, [2016], para 43.

[24] *X* (n 14).

[25] ibid, para 35.

[26] ibid, para 37.

able whether these terms provide more clarity than the notion of regularity, the Court refers to its jurisprudence on family reunification to highlight the necessity of administrative deliberative freedom: at a bare minimum, national migration authorities must be able to assess whether resources will be retained beyond the date of submission and that sufficiency of resources must be ascertained on the basis of an 'actual examination of the situation of each applicant'.[27]

In this vein, the Court effectively confers the requirement to carry out an individualised assessment from the field of family reunification to the acquisition of long-term resident status.[28] Accordingly, it is not the origin of the resources that is decisive, but the sustainability and sufficiency thereof in view of the individual situation of the person concerned, which is to be assessed by the competent migration authority. The legally binding commitment of a family member may be an important factor to be taken into account, but national migration authorities may equally consider the family relationship between the applicant and the family member prepared to bear her or his costs.[29] In addition, the Directive itself specifies that Member States 'may take into account the level of minimum wages and pensions'.[30] As guidance, this informs the decision-making of the competent immigration authority, albeit without prescribing its outcome. Nonetheless, the Court rejects the view that one factor alone, *in casu* the fact that the person does not have sufficient resources for himself, could be conclusive for the purpose of the administrative deliberation.

Conceptually, the ECJ seems to contrast individualised assessments with assessments that are 'automatic' in nature.[31] Automatic decision-making, in this sense, would be a mode of deliberation that rests solely on one factor or consideration that outweighs all other potential considerations. Accordingly, a European obligation to provide for an individualised assessment requires national legal systems to allow administrators to duly consider different aspects relating to the individual case before them. Such a legal requirement effectively ensures that national migration authorities are empowered to adjust their decisions to the specific case before them, proffering, at the very least, a choice between one of two options. Administrators may thus be authorised to self-programme their own assessment insofar as they may decide, within a certain range of feasible options, which decision may be the most appropriate in the light of the situation of the individual concerned.

[27] ibid, paras 38 ff, with a reference to *Chakroun (n 12), para 48.*

[28] See M Gerbaudo, 'The X Case: The Influence of the Resource Requirement on Long Term Residents' Integration and National Authorities' Discretionary Powers' (2019) 4 *European Papers Insight* 801.

[29] *X* (n 14), paras 40 ff.

[30] Council Directive 2003/109/EC of 25 November 2003 concerning the status of third-country nationals who are long-term residents (Long Term Residence Directive) [2003] OJ L16/44, art 5(1)(a) and *X* (n 14), para 36.

[31] For such an understanding in the context of EU free movement law, *Rendón Marín* (n 2), para 85; and in EU migration law specifically: Cases C-381/18 and C-382/18 *G.S. and V.G. v Staatssecretaris van Justitie en Veiligheid* ECLI:EU:C:2019:1072, [2019], para 65; Cases C-503/19 and C-592/19 *UQ and SI v Subdelegación del Gobierno en Barcelona* ECLI:EU:C:2020:629, [2020], para 42.

At first sight, the preclusion of automatic presumptions sounds like a technicality. In the practice of migration law in Europe, however, it has given rise to prominent litigation, specifically concerning the protection against expulsion of migrants who had been involved in criminal activities. The Long-Term Residence Directive permits Member States to expel a long-term resident only where (s)he constitutes an 'actual and sufficiently serious threat to public policy or public security'.[32] In this respect, the Directive codifies a list of aspects guiding Member States' deliberation in adopting an expulsion measure, which may be inspired by the jurisprudence of the Strasbourg court, requiring at any rate a fair balance of interests to be struck in the context of an expulsion measure.[33] In *López Pastuzano*, the ECJ confirmed that this provision in the Directive requires national migration authorities to carry out 'a case-by-case assessment which must, in particular, have regard to the elements mentioned'.[34]

The case concerned a long-term resident who had been the subject of two prison sentences, one of 12 and one of three months. After the competent Spanish migration authority adopted an expulsion decision against him for that reason, the referring Spanish court asked whether such a decision would fall within the scope of protection that Article 12 of the Directive affords. At that time, the Spanish Supreme Court interpreted national law in a manner that allowed national migration authorities to expel a long-term resident solely on the ground that (s)he had been criminally convicted, since this would, according to the Supreme Court, fall outside the scope of the Directive.[35] In its response, the ECJ made very clear that the protection afforded to long-term residents by the Directive applies to all expulsion measures concerning long-term residents. Member States are compelled to provide for an individualised assessment in this regard, which cannot merely be based on one single factor, such as a criminal conviction, but must rather include various aspects of consideration, such as the duration of residence in the territory, the person's age, the consequences of the expulsion on the person concerned and the family members and the links with the country of residence.[36] The Court highlighted that such an individualised assessment precludes that a criminal conviction would automatically lead to expulsion.

In the aftermath of the judgment in *López Pastuzano*, the Spanish Supreme Court still refused to accept the fact that EU law requires national authorities to carry out an individualised assessment. Accordingly, a lower court had to request the ECJ to articulate itself once again on the same provision.[37] By specifically

[32] Council Directive 2003/109/EC of 25 November 2003 concerning the status of third-country nationals who are long-term residents (Long Term Residence Directive) [2003] OJ L16/44, art 12.

[33] Seminally, *Boultif v Switzerland* ECHR 2001-IX, para 47 ff; the so-called 'Boultif criteria' were consequently applied and extended inter alia in *Üner v The Netherlands* ECHR 2006-XII, para 58.

[34] *López Pastuzano* (n 15), para 27.

[35] ibid, para 16.

[36] ibid, para 26.

[37] See D Acosta, 'Court of Justice of the European Union (Ninth Chamber), WT v Subdelegacíon Del Gobierno En Guadalajara: Case C-448/19, Judgment of 11 June 2020, EU:C:2020:467' (2020) 22 *European Journal of Migration and Law* 457, 460ff.

asking whether it may be acceptable that, in national law, an individualised assessment would be replaced by an 'automatic' assumption, the lower administrative court may be said to have hit the ECJ's conceptual trigger point. As highlighted already, the Luxemburg court considers automatic assumptions to constitute the antithesis to individualised assessments. In *WT*, accordingly, the ECJ unambiguously answered that the Long-Term Residence Directive precludes such automatic assumptions, highlighting that Member States are under an obligation to provide for an individualised assessment, based on various factors, as laid down in Article 12 (3) of the Directive.

It is in this vein that European requirements to carry out an individualised assessment serve as safeguards for national administrators' autonomy. By requiring national migration authorities to perform an *actual* examination of the case, this form of influence implies that individual administrators have the freedom, at least, to consider a variety of factors, and that none of these factors may 'automatically' outweigh all other factors. Additionally, depending on the EU legal framework and the Court's guidance, an individualised assessment may likewise entail the power to decide which aspects may be of relevance in a specific situation. While EU secondary law instruments or the case law of the ECJ or the ECtHR may indicate which factors may qualify as such,[38] national migration authorities preserve a degree of autonomy in relation to deciding the individual case before them.

ii. National Lawmakers and European Individualisation Requirements

The requirement to carry out an individualised assessment presupposes that national administrative actors are authorised, by virtue of their respective national legal framework, to perform such an assessment in the first place. It is in this way that European individualisation requirements affect national lawmakers. By safeguarding administrators' ability to adjust their decision in the light of the specificities of the individual case, such a requirement at EU level prevents national lawmakers from pre-empting the ability of administrators to perform such an assessment.[39]

While national lawmakers are therefore obliged to ensure that administrators have some flexibility, this does not imply that they would be barred entirely from adopting rules governing administrative conduct. Quite to the contrary, in European migration law, national lawmakers have designed a variety of legal arrangements to steer administrative deliberations. This does not ultimately forego the ability of administrators to consider the specificities of the individual case but draws their deliberation to the consideration of certain factors or attributes

[38] See J Bornemann, 'The Guises of and Guidance to Administrative Discretion in the European Court of Justice's Interpretation of EU Immigration Law' (2019) 12 *Review of European Administrative Law* 97, 116 ff.

[39] See Wendel (n 3) 77 ff.

relative weight to these decision-making factors. Dutch lawmakers have excelled in designing legal frameworks that programme administrative conduct without pre-empting a measure of administrative flexibility.

Integration conditions are a case in point. On several occasions, EU Directives on legal migration include provisions that allow Member States to adopt measures aimed at integration of third country nationals. Since these provisions do not lend themselves to an unequivocal interpretation as to how the term integration should be conceptualised,[40] some Member States have relied on these provisions to effectuate a policy shift towards more restrictive migration policies.[41] While the ECJ ultimately endorsed an interpretation of the Family Reunification Directive and the Long-Term Residence Directive that accepts, in principle, the introduction of integration measures (or respectively: integration conditions) by Member States with the intention of restricting the legal position of migrants, it equally added that this option must nevertheless allow for 'considerations of the specific circumstances of the person concerned, such as age, illiteracy or level of education'.[42] This can be viewed as a requirement to provide for an individualised assessment, albeit one that is limited to specific considerations of individual hardship.

Dutch lawmakers have undertaken significant efforts to adopt rules that pre-programme this assessment without foregoing the ability of administrators to duly consider individual hardship. This gave rise to an intense interaction between national courts and the Court of Justice, requiring the latter to elaborate in detail how national legal systems should incorporate this individualisation requirement.[43]

The Netherlands had introduced a legal arrangement in domestic law that imposed a general requirement to pass an integration test as a condition for family reunification, subject to a hardship clause that would have allowed derogations only in very exceptional situations of mental or physical disability.[44] In *K and A*, the Court relied on the principle of proportionality to clarify that the incorporation of a hardship clause may not per se satisfy the requirement to carry out an individualised assessment.[45] The Court found that if the requirements to pass an integration test were to 'systematically . . . prevent family reunification', they would

[40] For an overview, see T Kostakopoulou, '"Integrating" Non-EU Migrants in the European Union: Ambivalent Legacies and Mutating Paradigms' (2002) 8 *Columbia Journal of European Law* 181, 184 ff.; T Waal, *Integration Requirements for Immigrants in Europe: A Legal-Philosophical Inquiry* (Hart, 2021) 16 ff.

[41] See on that phenomenon, L Block, 'Regulating Membership: Explaining Restriction and Stratification of Family Migration in Europe' (2015) 36 *Journal of Family Issues* 1433, 1437 ff; and for criticism, see S Carrera and A Wiesbrock, 'Civic Integration of Third-Country Nationals: Nationalism versus Europeanisation in the Common EU Immigration Policy' [2009] *CEPS Papers in Liberty and Security in Europe* 1, 31 ff.

[42] Case C-579/13 *P and S v Commissie Sociale Zekerheid Breda and College van Burgemeester en Wethouders van de gemeente Amstelveen* ECLI:EU:C:2015:369, [2015], para 49; this line of argument was subsequently reproduced in the context of the Family Reunification Directive; Case C-153/14 *Minister van Buitenlandse Zaken v K and A* ECLI:EU:C:2015:453, [2015], paras 53 and 58.

[43] See J Krommendijk, 'The Preliminary Reference Dance between the CJEU and Dutch Courts in the Field of Migration' (2018) 10 *European Journal of Legal Studies* 101, 145.

[44] Vreemdelingenbesluit 2000, art 3.71a(2)(d) (NL).

[45] *K and A* (n 42), para 51.

exceed what is necessary. It is therefore the willingness to pass the integration exam as well as the applicants' efforts that should guide the assessment of the application.[46] In particular, proportionality demands specific individual circumstances of hardship to be given due consideration, regarding in particular age, illiteracy, level of education, economic situation or health of the person concerned,[47] and that fees must not be too high to render family reunification impossible or excessively difficult. Against this backdrop, the Court found the Dutch national legal arrangement to conflict with the Family Reunification Directive.[48] Although domestic law included a hardship clause, this clause was too narrowly drafted, to the effect that it only applied to *very* exceptional circumstances of hardship which were incongruent with those envisioned by the ECJ. Accordingly, the Dutch legislature had pushed the limits of restricting the requirement to carry out an individualised assessment too far. By devising a hardship clause that merely applied to situations of mental or physical disability, Dutch domestic law effectively excluded situations that should, in the light of Union law, be covered by an individualised assessment.

Not long after the Court indicated that the national legal arrangement conflicted with the Family Reunification Directive in *K and A*, it had to pronounce itself on the same policy in *C and A*.[49] In the case, the Netherlands had imposed an integration requirement on third country nationals who wished to apply for an autonomous residence permit under Article 15 of the Directive. Whereas such an autonomous residence permit should, at the latest, be granted to a family member after five years of residence, Article 15 (4) stipulates that the conditions to that end 'are established by national law'. This motivated the Netherlands to introduce a requirement in domestic law that family members must pass a civic integration test before obtaining such a residence permit. However, Dutch lawmakers, in the meantime, had incorporated the Court's jurisprudence in *K and A* into national law. Accordingly, the hardship clause had been extended to include persons who 'cannot reasonably satisfy the civic integration requirement'.[50]

The Court's reasoning in this case is based on the assertion that the EU legislature (*in casu* the Council) had explicitly authorised Member States to subject the grant of an autonomous residence permit to conditions which are to be defined in national law.[51] The Court intimated that the situation of granting an autonomous residence permit, for that reason, differed from the rules relating to authorisation of family reunification, which include specific positive obligations and thus require Member States, as a rule, to authorise family reunification.[52] Nonetheless, the Court infers from Article 15 that the granting of an autonomous residence

[46] ibid, para 56.
[47] ibid, para 58.
[48] ibid, para 63.
[49] Case C-257/17 *C and A v Staatssecretaris van Veiligheid en Justitie* ECLI:EU:C:2018:876, [2018].
[50] Wet inburgering 2021, art 6(1) (NL).
[51] *C and A* (n 49), para 48.
[52] ibid, para 50; even though it may be noted that both provisions, Arts 7 (2) and 15, explicitly refer to Member States national laws; cf. *K and A* (n 42), para 47.

permit constitutes the rule and that, accordingly, the provision must not be used by the Member States to undermine the objective and effectiveness thereof. 'By analogy', this reproduces the test spelled out in *K and A*, despite the Court's emphasis of contextual differences.[53] Whilst the Court goes to length to explicate the contextual differences of integration measures pertaining to the authorisation of family reunification and for issuing an autonomous residence permit – it applies the same test in substance.

Accordingly, conditions introduced by Member States may not be so onerous as to prevent, in practice, a third country national from validly obtaining such a permit.[54] On the one hand, the Court thus acknowledges the EU legislature's decision to allow Member States to introduce in their national laws such an option; a legislative determination that cannot be overturned by virtue of judicial interpretation.[55] On the other hand, the Court insists that the detailed rules laid down in national law must be capable of furthering the objective of that provision and be exercised in accordance with the principle of proportionality.[56] In accordance with that principle, civic integration tests must be at a basic level, fees must not be excessive and the national administrative authority should be able to take due account of the specific circumstances of the individual case.[57] In another judgment, rendered the very same day, the Court appears to accept the legal framework put in place by the Netherlands, which provides for an extended hardship clause.[58]

Against this background, it can be concluded that Dutch lawmakers have adopted a trial and error-strategy to assert in how far they may be able under Union law to narrow the scope of the individualised assessment. Since the original national framework provided for a very limited hardship clause, the Court's initial intervention found this to conflict with the requirements of Union law. Consequently, Dutch lawmakers amended the respective clause to include other situations of hardship as well, to the effect that this national provision appears to be in line with the Court's interpretation of the Directive. Such a strategy has been effectuated by national courts' active use of the preliminary reference procedure and the ECJ's willingness to spell out the implications of the requirement to provide for a hardship clause in that regard.

Another illustration of Dutch lawmakers' efforts to pre-programme administrative decision-making without foregoing the individualised nature of assessment can be detected in the context of decisions based on public policy, public security or public health grounds. All instruments of legal migration permit Member States to adopt such decisions in certain situations, subject to an individualised assessment. Against this backdrop, the Netherlands had introduced a system of 'sliding

[53] *C and A* (n 49), para 51.
[54] ibid, para 52.
[55] In this sense, ibid, paras 53 ff.
[56] ibid, para 60.
[57] ibid, para 63, all by way of reference to the judgment in *K and A* (n 42), paras 54 ff.
[58] Subject, however, to the national courts' proportionality assessment; Case C-484/17 *K v Staatssecretaris van Veiligheid en Justitie* ECLI:EU:C:2018:878, [2018], para 24.

slopes', devised for the purpose of guiding national decision-makers in the deliberation whether a prison sentence would qualify as a ground for withdrawal of a residence permit for the purpose of family reunification. This legal arrangement was brought to the attention of the Court of Justice in *G.S. & V.G.*[59]

The Dutch government emphasised time and time again in the litigation that this complicated national legal arrangement would not allow for any conclusions to be drawn 'automatically' but rather for an attribution of relative weight to grounds of public security corresponding to the severity of the offence.[60] In substance, the case concerned two individuals: first, an Indian national who had been sentenced to four years and three months imprisonment in Switzerland and whose extension of a residence permit in the Netherlands for the purpose of family reunification was rejected for that reason. The second individual was an Armenian national who had been sentenced repeatedly for drug offences and whose application for family reunification had been refused on the same ground.

In its judgment, the Court acknowledged that the term 'grounds of public policy' resonates with its settled case law in the context of free movement law.[61] This case law requires the conduct of the EU citizen or a citizen's family member to represent a genuine, present and sufficiently serious threat affecting one of the fundamental interests of the society of the Member State concerned. In relation to the Family Reunification Directive, however, the ECJ departed from such a strict formula. Instead, it ruled that national authorities may, under Article 6 of the Family Reunification Directive, rely solely on the fact that the person concerned has been convicted of a criminal offence.[62] The Court, however, added that national migration authorities must, in their deliberation, respect the principle of proportionality. As a corrective, proportionality thus precludes 'automatic' inferences from the fact that a person has been convicted of a criminal offence.[63] Rather, the offence must be serious enough, or of such a type, that it is necessary to rule out residence of the third country national concerned. Accordingly, national migration authorities are required to base their decision on an 'individual assessment', which takes due account of the situation of the person concerned, even though they may rely solely on the fact that a third country national has been convicted of a criminal offence where that offence is sufficiently severe to justify the termination of stay.[64]

At first sight, this seems to be a contradictory conclusion. The Court's acknowledgement that national migration authorities may rely solely on a person's criminal

[59] *G.S. and V.G.* (n 31).

[60] See Cases C-381/18 and C-382/18 *G.S. and V.G. v Staatssecretaris van Justitie en Veiligheid* ECLI:EU:C:2019:608, [2019], Opinion of AG Pitruzella, para 61.

[61] On this type of inspiration between fields of EU law, see Thym, '"Public Policy" as a Chameleonlike Concept: The Quest for Coherence in the CJEU Case Law On Migration and Union Citizenship' (n 8) 1375.

[62] *G.S. and V.G.* (n 31), paras 63 ff.

[63] ibid, para 65.

[64] ibid, para 68.

conviction appears to logically rule out an individual assessment based on several factors, as ordained inter alia by Article 17 of the Family Reunification Directive. A closer investigation, however, warrants a different conclusion. In *G.S. & V.G.*, the Court does not set aside the need to carry out an individualised assessment but rather highlights that Member States may attribute relative weight to the interests that need to be balanced. Very severe criminal offences may justify, in the light of a proportionality assessment, the immediate termination of a third country national's stay in a Member State, even if other factors of family life may rally against such a conclusion. Criminal offences that do not reach such a threshold of severity may be weighed against interests of the individual to the end that a restriction to family reunification may or may not be warranted with a view to the individual situation of the person concerned. Accordingly, the Court's assertion that national migration authorities may rely 'solely' on one factor, namely a person's criminal conviction, constitutes the outcome of a weighing of interests, not its substance.

In analytical terms, the Court's jurisprudence in this regard highlights that it is necessary to distinguish an automatic assessment based 'solely' on one factor, and deliberations that appraise and weigh various elements before drawing the conclusion that one factor outweighs all other considerations. Whereas the former is precluded by virtue of an individualised assessment, the Court accepted the latter in *G.S. & V.G.* Accordingly, in this situation, the principle of proportionality instructs the requirement to carry out an individualised assessment. National migration authorities may reject an application for family reunification or withdraw a residence permit on that ground where the 'offence is so serious, or of such a type, that it is necessary to rule out residence'.[65] Accordingly, to ascertain whether a criminal conviction may justify the adoption of an unfavourable decision, national migration authorities must take various factors into consideration. A sufficiently serious criminal conviction may constitute the sole factor that outweighs all other aspects but does not amount to an 'automatism' that would conflict with the requirement to carry out an individualised assessment.

This reading of the Court's interpretation has been corroborated in subsequent case law regarding the Long-Term Residence Directive. In *UQ & SI*, the ECJ was asked to interpret the broadly termed provision in Article 6 thereof.[66] The case concerned a national legal arrangement that allowed migration authorities to cross-check, in assessing an application for long-term resident status, whether an applicant had been convicted of an offence. The litigation arose against the backdrop of two unfavourable decisions in this regard by the competent Spanish authorities. In the first place, Spanish migration authorities refused issuance of long-term resident status to a third country national who had been caught

[65] ibid, para 66.

[66] For criticism of the Directive in this regard, see L Halleskov, 'The Long-Term Residents Directive: A Fulfilment of the Tampere Objective of Near-Equality?' (2005) 7 *European Journal of Migration and Law* 181, 187, even though that view appears to downplay the limits imposed on Member States in the second limb of art 6(1) and in art 6(2).

drink-driving and who was sentenced to 40 days' community service for that reason. The second case concerned an applicant for long-term resident status who had been sentenced to 11 months in prison for forgery of public documents, but whose sentence had been suspended.

In its response, the ECJ focused on the affirmation of an individualised assessment. Unlike national legal arrangement that provided for one sole factor, *in casu* the existence of a conviction, to suffice for the purpose of refusing an application, national migration authorities must weigh up 'a certain number of factors'; specifically, the seriousness or nature of offence committed by the person, the threat that (s)he presents to public policy or security and the length of residence in and ties to the host Member State.[67] Such a 'case-by-case' assessment precludes a refusal to grant long-term resident status solely on the ground that the person concerned had been convicted, irrespective of the nature of the offence. In this regard, the Court stressed that national migration authorities cannot automatically refuse long-term resident status on grounds of public policy, merely because the person concerned had been convicted of a criminal offence.[68]

While national migration authorities may, in certain situations, attribute such a weight to a person's conviction that it outweighs all other factors, such a conclusion may not be drawn automatically. Rather, this reflects the result of the weighing exercise carried out by national immigration authorities. Initially, national authorities must consider various aspects, amongst which a person's conviction may be one factor. Where a criminal offence is very severe, this may lead the national migration authority to refuse long-term resident status to the person concerned solely based on that ground. In this case, it is obliged to appraise aspects of deliberation that may rally against a negative decision but draw the conclusion that the criminal offence outweighs any other aspects.

C. Individualised Assessments and Discretionary Power: Two of a Kind?

The preceding chapters elucidated how European law may spell out a guarantee of administrative self-programming power in national legal systems. In European migration law, this constitutes a particularly prominent form of influence, due to the human rights obligations that follow from Article 8 ECHR and the supranational invigoration thereof. These influences culminate in a relatively coherent requirement for national legal systems to provide for an individualised assessment. Conceptually, however, this avenue of European legal influence does not, in and of itself, amount to a safeguard of discretionary power. Rather, the present investigation endorses a definition of discretion that rests on several aspects, including the absence of judicial review that would effectively supersede an initial decision.

[67] *G.S. and V.G.* (n 31), para 38.
[68] ibid, paras 40 ff.

An individualisation requirement does not predetermine the intensity of judicial control as such and may therefore not necessarily give rise to discretion.

In EU law, this form of influence takes effect against the backdrop of Member States' procedural autonomy, allowing for principled pluralism in the choice of a model of judicial control, including the intensity of review.[69] This is not to say, however, that a European individualisation requirement would create no ramifications for the intensity of judicial control in national legal systems whatsoever. Rather, in the literature, the view has been posited that the requirement to carry out an individualised assessment precludes national courts from carrying out a standard of marginal review.[70] Instead, such a requirement enables judges to examine the merits and facts of the case and thus to effectively supersede the initial administrative decision.[71] This understanding is supported, for instance, by the Commission's guidance on the Family Reunification Directive, which stipulates that the right to mount a legal challenge pursuant to Article 18 thereof, read in light of Article 47 of the Charter, 'implies that full judicial review must be available concerning merits and legality'.[72] Nevertheless, this perception would jump to conclusions. Doubts should be harboured as to the view that national courts would be under an obligation to carry out 'full review' of individualised assessments in the field of legal migration.

However, this position cannot readily be inferred from the jurisprudence of the ECJ. It neither follows from Article 18 of the Family Reunification Directive and, respectively, Article 20(2) of the Long-Term Residence Directive; nor from Article 47 of the Charter. To the contrary, in addition to the fact that the Court routinely treats the intensity of control as a matter of Member States' procedural autonomy, the second subsection of Article 18 of the Family Reunification Directive specifically points to the fact that the 'procedure and the competence according to which the right [to mount a legal challenge] is exercised shall be established by the Member State concerned'.

i. Implications for the Intensity of Review

Nonetheless, it is true that the requirement to carry out an individualised assessment which takes account of all the relevant aspects of the individual case creates repercussions for the reviewing court. It allows judges to verify whether the national decision-maker has taken due account of all the interests at stake, including the

[69] See R Widdershoven, 'National Procedural Autonomy and General EU Law Limits' (2019) 12 *Review of European Administrative Law* 5, 24.

[70] For an analysis of divergent conceptions of 'limited' judicial review, see above at ch 2, s II.C.i.

[71] For this argument, see K Groenendijk and T Strik, 'Family Reunification in Germany, Netherlands and the EU since 2000: Reciprocal Influence and the Role of National and EU Actors' in S Beichel-Benedetti and C Janda (eds), *Hohenheimer Horizonte: Festschrift für Klaus Barwig* (Nomos, 2018) 364.

[72] Communication from the Commission to the European Parliament and the Council on guidance for application of Directive 2003/86/EC on the right to family reunification, COM(2014) 210 final, at 29; the argument may be applied mutatis mutandis to the Long-Term Residence Directive's art 20 (2).

interests that individuals derive from fundamental rights. In this vein, a standard of proportionality may genuinely increase the intensity of judicial review.[73] Accordingly, a European individualisation requirement permits national courts to explore, to some extent, the merits of that assessment. Against this background, it may be correct to presume that the requirement to carry out an individualised assessment precludes very marginal standards of review by national courts. Yet, this does not conceptually imply that national courts would exercise 'full review'.

In summary, this suggests that administrative self-programming and discretionary power are not two of a kind. Rather, on a conceptual level, a European guarantee of administrative self-programming power need not necessarily coincide with a standard of judicial review that precludes a court to supersede the initial decision in substance.[74] While this avenue of European influence may therefore corroborate the existence of one property of discretionary power, it does not premeditate another. Against this backdrop, close analytical attention is warranted. National legal systems may have various options at their disposal to accommodate this requirement of European law. It should therefore not be a foregone conclusion that a European guarantee of administrative self-programming power would give rise, in national law, to the existence of discretion.

ii. Proliferation of Discretion as a Means to Allow for Administrative Autonomy

Conceptually, European guarantees of administrative self-programming need not necessarily give rise to discretionary power. Empirically, however, discretionary power may be the most common and intuitive option for national lawmakers to accommodate such a requirement in their legal systems. The need to allow administrators to duly consider the specificities of the individual case constitutes one of the prominent topoi underscoring the existence of discretion in legal systems in Europe.[75] This is empirically borne out by the practices of integrating this avenue of influence in national laws explored above.

As had been explored, Dutch lawmakers opted for a legal arrangement providing for 'sliding slopes', that attaches a fixed legal consequence, that is, rejection of an application of family reunification or withdrawal of residence permit, to a discretionary deliberation whether a criminal conviction may outweigh other reasons.[76] A similar legal structure was adopted in the context of the revised

[73] In so far, it is correct that the powers of courts have increased under the influence of the Family Reunification Directive, as has been argued by S Bonjour, 'The Power and Morals of Policy Makers: Reassessing the Control Gap Debate' (2011) 45 *International Migration Review* 89, 92.

[74] In this sense, it may be confusing that the ECJ occasionally speaks of 'discretion' in contexts where national courts fully review a decision, ECJ, C-159/21, *GM v Országos Idegenrendészeti Főigazgatóság and Others*, ECLI:EU:C:2022:708, para 81.

[75] This can be traced back to the classical understanding of bureaucracy formulated by Weber, see P Hupe and T Evans, 'Discretion in Governance: An Introduction' in T Evans and P Hupe (eds), *Discretion and the Quest for Controlled Freedom* (Palgrave Macmillan, 2020) 214.

[76] Opinion of AG Pitruzella, *G.S. and V.G.* (n 60), para 6.

hardship clause with a view to integration measures. In this case, Dutch law stipulated that the competent Minister was obliged to exempt a person from the integration requirement where that person was either permanently incapable of passing the integration exam or where the Minister comes to the view that the person concerned 'cannot reasonably satisfy the civic integration requirement'.[77]

In both legal contexts, Dutch lawmakers designed national law in a way that casts the legal consequence in mandatory terms but acknowledges that the establishment of pre-conditions for a decision is left to the migration authority's assessment, subject to a verification of 'reasonableness'. From the conceptual perspective of Dutch law, this may be viewed as an instance of decision-making autonomy that coincides with limited judicial review.[78] While the existence of discretion in this context is not imperative from a legal perspective, this illustrates that, empirically, national lawmakers may often opt for legal arrangements that allow for discretionary decision-making to accommodate a European individualisation requirement. Where legal arrangements previously prescribed a non-discretionary decision – like the Spanish legal framework on the refusal to afford or prolong long-term residence status[79] – this influence will bring about a proliferation of discretionary power.

II. EU Migration Law's Vested Interest in Discretion

As the previous sections suggest, European law tends to contribute to the persistence of discretion in national legal systems in a rather implicit fashion. Occasionally, however, the existence of discretionary decision-making is commanded in more explicit terms. Particularly, the Court of Justice has repeatedly ruled that national migration authorities should have 'wide discretion' in the implementation of EU migration law.[80] Not unlike European individualisation requirements, this constitutes a form of 'transversal influence', whereby European legal requirements shield national administrative decision-makers from interferences by national lawmakers.[81] What distinguishes this form of influence from individualisation requirements, however, is that it explicitly employs the term 'discretion' to refer to this degree of administrative freedom.

In EU migration law, explicit references to national migration authorities' discretion feature in the context of Schengen law, and specifically in decision-making

[77] *C and A* (n 49), para 11.

[78] For an overview of the evolution of judicial review in Dutch administrative law in this regard, see T Barkhuysen and M van Emmerik, 'Judicial Review in Dutch Environmental Law: General Observations' in J Poorter, E Hirsch Ballin and S Lavrijssen (eds), *Judicial Review of Administrative Discretion in the Administrative State* (Asser; Springer, 2019) 109.

[79] See above at ch 3, s I.B.ii.

[80] Amongst others, Case C-84/12 *Rahmanian Koushkaki v Bundesrepublik Deutschland* ECLI:EU:C:2013:862, [2013], para 60.

[81] The author's approximated translation of 'diagonaler Zugriff', Wendel (n 3) 89.

in relation to short-term visas. In this field of law, executive decision-making is often linked to vast or even unfettered deliberative freedom which can be traced back to the earlier phases of intergovernmental cooperation in this field.[82] Against this backdrop, it may be argued that the ECJ's repeated affirmation of national migration authorities' discretion would merely reiterate the *status quo ante*. The following analysis, however, begs to differ. It argues that this form of influence established discretion as a targeted phenomenon, linked to specific instances of deliberation that can be labelled complex in nature (subsection A). It suggests that EU migration law may have a vested interest in ensuring that national migration authorities have discretion in certain situations, especially in the context of measures adopted to safeguard public order and national security (subsection B). This vested interest may explain why the Court departed from the principled pluralism in relation to the intensity of judicial review, exceptionally prescribing a form of limited judicial review on national courts on some occasions (subsection C).

A. The Reproduction of an EU-level Tradition of Discretion in National Administrative Contexts

Supranational acknowledgements of national administrations' 'wide discretion' feature in a variety of contexts in EU migration law. Routinely, these characterisations are based on the finding of the Court that an administrative deliberation would entail some degree of 'complexity'.[83] For scholars of EU administrative law, this reference to complexity will come as no surprise. The idea that the existence of discretion should be linked to judicial acknowledgements of complexity is a characteristic feature of the Court's jurisprudence in relation to decision-making of EU institutions and agencies.[84] In the field of EU migration law, this understanding is effectively reproduced in national administrative contexts.

Supranational affirmations of national administrative discretion first featured in the context of visa law proper, that is, in the Court's interpretation of the EU Visa Code.[85] Successively, however, the Court applied the same reasoning in other, closely related fields of law, such as students' and researchers' mobility and Schengen short-term stays (subsection i). This indicates that the Court's acknowledgement of 'wide discretion' has effectively spilled from one area of EU migration

[82] This conclusion is routinely drawn on a side note and not so much on the basis of an analysis of historical legal arrangements; see, for instance, G Cornelisse, 'What's Wrong With Schengen? Border Disputes and the Nature of Integration in the Area Without Internal Borders' (2014) 51 *Common Market Law Review* 1, 25; S Peers, *EU Justice and Home Affairs Law: Volume I: EU Immigration and Asylum Law* 4th edn (Oxford University Press, 2016) 209.

[83] See Bornemann (n 38) 113.

[84] For a discussion, see M Prek and S Lefèvre, '"Administrative Discretion", "Power of Appraisal" and "Margin of Appraisal" in Judicial Review Proceedings before the General Court' (2019) 56 *Common Market Law Review* 339, 347.

[85] Regulation (EC) No 810/2009 of the European Parliament and of the Council of 13 July 2009 establishing a Community Code on Visas (Visa Code) [2009] OJ L243/1.

law to another. This knock-on effect may be explained through the ECJ's versatile use of the complexity label that is central to a supranational tradition of discretionary power (subsection ii).

i. Affirmations of Wide 'Discretion' in the Jurisprudence of the ECJ

The Court confirmed national migration authorities' wide discretion for the first time in relation to the EU Visa Code in the case *Koushkaki*. The case concerned an Iranian national who had applied for a visa at the German embassy in Tehran but was unable to dispel the authority's doubts as to his willingness to return to Iran before the expiry of the visa.[86] The case therefore revolved around the question under which circumstances national visa authorities could refuse to issue a visa on the ground that the person may overstay.[87] In the first place, the Court interpreted the list of criteria on the basis of which a national authority may refuse the issuance of a visa to be exhaustive. The Visa Code lays down a harmonised list of criteria for refusal which preclude national visa authorities from relying on another ground.[88] In the second place, however, it added that, in the application of those exhaustively listed grounds, national authorities have 'a wide discretion'.[89] That discretion relates to the conditions for the application of grounds for refusal as well as to the assessment of the relevant facts to determine whether one of these grounds would preclude the issuing of a visa.[90]

The Court's affirmation of national authorities' wide discretion reproduces, in national contexts, a characteristic element of the tradition of discretionary power in Union law. It focuses on the Court's assertion of the 'complexity' of assessment. In *Koushkaki*, the Court considered this complexity to pertain to several aspects of the visa applicant's individual position, such as the person's social and economic situation in the country of origin, predictions as to her or his foreseeable conduct and the processing of various documents.[91]

To substantiate that finding, however, the Court additionally referred to the intention of the EU legislature to leave wide discretion to national visa authorities. The wording of the Visa Code may suggest as much, stipulating that said authorities would have to give 'particular consideration' or maintain 'reasonable doubts' with a view to an element of assessment.[92] Whereas it is not self-evident that such wording would unambiguously hint at a specific legislative intention, the Court's effort in this regard may be viewed as a hallmark of the pluralism inherently built into the tradition of discretion in Union law. The Court is eager to accommodate situations of direct and indirect administration alike. The tradition of discretion

[86] *Koushkaki* (n 80), paras 19 ff.
[87] ibid, para 23.
[88] ibid, paras 45 ff.
[89] ibid, para 60.
[90] ibid.
[91] ibid, paras 56 ff.
[92] ibid, para 61.

that the Court of Justice applies therefore appears to be responsive to diverging national contexts – in the case of *Koushkaki*, to the German tradition of discretionary power, which rests on normative authorisations.[93] By linking the 'wide discretion' that is directly imposed on national visa authorities to the intention of the EU legislature, the Court tosses a conceptual lifeline to national actors, inter alia national courts, to view this 'wide discretion' as a 'Beurteilungsspielraum' and hence, an embodiment of discretion.[94]

ii. Complexity as a Functional Reason Underpinning Discretion'

The Visa Code is not the only instrument in the interpretation of which the Court has acknowledged national migration authorities' wide discretion. It likewise did so with a view to related instruments of EU migration law, particularly, the Students Directive and the Schengen Borders Code.[95] In both legal contexts, national migration authorities are said to benefit from a wide measure of discretion. However, the arguments employed to that end differ notably. On the one hand, the Court routinely refers to its judgment in *Koushkaki* as a precedent to emphasise the complexity that the immigration authorities' assessment entails.[96] On the other hand, the Court's reasoning may occasionally do without the label of complexity. In *Ben Alaya*, for instance, the Court confirmed that national migration authorities should 'exercise a measure of discretion when considering applications for admission',[97] albeit without any reference to the complexity that such a deliberation may entail.

In *Fahimian*, the ECJ was more explicit in acknowledging national migration authorities' wide discretion in the context of the Students Directive.[98] The case arose with a view to an Iranian doctoral student, whose application for a residence permit was refused by German authorities on public security grounds.[99] The EU had imposed restrictive measures on Ms Fahimian's home university and on persons associated with it, on account of the university's cooperation with the Iranian Ministry of Defence. Against this background, the German migration authorities refused her application, arguing that the knowledge she might acquire during her research stay may be used by the Iranian government to endanger the

[93] See above at ch 2, s II.B.

[94] BVerwG, Urteil vom 17 September 2015, 1 C 37.14, paras 19 ff (DE); on the flipside, this caters to a pluralisation of normative authorisations, as described by Wendel (n 3) 190 ff.

[95] Council Directive 2004/114/EC of 13 December 2004 on the conditions of admission of third-country nationals for the purposes of studies, pupil exchange, unremunerated training or voluntary service [2004] OJ L375/12, art 6(1)(d); and Regulation (EU) 2016/399 of the European Parliament and of the Council of 9 March 2016 on a Union Code on the rules governing the movement of persons across borders (Schengen Borders Code) [2016] OJ L77/1, art 6(1)(e).

[96] Case C-544/15 *Sahar Fahimian v Bundesrepublik Deutschland* ECLI:EU:C:2017:255, [2017], para 41; Case C-380/18 *Staatssecretaris van Justitie en Veiligheid v E.P* ECLI:EU:C:2019:1071, [2019], para 37.

[97] Case C-491/13 *Mohamed Ali Ben Alaya v Bundesrepublik Deutschland* ECLI:EU:C:2014:2187, [2014], para 33.

[98] *Fahimian* (n 96).

[99] ibid, para 22 ff.

security of the Federal Republic of Germany.[100] In its response, the Court relied heavily on its reasoning in *Koushkaki* to highlight the complexity surrounding the consideration whether admission of such a person may pose a potential threat to public security, including the necessity to assess the risk admission may cause.[101] Accordingly, in those deliberations, national migration authorities should have wide discretion.[102]

The Court equally acknowledged national migration authorities' wide discretion in the context of the Schengen Borders Code. The case of *E.P.* concerned an Albanian citizen who claimed to stay as a tourist in the Netherlands, where he was arrested during a police raid which led to the impounding of large amounts of drugs.[103] When he was apprehended, the police assumed that *E.P.* had indeed been caught red handed and, on that suspicion, he was ordered to leave EU territory as he no longer fulfilled the conditions for stay according to the Schengen Borders Code.[104] Against this background, the Court firstly noted that the conditions for stay are closely connected to the Visa Code. For that reason, the complexity that marks national migration authorities' deliberations should permeate the application of the criteria in the Schengen Borders Code as well.[105] The Court accordingly relied on its reasoning in *Koushkaki* to corroborate national migration authorities' wide discretion in determining whether a short-term stay would have to be terminated on the ground that a third country national posed a threat to public policy.[106]

All this illustrates that the Court's characterisation of national migration authorities' 'wide discretion' relies of a characterisation of situations as complex and that the Court's conceptualisation of complexity in this regard varies. Aside from the reasoning in *Ben Alaya* where the Court did not justify the existence of discretion altogether, complexity relates to different types of deliberation. In the jurisprudence discussed, at least three conceptions of complexity may be discerned.

First, complexity appears to result from prospective assessments. In the field of visa law, complexity links to the need to predict whether the person concerned will overstay her or his visa.[107] Similarly, in the context of the Students Directive, the personality and the future conduct will inform the assessment whether the student's knowledge may be used for purposes that may endanger the future security of a Member State.[108] This links to a feature more generally associated with the existence of wide discretionary power, namely that prospective assessments may often be viewed as requiring a measure of discretion.[109] In fact, this specific

[100] ibid, para 23.
[101] ibid, para 41.
[102] ibid, para 42.
[103] *E.P.* (n 96).
[104] ibid, para 15.
[105] ibid, paras 36 ff.
[106] ibid, para 37.
[107] *Koushkaki* (n 80), para 57.
[108] *Fahimian* (n 96), para 42.
[109] See BG Mattarella, 'Law and Discretion. A Public Law Perspective on the EU' in J Mendes (ed), *EU Executive Discretion and the Limits of Law* (Oxford University Press, 2019) 32.

form of complexity may be a hallmark of decision-making in the field of human mobility and may serve as a general argument rallying in favour of discretionary decision-making.

Second, complexity may arise out of the sheer amount of information and documents in need of being verified and assessed for the purpose of visa examination.[110] In this sense, complexity calls for a high degree of expertise. This may resonate with an understanding of relative authority.[111] Legal systems tend to afford discretionary power to national administrative bodies where the latter are, by virtue of their expertise, best placed to take an appropriate decision in situations of intricacy.

In addition, there may be a third aspect that motivates the Court to acknowledge complexity in the national migration authorities' assessments. In his opinion in *E.P.*, AG Pitruzella pointed to a practical consideration that may motivate the Court to consider an evaluation as complex. Where national migration authorities must take a decision concerning a third country national but lack reliable information to that end, this may be said to invite complexity. This was the case in *E.P.*, where the competent national authorities were obliged to take a decision, even though the information available to them was limited, since the third country national concerned was not obliged to obtain a visa prior to entry. Although the Court did not explicitly endorse the AG's view, it nonetheless found that national migration authorities may be faced with complexity in that regard.

B. Wide Discretion to Safeguard Public Order and Security

In the practice of the Court, explicit references to the discretion of national migration authorities typically concern measures designed to safeguard public order and security.[112] The prominence of discretionary decision-making in European migration law is therefore closely tied to the centrality of security considerations in this field. National authorities are routinely empowered to adapt their decisions where public order or security so require, and such instances of decision-making are habitually framed in terms of discretion.[113]

While the Court's jurisprudence suggests that migration authorities' discretion in this regard should be 'wide', the exact width of that power may vary from one situation to another. Unlike the Court's case law in the field of EU free movement law, where measures taken for the purpose of safeguarding public security must be based exclusively on the personal conduct of the individual concerned, posing a 'genuine, present and sufficiently serious threat' to a fundamental interest

[110] *Koushkaki* (n 80), para 57.

[111] See above at ch 2, s I.B.

[112] See J Chlebny, 'Public Order, National Security and the Rights of Third-Country Nationals in Immigration Cases' (2018) 20 *European Journal of Migration and Law* 115, 120.

[113] See above at ch 1, s II.C.

of society,[114] the wide discretion that authorities are afforded in EU migration law instruments appears not to be subjected to the same strict limitations. While the ECJ adopts the same definition of public policy or public security in both contexts, the conditions upon which the existence of a threat may be presumed differ.[115] At the heart of it, the Court adjusts the conditions upon which a national authority may act to thwart a threat to public security or public order. In contrast to the strict standard of a 'genuine, present and sufficiently serious threat' applicable in free movement law, the Court acknowledged that national migration authorities may rely on 'potential' threats to restrict the mobility rights of third country nationals.[116]

By confirming that potential threats may qualify as threats to public order and security, the Court's jurisprudence in *Fahimian* and in *E.P.* adopts a rather lenient approach in delimiting the power of migration authorities' wide discretion. This finding notwithstanding, the precise boundaries of national migration authorities' wide discretion will be determined by the respective legal instrument from which this power derives. In *Fahimian*, for instance, it pointed to the fact that the Students Directive, and particularly recital 14 thereof, indicated that national migration authorities may refuse a third country national entry where they consider that person a threat, if only a potential one, to public security.[117] In *E.P.*, the Court drew a similar conclusion with a view to the Schengen Borders Code. Since recital 6 thereof suggests that Member States should be able to thwart 'any threat' to public policy or internal security,[118] the Court inferred that the Code allowed Member States to combat 'all threats to public policy', thus including potential threats.[119]

Although the Court highlighted the principle of proportionality as a corrective to this wide discretion,[120] there can be no doubt that the lenient standard employed in *Fahimian* and *E.P.* affords national migration authorities a wider margin of administrative autonomy than compared to the requirements in free movement law. In *E.P.*, for instance, the national authorities did not have to demonstrate that the individual concerned would pose a genuine threat to public order but instead accepted that the Dutch authorities had a suspicion to that end. The person concerned was apprehended in the context of a drug-related crime, but it was not established beyond doubt that he was involved therein. Accordingly, the Dutch authorities acted on the suspicion that he posed a potential threat, and the Court,

[114] Case 41/74 *Yvonne van Duyn v Home Office* ECLI:EU:C:1974:133, [1974] ECR 1337, para 13; nowadays codified in Directive 2004/38/EC of the European Parliament and of the Council of 29 April 2004 on the right of citizens of the Union and their family members to move and reside freely within the territory of the Member States amending Regulation (EEC) No 1612/68 and repealing Directives 64/221/EEC, 68/360/EEC, 72/194/EEC, 73/148/EEC, 75/34/EEC, 75/35/EEC, 90/364/EEC, 90/365/EEC and 93/96/EEC [2004] OJ L158/77, art 27 ff.

[115] See for the definition of public security, *Fahimian* (n 96), para 39; similarly, with regard to the concept of 'threat to public security', *E.P.* (n 96), para 32.

[116] *Fahimian* (n 96), para 40.

[117] ibid, para 40.

[118] *E.P.* (n 96), para 44.

[119] ibid, para 45.

[120] ibid, para 48.

by accepting such conduct, confirmed the wide decision-making power that national authorities have in this regard.

The ECJ's reasoning in *Fahimian* furthermore illustrates that national migration authorities' discretion may extend to measures less directly linked to the personal conduct of the individual concerned. Unlike the standard formula in free movement law, which focuses exclusively on the personal conduct of the individual concerned, the Court accepted that German authorities could ground a threat to public security in the activities of the Iranian university and not, for that matter, in Ms Fahimian's personal conduct.[121]

The different thresholds for tackling threats to public order or internal security bring to bear a distinction of constitutional provenance.[122] Individuals derive subjective rights from EU citizenship or the fundamental freedoms by virtue of primary law. Accordingly, the Court has repeatedly ruled that a strict interpretation is merited in the light of the constitutional right of residence of Union citizens.[123] Effectively, this renders restrictions thereto a rare, exceptional encounter. In contrast, third country nationals travelling to the EU by virtue of instruments of EU migration law may not have a comparable – constitutionally warranted – safeguard at hand. The Court's interpretation in this regard suggests that, in such a situation, the limitations to invoking public order grounds should be more lenient, to the effect that derogations may be applied more frequently.

Underlying this distinction between free movement and EU migration law may be a principled view holding that the granting of a residence permit in the context of the temporary, legal immigration 'constitutes a favour and not a right'.[124] Even though this view is technically not entirely correct,[125] as an impulse, it may explain the more lenient standards employed in *Fahimian* and *E.P.*[126] This is not to say, however, that third country nationals would categorically be barred from a standard of protection otherwise applied in free movement law. In the context of detention of migrants for the purpose of return, for instance, the Court has no difficulty reproducing the strict standard of a 'genuine, present and sufficiently serious threat' in EU migration law.[127] What sets this situation apart from the wide discretion of migration authorities, however, is that detention engages

[121] *Fahimian* (n 96), para 40.

[122] See Thym, '"Public Policy" as a Chameleonlike Concept: The Quest for Coherence in the CJEU Case Law On Migration and Union Citizenship' (n 8) 1374.

[123] Prominently, for instance, *Rendón Marín* (n 2), paras 82 ff.

[124] This description was coined by Belgian Constitutional Court, Judgment No 123 at 7, 26 September 2013 (BE), the author's translation of 'l'autorisation de séjour . . . constitué une faveur et non un droit', cited from F Strumia, 'European Citizenship and EU Immigration: A Demoi-Cratic Bridge between the Third Country Nationals' Right to Belong and the Member States' Power to Exclude' (2016) 22 *European Law Journal* 417, 430.

[125] See, for instance, *Ben Alaya* (n 97), para 31.

[126] For a similar explanation, see S Iglesias Sánchez, 'The Constitutional Status of Foreigners and European Union Citizens: Loopholes and Interactions in the Scope of Application of Fundamental Rights' in D Thym (ed), *Questioning EU Citizenship: Judges and the Limits of Free Movement and Solidarity in the EU* (Hart, 2017) 252.

[127] To this effect, Case C-18/19 *WM v Stadt Frankfurt am Main*, ECLI:EU:C:2020:51, [2020], para 46.

weighty fundamental rights safeguards, whereas restrictions to students' mobility or short-term travels may cause nuisance but will not, routinely, raise comparable fundamental rights considerations.

At the same time, a lenient interpretation of threats to public order and internal security in the field of EU migration law may equally follow from the division of powers between the Union and its Member States in this field of law. Despite a lack of explicit references thereto in the jurisprudence discussed, the Court's interpretation may be informed by Article 72 TFEU.[128] This constitutional provision stipulates that Union law 'shall not affect the exercise of the responsibilities incumbent upon Member States with regard to the maintenance of law and order and the safeguarding of internal security'. Although the repercussions of that provision are not yet established unequivocally,[129] it may be argued that Article 72 TFEU commands a broad interpretation of public order derogation clauses in secondary law, to the effect that national authorities may have wider discretion in the application thereof. On a conceptual level, however, it should be borne in mind that Article 72 TFEU draws a vertical line of division of competences, that is, between the Union and its Member States. Therefore, it does not relate to national executives specifically but may equally benefit national actors other than executives.

C. Abandoning Conceptual Pluralism? Limited Judicial Review Prescribed

In relation to foundational legal concepts of administrative law such as discretion, EU law tends to frequently accommodate different national perceptions and traditions. This principled pluralism can equally be detected in the context of the Court's affirmation of national migration authorities' wide discretion. While such a supranational label reproduces some of the characteristics of a supranational tradition of discretion,[130] the ECJ does not principally specify which ramifications should follow from the fact that a national migration authority has 'wide discretion'. Specifically, it equally applies to the question which intensity of control national courts should apply. The intensity of judicial review is treated, in this regard, as a matter of national procedural autonomy, allowing for a notable degree of variance between Member States.

In *Fahimian*, however, the Court explicitly departed from its pluralist stance. When pressed on the matter by the referring court, the ECJ scantly explicated that 'since the competent national authorities have a wide discretion in assessing the facts, judicial review is limited, as far as that assessment is concerned, to

[128] In this sense, Case C-544/15 *Sahar Fahimian v Bundesrepublik Deutschland* ECLI:EU:C:2016:908, [2016], Opinion of AG Szpunar, para 61.

[129] See H de Verdelhan, 'Art. 72 TFEU as Seen by the Court of Justice of the EU: Reminder, Exception, or Derogation?' (2024) 9 *European Papers* 1330.

[130] See above at ch 3, s II.B.

the absence of manifest error'.[131] In doing so, the Court effectively superimposed a supranational tradition of discretion onto national legal systems. By requiring national courts to limit their review of administrative discretion to manifest errors, the Court imported into national legal contexts its own understanding of how discretionary decision-making should be reviewed. Effectively, this judgment therefore marks a departure from the Court's principled pluralist approach.

On a more conceptual level of analysis, the ECJ's imposition of a specific intensity of control in *Fahimian* raises several questions. It may resemble an instance of 'imposed uniformity' that is rather uncharacteristic for the Luxemburg court's jurisprudence in this regard.[132]

In the first place, it may be worth asking whether a standard of limited judicial review should always follow from the Court's affirmation of national authorities' wide discretion, and not just in the rather peculiar situation of the case in *Fahimian*. In his opinion of the case, AG Szpunar argued along these lines, stipulating that a wide discretion should inevitably imply limited judicial review; '[o]therwise the margin of discretion would be frustrated, and the judiciary would be doing the job of the executive'.[133] From the perspective of the tradition of discretion in Union law, this view is entirely warranted. Nonetheless, it appears to disregard the fact that, in situations of indirect administration, the ECJ's understanding of discretion applies cheek-by-jowl with national traditions of discretion, which may engender certain conceptual idiosyncrasies. The case in *Fahimian*, for instance, concerned a particularity of the German tradition of discretion, namely the fact that undetermined legal terms would routinely not be viewed as entailing discretion and thus be subject to full review.[134] Accordingly, the situation in *Fahimian* would originally not have given rise to discretionary power in the German tradition thereof, despite the ECJ's affirmation to that end.

In his opinion in *Koushkaki*, to the contrary, AG Mengozzi seemed more aware of the conceptual divergence existing among the traditions of discretion concerned. Although the AG acknowledged that it was 'a specific point of contention in national law' whether German courts could fully review national migration authorities' wide discretion, he added that it was 'not for the Court to enter into such a debate', as this matter fell within the procedural autonomy of the Member State.[135] In *Fahimian*, however, the Court followed AG Szpunar's view, stipulating that a supranational characterisation of 'wide discretion' should conceptually call for limited judicial review by national courts. It did not provide any details for why, in this case, it deemed it necessary to interfere in the German debate, whereas it had refrained from doing so in the past. This case illustrates that the ECJ may

[131] *Fahimian* (n 96), para 46.
[132] R Widdershoven, 'Developing Administrative Law in Europe: Natural Convergence or Imposed Uniformity?' (2014) 7 *Review of European Administrative Law* 5, 10.
[133] Opinion of AG Szpunar, *Fahimian* (n 128), para 72.
[134] See above ch 2, s II.A.ii.
[135] Case C-84/12 *Rahmanian Koushkaki v Bundesrepublik Deutschland* ECLI:EU:C:2013:232, [2013], Opinion of AG Mengozzi, paras 26 ff.

exceptionally prescribe a method of limited judicial review to national courts, thus departing from its principled pluralist stance with a view to the intensity of judicial control.

i. De-Judicialisation by Judicial Means?

A second question arising in the fairway of the Court's imposition of a standard of limited review on national courts may relate to the precise nature of the standard thus imposed on national courts. What does 'limited' review mean in this regard? The Court's judgment in *Fahimian* may leave the impression that Union law caters to a reduction of a previously intense standard of control – a de-judicialisation by judicial means as it were. By requiring German courts to exercise limited judicial review in spheres where they would otherwise fully review administrative action, the position of courts vis-á-vis administrations is effectively weakened. Conceptually, however, the Court's understanding of limited review should not be mistaken for no judicial control at all.[136] Rather, there is more to the ECJ's conception of 'limited review' than would first meet the eye. It imposes on judges a specific form of control that centres on at least three aspects, which create noticeably avenues for judicial control, namely, verification that no procedural error occurred, that the factual basis for administrative action is correctly appraised, and the relevant standards of legality interpreted accurately.

In this sense, the limited nature of review of discretion is firstly compensated for by virtue of thorough review of procedural safeguards.[137] Where Union law prescribes national courts a standard of limited review, such procedural safeguards offer an opportunity to scrutinise national migration authorities' conduct, even where the latter is authorised by virtue of Union law to exercise 'wide discretion'. With a view to situations of direct administration, the ECJ has held that these standards are of 'even more fundamental importance' where the decision-maker exercised discretion.[138] Where national migration authorities are tasked to give effect to Union law through 'wide discretion', this particular significance of procedural standards is ferried over into national contexts.[139] In *Fahimian*, for instance, the Court ruled that those procedural guarantees include the obligation for

[136] Expressly, in this sense, Case C-723/17 *Lies Craeynest and Others v Brussels Hoofdstedelijk Gewest and Brussels Instituut voor Milieubeheer* ECLI:EU:C:2019:533, [2019], para 45: 'the existence of such discretionary powers does not in any way mean that the decisions taken by those authorities in that connection are exempt from judicial review, in particular in order to verify whether they have exceeded the limits set for the exercise of those powers'.

[137] See R Widdershoven, 'The European Court of Justice and the Standard of Judicial Review' in J Poorter, E Hirsch Ballin and S Lavrijssen (eds), *Judicial Review of Administrative Discretion in the Administrative State* (Asser; Springer, 2019) 57.

[138] Seminally, Case C-269/90 *Technische Universität München v Hauptzollamt München-Mitte* ECLI:EU:C:1991:438, [1991] ECR I-05469, para 14.

[139] *Fahimian* (n 96), para 46; see, on the significance of procedural aspects of an integrated European administration, W Weiß, *Der Europäische Verwaltungsverbund: Grundfragen, Kennzeichen, Herausforderungen* (Duncker & Humblot, 2010) 82 ff.

national migration authorities to act 'carefully and impartially' and to state the reasons motivating their decision.[140]

The statement of reasons for a decision is particularly relevant for a second avenue of judicial control, namely the assertion that all the factual and legal elements for exercising 'wide discretion' were present. This form of control was already evident in the Court's jurisprudence in other fields of EU law, where the ECJ held that national courts are to ascertain 'the accuracy of the findings of fact and law made by the authority concerned'.[141] This safeguard is not equally mentioned in *Fahimian*. On the one hand, it is true that national courts are tasked to merely verify that the decision is based on 'a sufficiently solid factual basis',[142] which points to a certain 'fact-finding discretion' barring national courts from fully reviewing the relevance of information gathered by the individual decision-maker.[143] On the other hand, the ECJ still insists that national courts verify that factual and legal elements giving rise to 'wide discretion' were present, which may allow for some form of judicial control over national migration authorities' assessment.

Third, national courts are moreover compelled to verify the accuracy of the findings of law. It is evident from the Court's reference to 'wide discretion' that national migration authorities' deliberations are not strictly circumscribed by standards of legality in such instances. Nonetheless, where Union law entails substantive standards instructing the exercise of wide discretion, national courts are obliged to review the measure in the light thereof, as is prominently borne out by the principle of proportionality. As a ground for review, the principle of proportionality allows national courts a more thorough investigation into the substance of the initial decision than the reference to limited judicial review would suggest at first.

The judgment in *E.P.* is emblematic in this regard.[144] The Court asserted that the national migration authorities are obliged, by virtue of the proportionality principle, to establish that the termination of a short-term stay was justified with a view to the seriousness of the alleged misconduct.[145] In this vein, the proportionality principle enables courts to review whether the relationship of preliminary facts, that is, the third country national's misconduct, and the content of the decision, *in casu* the immediate termination of short-term stay, relate reasonably to one

[140] *Fahimian* (n 96), para 46.

[141] Case C-120/97 *Upjohn Ltd v The Licensing Authority established by the Medicines Act 1968 and Others* ECLI:EU:C:1999:14, [1999], ECR I-00223, para 34.

[142] *Fahimian* (n 96), para 45.

[143] R Lehner and S Gies, 'Students and Researchers Directive (EU) 2016/801' in D Thym and K Hailbronner (eds), *EU Immigration and Asylum Law: Article-by-Article Commentary* 3rd edn (Beck; Hart; Nomos, 2022) 1071; K Hailbronner and S Gies, 'Council Directive 2004/114/EC of 13 December 2004 on the Conditions of Admission of Third-Country Nationals for the Purposes of Studies, Pupil Exchange, Unremunerated Training or Voluntary Service' in K Hailbronner and D Thym (eds), *EU Immigration and Asylum Law. A Commentary* 2nd edn (Beck; Nomos; Hart, 2016) 589 which made its way into Case C-544/15, *Sahar Fahimian v Bundesrepublik Deutschland* ECLI:EU:C:2016:908 [2016], para 67, Opinion of Advocate General Szpunar.

[144] *E.P.* (n 96), para 47.

[145] ibid, para 48.

another.[146] Whereas this ultimately leaves the rigour of proportionality review to the reviewing national court, proportionality may nonetheless impel national judges to invest in more intensive review.[147] By establishing proportionality as a substantive ground for review, the ECJ thus enables national courts to effectively step up the intensity of review vis-á-vis migration authorities' wide discretion.

Finally, the ECJ's later references to the judgment in *Fahimian* suggest that this judgment was not intended to lead to a de-judicialisation of discretionary powers. Rather, it appears to emphasise the Court's effort to establish a specific method of judicial oversight that is limited in substance but rigorous in ascertaining factual and procedural requirements. Albeit in a different context, in *Banger*, the Court referred to *Fahimian* to reiterate that Union law entitles individuals to a review by a court to verify whether the competent national authorities remains within the limits of their discretionary power – with no mention, however, of the fact that this constituted a form of 'limited' review.[148] Accordingly, *Fahimian* served as a reminder that the national court must ascertain in particular whether the discretionary decision was based on a sufficiently solid factual basis and whether the factual and legal elements on which the exercise of the discretionary power depends were present.[149] If it is presumed that the Court proceeds in a step-by-step fashion,[150] this may put the rather exceptional jurisprudence in *Fahimian* in context.

ii. Effective Remedy and the Preclusion of Uncontrolled Discretion

The repercussions that European legal influences create for national laws are contingent on the legal arrangements formerly prevalent in national legal systems. While from the perspective of one legal system, prescribed limited judicial review may appear as de-judicialisation by judicial means, other legal systems may get a very different experience. Quite the opposite to German law in *Fahimian*, for instance, the Court's affirmation of 'wide discretion' may call into question national legal arrangements that previously precluded national courts from reviewing administrative discretion altogether. In such a situation, European law caters to a relative invigoration of judicial control. A form of 'limited review' may thus mark the effective empowerment of national courts *vis-á-vis* national migration authorities, as the litigations in *El Hassani* and *Konsul Rzeczypospolitej Polskiej* illustrate.[151]

[146] ibid, para 48.

[147] On that phenomenon, see M Eliantonio, 'Deference to the Administration in Judicial Review: The European Union' in G Zhu (ed), *Deference to the Administration in Judicial Review: Comparative Perspectives* (Springer, 2019) 175 ff.

[148] Case C-89/17 *Secretary of State for the Home Department v Rozanne Banger* ECLI:EU:C:2018:570, [2018], para 50.

[149] ibid, para 51.

[150] See K Lenaerts, 'The Court's Outer and Inner Selves: Exploring the External and Internal Legitimacy of the European Court of Justice' in M Adams, H Waele and J Meeusen and G Straetmans (eds), *Judging Europe's Judges: The Legitimacy of the Case Law of the European Court of Justice* (Hart, 2013) 46.

[151] Case C-403/16 *Soufiane El Hassani v Minister Spraw Zagranicznych* ECLI:EU:C:2017:960, [2017] and Case C-949/19 *M.A. v Konsul Rzeczypospolitej Polskiej w N.* ECLI:EU:C:2021:186, [2021].

The case in *El Hassani* concerned the Polish legal framework on visas, which ruled out review by administrative courts altogether if a visa was issued by a consul.[152] This legal arrangement applied to national and Schengen visas alike.[153] Accordingly, the referring national court asked the ECJ whether such a legal arrangement could be in conformity with EU law, specifically the Visa Code, which obliges Member States to provide for an appeal and must be read in the light of Article 47 of the Charter of Fundamental Rights, that is, the right to an effective remedy before a court. Unlike the case in *Fahimian*, which concerned the reduction of the intensity of control, *El Hassani* revolved around the question whether judicial control had to be introduced in the first place.[154]

In its response, the ECJ emphasised that the Visa Code left to the Member States the task of determining the nature and conditions of remedies available to visa applicants, referring in this regard to the principle of procedural autonomy.[155] Nonetheless, it added that the Visa Code must be interpreted in accordance with the Charter of Fundamental Right. Whereas national migration authorities, *in casu* the Polish consul placed at an embassy abroad, have 'wide discretion' by virtue of the Visa Code,[156] this does not factor out the applicability of the Charter in these situations.[157] Accordingly, the respective legal framework must therefore provide for an effective remedy before a court, as Article 47 of the Charter stipulates. Union law does not specify at which moment in the proceedings such a remedy must be permitted, but, at a certain stage, there must be a possibility to bring a case against a final decision.[158] The judgment compelled the Polish legislature to reform the national framework on visas, so as to accommodate the requirements of Union law in this respect.[159] By virtue of Article 47 of the Charter of Fundamental Rights, the ECJ thus subjugated the previously uncontrolled decision-making of Polish consuls in visa matters to the jurisprudence of national administrative courts, without however specifying that this would imply limited judicial review.

The ECJ subsequently conferred this jurisprudence to the Students and Researchers Directive.[160] It reiterated, in this regard, that Member States are under an obligation, in situations governed by that instrument, to provide for an effective remedy. Although the Court essentially left the question whether the Directive would apply to the situation at hand to the referring national court, it explicated

[152] The original version of Prawo o postępowaniu przed sądami administracyjnymi 2002 [Law on Proceedings before Administrative Courts] (Dz. U. 2002, no 153, item 1270), art 5(4).

[153] *El Hassani* (n 151), para 19.

[154] See W Piątek, 'The Right to an Effective Remedy in European Law: Significance, Content and Interaction' (2019) 6 *China-EU Law Journal* 163, 170 ff.

[155] *El Hassani* (n 151), paras 25 ff.

[156] ibid, para 36.

[157] ibid, paras 32 ff.

[158] ibid, para 41.

[159] See Piątek (n 154) 171.

[160] *Konsul Rzeczypospolitej Polskiej* (n 151); referring to Directive (EU) 2016/801 of the European Parliament and of the Council of 11 May 2016 on the conditions of entry and residence of third-country nationals for the purposes of research, studies, training, voluntary service, pupil exchange schemes or educational projects and au pairing [2016] OJ L132/21.

that absence of judicial review in this regard would be incompatible with EU law.[161] This being noted, the Court highlighted that the intensity of judicial review would be a matter of Member States' procedural autonomy.[162] In contrast to its ruling in *Fahimian*, the ECJ thereby returns to a pluralist tenor regarding the intensity of judicial control, refuting however, instances of discretionary power that would preclude judicial control altogether.

In *XXX v État belge*, the Court of Justice was moreover asked to clarify whether a cassation model of review would satisfy the requirements that flow from the right to an effective remedy.[163] In this case, Belgium had implemented a legal framework that allowed national courts to review and annul the decision refusing to grant a visa, but not to vary the initial decision by the competent migration authorities. In its reasoning, the Court again starts from a pluralist premise. It points out that, in principle, Article 47 of the Charter does not preclude a legal arrangement whereby the reviewing court is competent 'only to rule on the annulment of the decision . . . , without being able to substitute its own assessment for that of [the competent authority]'.[164] This principled pluralism notwithstanding, the Court emphasised that such a legal arrangement may not be used to render the right to an effective remedy illusory.[165] Rather, national legal systems must ensure that the competent administrative body to which the court remits the case complies with the assessment of the court and adopts its decision swiftly.[166] This goes to show that the Court is principally willing to keep national traditions of judicial review intact, at least insofar as they are not designed in a way that would frustrate the right to an effective remedy in practice.

III. Discretion as a Compensation Valve for Dysfunctional Transnational Administrative Systems

When discussing discretion in European Migration law, the Dublin system's discretionary clause is often the first instance that springs to mind. The provisions prominence is hardly surprising: during the so-called refugee crisis, the Dublin discretionary clause became a central legal basis for ad hoc crisis management and relocation efforts among Member States. Much of its significance, therefore, derives from the makeshift solutions to which it gave rise in recent crisis moments.

Against this backdrop, it can be argued that the Dublin discretionary clause provided the flexibility necessary to keep the Dublin system intact during times of severe crisis.[167] Through its activation, national migration authorities were able to

[161] ibid, para 41.
[162] ibid, para 43.
[163] For this form of judicial control, see above at ch 2, s II.C.ii.
[164] Case C-14/23 *XXX v État belge* ECLI:EU:C:2024:647, [2024], para 65.
[165] ibid, para 62.
[166] ibid, para 64.
[167] For a similar conclusion, see D Thym, 'Judicial Maintenance of the Sputtering Dublin System on Asylum Jurisdiction: Jafari, A.S., Mengesteab and Shiri' (2018) 55 *Common Market Law Review* 549, 561.

compensate for some of the shortcomings and dysfunctionalities that characterise administrative cooperation. In this sense, the Dublin discretionary clause can be likened to a compensation valve, enabling national administrators to relieve some of the pressure put on a transnational administrative system in moments of crisis.

In analytical terms, it is important to highlight that the discretionary clause in the Dublin system constitutes a form of faculty afforded to Member rather than to national administrators specifically. Yet, as will be illustrated in the following analysis, national lawmakers routinely entrust the freedom to decide whether to activate this discretionary clause to national administrative authorities (subsection A). While national lawmakers remain free, in principle, to opt for different legal arrangements in this regard, it will be argued that administrative discretion may have emerged as a prerequisite for ad hoc crisis responses seeking to mitigate some of the dysfunctionalities of the transnational administrative system of responsibility allocation (subsection B).

A. The Dublin Discretionary Clause

The Dublin system establishes a legal framework for the purpose of attributing responsibility among the Member States for the examination of asylum applications. With the entry into force of the New Pact on Migration and Asylum, this system is nowadays enshrined in the Asylum and Migration Management Regulation (AMMR).[168] Not unlike its predecessor, the Dublin III Regulation,[169] the AMMR system spells out a list of 'objective' criteria on the basis of which the Member State responsible for examining an asylum application is to be determined. Essentially mirroring the legal arrangement under the Dublin III Regulation, the determination of the Member State responsible follows from the hierarchy set out in Articles 24 ff AMMR.

The list places the interests of unaccompanied minors to be united with their family members at the top, spelling out detailed rules which Member State should be responsible for these persons. For other applicants of international protection who have family members legally residing in another Member State, that other Member State should be responsible for the examination of their application. If these family-related criteria do not apply to an applicant for international protection but a Member State had issued a residence document or a visa to that person, it should be this latter Member State that is responsible for the application. Although this situation may be pertinent with a view to some third country

[168] Regulation (EU) 2024/1351 of the European Parliament and of the Council of 14 May 2024 on asylum and migration management, amending Regulations (EU) 2021/1147 and (EU) 2021/1060 and repealing Regulation (EU) No 604/2013 (AMMR) [2024] OJ L 1351 (henceforth: AMMR).

[169] Regulation (EU) No 604/2013 of the European Parliament and of the Council of 26 June 2013 establishing the criteria and mechanisms for determining the Member State responsible for examining an application for international protection lodged in one of the Member States by a third-country national or a stateless person [2013] OJ L180/31.

nationals, it should be noted that Member States are regularly reluctant to issue such documents to potential asylum seekers.[170] While the AMMR adds a new criterion relating to the issuing of a diploma or a qualification and maintains some additional criteria that were already mentioned in the Dublin III Regulation, such as visa-waived entry and applications filed in international transit areas, the criterion that is the most relevant in practice is the criterion of first entry: where no higher-ranking criterion applies, it will be the Member State in which the applicant first entered the EU that is responsible for the examination of her or his application for international protection.

Technically, this system is seamless. The criteria listed always allow for the identification of one Member State responsible for examining the asylum application. In this vein, the Dublin system may be said to create a system in which responsibility is vested with one single Member State, based on criteria that are (arguably) fair regarding Member States and third country nationals concerned.[171] The practice within the Dublin system, however, betrays these objectives,[172] and it may reasonably be questioned whether the innovations in the system of hierarchical criteria following the entry into force of the AMMR would improve this situation. In the past, at least, the Dublin system has been beset by severe asymmetries.[173] This has significantly elevated the practical prominence of the Dublin discretionary clause, which emerged as the key legal tool to enable Member States to avoid transfer of applicants for international protection to other Member States where legal or factual reasons precluded this.

Not unlike the Dublin III Regulation, the AMMR includes a broad discretionary clause that provides that a Member State 'may decide to examine an application for international protection ... registered with it, even if such examination is not its responsibility according to the criteria laid down in this Regulation'.[174] This discretionary clause formed part of the Dublin system since its inception and has prominently been labelled the 'sovereignty clause'.[175] Although such terminology may be misleading,[176] it nonetheless resonates with the provision's principal objective, namely to 'maintain the prerogatives of the Member States'.[177] Moreover,

[170] See M Mouzourakis and C Costello, 'The Common European Asylum System: Where Did It All Go Wrong?' in M Fletcher, E Herlin-Karnell and C Matera (eds), *The European Union as an Area of Freedom, Security and Justice* (Routledge, 2017) 270.

[171] In this sense, AMMR, recital 1.

[172] For analyses of these deficits, see amongst others F Maiani, 'The Reform of the Dublin System and the Dystopia of "Sharing People"' (2017) 24 *Maastricht Journal of European and Comparative Law* 622, 625.

[173] See D Dreyer-Plum, 'Dublin Revisited: Geographic Asymetry and Corrective Allocation Mechanisms' (2020) 22 *European Journal of Migration and Law* 386, 389.

[174] AMMR, art 35 (1).

[175] See S Morgades-Gil, 'The Discretion of States in the Dublin III System for Determining Responsibility for Examining Applications for Asylum: What Remains of the Sovereignty and Humanitarian Clauses After the Interpretations of the ECtHR and the CJEU?' (2015) 27 *International Journal of Refugee Law* 433, 441.

[176] See ibid 454.

[177] Case C-661/17 *M.A. and Others v The International Protection Appeals Tribunal and Others* ECLI: EU:C:2019:53, [2019], para 60, with further references.

again mirroring the previous legal framework in the Dublin III Regulation, the AMMR includes a second discretionary clause, aimed at bringing together family members.[178] Both provisions are 'optional' and, on that note, 'grant a wide discretionary power to Member States'.[179]

i. Devolvement to Administrative Bodies

Following the express wording of Article 35 AMMR, these discretionary clauses are addressed to the Member States in their own right. Against that background, it may be questioned whether these avenues of discretion specifically benefit national administrations or rather, a Member State in its entirety. On the one hand, the AMMR is directly applicable law which, in principle, does not require national measures of transposition. In this regard, the normative context of the discretionary clause would rally for an interpretation that procedurally links its exercise to the individual case of an applicant for international protection.[180] The wording of Article 35 AMMR, on the other hand, suggests that this form of discretion is aimed at Member States as such, without a specification as to which national actor should exercise this power. In keeping with the principal motive of 'maintaining the prerogatives of the Member States',[181] the Dublin discretionary clauses should therefore be viewed as a form of latitude afforded to the Member States in their own right.

Accordingly, Member States are principally free to assign the tasks of activating the Dublin discretionary clause to national bodies as they deem appropriate. The Irish Supreme Court, for instance, was uncertain whether the Member States could adopt a national legal framework that, for the regularities of the Dublin procedure, tasked an administrative authority – the national Refugee Applications Commissioner[182] – but for the exercise of the discretionary clauses, a governmental institution, namely the Minister of Justice and Equality. The ECJ had no difficulty to accept this legal arrangement, to the effect that Member States may attribute tasks arising from the Dublin III Regulation and, nowadays, the AMMR,

[178] AMMR, art 35 (2), largely mirroring Regulation (EU) No 604/2013 of the European Parliament and of the Council of 26 June 2013 establishing the criteria and mechanisms for determining the Member State responsible for examining an application for international protection lodged in one of the Member States by a third-country national or a stateless person (Dublin III Regulation) [2013] OJ L180/31, art 17 (2).

[179] With regard to the previous Dublin II Regulation; Council Regulation (EC) No 343/2003 of 18 February 2003 establishing the criteria and mechanisms for determining the Member State responsible for examining an asylum application lodged in one of the Member States by a third-country national (Dublin II Regulation) [2003] OJ L50/1, Case C-394/12 *Shamso Abdullahi v Bundesasylamt* ECLI:EU:C:2013:813, [2013], para 57; reaffirmed for the Dublin III Regulation, *M.A.* (n 177), para 60.

[180] See Wendel (n 3) 327.

[181] *M.A.* (n 177), para 60.

[182] Admittedly, this qualification of the Commissioner's mandate as administrative may be questioned. However, before its resolution and replacement by the International Protection Office, its task predominantly concerned decision-making vis-á-vis individuals, which corresponds to the definition of administrative power used in this investigation; see above at the introductory section to ch 1.

to different institutions.[183] It may be noted that the institutional arrangement adopted by Ireland illustrates how traditioned perceptions on administrative power may influence the manner of implementation of Union law in the Member States. While Ireland tasked an administrative body with the responsibility to apply this directly applicable Regulation, it felt that the exercise of wide discretionary power was better placed in the hands of a politically more directly responsible authority such as a minister.[184]

While the Dublin discretionary clauses are formally addressed to Member States as such, national legal systems tend to attribute the task of activating the discretionary clause to administrative authorities.[185] The Dublin system may thus serve as a good example of a practice in which Member States devolve their latitude to administrative actors. A cursory analysis of Member States' institutional arrangements corroborates this. In Germany, the decision whether to activate the discretionary clauses in the Dublin system is assigned to the Bundesamt für Migration und Flüchtlinge, the administrative federal office responsible for asylum examinations,[186] and the French legal system assigns this responsibility to *préfectures*, the local representation of the ministry of interior.[187]

ii. Devolvement and Discretion

On an analytical level, it should be noted that the devolvement of Member States' deliberative freedom to administrative bodies may not, in and of itself, give rise to legal arrangements that qualify as discretion for the purposes of the present investigation. Particularly, by attributing the power to activate the Dublin discretionary clause to administrative bodies, Member State legal systems do not specify what intensity of judicial control should be exercised. For that reason, it may not be inconceivable that national courts would fully review the decision to activate or refuse to activate the Dublin discretionary clauses. Empirically, however, it may be noted that national legal systems frequently reproduce standards of limited judicial review in relation to these instances of devolved freedom.

In the Netherlands, the power to decide whether to apply one of the discretionary clauses lies with the Immigration and Naturalisation Service (IND). The authority acts on the basis of instructions set out in a ministerial circular, which stipulate that the discretionary clauses may be activated in situations involving special circumstances in which the transfer to the responsible Member State would result in particular hardship or where there are concrete indications that the responsible Member State does not comply with its international obligations

[183] *M.A.* (n 177), paras 62, 64 ff.

[184] On this point, see ch 2, s I.A.ii.

[185] See M Wendel, 'The Refugee Crisis and the Executive: On the Limits of Administrative Discretion in the Common European Asylum System' (2016) 17 *German Law Journal* 1005, 1012.

[186] Asylgesetz 2008, § 5 (1) (BRD).

[187] *Code de l'entrée et du séjour des étrangers et du droit d'asile*, art R741-1 (FR).

in relation to international protection.[188] What is worth noticing in this context is that the Dutch Council of State has confirmed that this decision should be subject to limited judicial review.[189] When reviewing the (non-)activation of the Dublin discretionary clause, the reviewing national court should not supersede the decision of the IND and instead carry out restraint review. Analytically, this suggests that national legal systems tend to integrate the Dublin discretionary clauses through national legal arrangements that qualify, for the purposes of this investigation, as discretion.

Before the UK's withdrawal from the EU, a similar development could be witnessed in English law. In a landmark judgment concerning the situation of minors in the so-called jungle of Calais, Lord Justice Beatson clarified that the exercise of the Dublin discretionary clause would be 'subject to the ordinary public law principles of propriety of purpose, relevancy of considerations, and the longstop *Wednesbury* unreasonableness category' and, following from the UK's obligations pursuant to Article 8 ECHR, an appropriate intensity of review in the assessment of proportionality.[190] The was later picked up in Upper Tribunal in *R (BAA & Anor)*, confirming that judicial review of this decision-making power should be based, amongst other things, on the Wednesbury unreasonableness test.[191] This goes to show that the Dublin discretionary clause, when integrated into national legal systems, may be associated with traditioned understandings of administrative discretion, to the effect that national courts will apply a standard of limited judicial review.

B. Dublin Discretion and Makeshift Crisis Responses

The discretionary clause of the Dublin system has hogged the limelight of political attention in the fairway of the so-called refugee crisis.[192] Events that unfolded in September 2015 – difficult as they are to analytically discern in all detail – showcased the transnational effects of unilateral assumption of responsibility by some Member States.[193] In this regard, excessive use of the discretionary clause has occasionally been interpreted as hammering a nail in the coffin of the Dublin system. This view is inaccurate, given the vast nature of latitude afforded to Member States by virtue of what is now Article 35 AMMR. Nonetheless, the Dublin discretionary

[188] Vreemdelingencirculaire 2000, Section C2/5 (NL)

[189] Council of State, Decision no 201806712/1, ECLI:NL:RVS:2018:3246 (10 October 2018), point 1, 2 (NL).; Council of State, Decision no 201908101/1/V3, ECLI:NL:RVS:2020:545, point 3 (NL).

[190] *Secretary for the Home Department v ZAT* [2016] EWCA Civ 810 (UK).

[191] *R (BAA & Anor) v Secretary of State for the Home Department* [2020] UKUT 227 (IAC) (UK), para 27, para 31, with reference to the precedence provided by Lord Justice Beatson in *Secretary for the Home Department v ZAT* [2016] EWCA Civ 810 (UK), para 85.

[192] See Wendel (n 3) 129 ff.

[193] Transnational effects, in this sense, may refer to transnational *legal* effects, but equally to factual developments. Regarding the latter, see L Pries, '"We Will Manage It": Did Chancellor Merkel's Dictum Increase of Even Cause the Refugee Movement in 2015?' (2019) 58 *International Migration* 18, 24 ff.

clauses have been instrumental in the creation and legal justification of makeshift crisis responses in two contexts. First, the excessive use of the discretionary clause by Germany in September 2015 may serve as a prominent and tirelessly discussed example of unilateral activation of the discretionary clause (subsection i), whereas the so-called Malta declaration provided for negotiated but limited framework for assuming responsibility by virtue of the discretionary clause (subsection ii).

i. Suspending Dublin by Exercising the Discretionary Clause?

The Dublin discretionary clause has gained notoriety in the context of the so-called refugee crisis. Although Member States are generally reluctant to exercise the discretionary clause, exceptional circumstances may impel them to do so, nonetheless. Faced with a sharp increase of applications for international protection, German immigration authorities, for instance, decided to 'suspend' Dublin procedures for Syrian applicants to free capacities for the examination of large numbers of claims in substance.[194] Initially, commentators wondered how to construe this suspension in legal terms. A prominent reading of this step stipulated that German authorities – and Chancellor Merkel personally – blatantly violated the Dublin rules as well as the Grundgesetz.[195] In this sense, it was portrayed as cold-blooded disapplication of the Dublin III Regulation altogether. A more benevolent reading, however, interprets this suspension as a generalised application of the discretionary clause in Article 17(1) of the Dublin III Regulation by the German authorities.[196]

A generalised application of Article 17(1) complies with the spirit and letter of the Dublin III Regulation. In the first place, the Court has prominently conceptualised the discretionary clause to form an integral part of the Dublin system.[197] From this perspective, it would be inapt to describe its application as a suspension thereof. In the second place, however, such a crisis response effectively pushes the rule-exception relationship inherent in the Dublin system to a limit. It partially replaces the system of objective criteria for determining the Member State responsible with a generalised exercise of the discretionary clause, which should apply '[b]y virtue of derogation' therefrom.

The ECJ put an end to the debate whether German authorities' excessive use of the discretionary clause in times of crisis was acceptable from the perspective of Union law. In *Jafari*, the Court ruled that one Member State may assume responsibility by virtue of Article 17(1), where another Member State experiences an unusually large number of third country nationals seeking international protection.[198] In such a situation, it may be appropriate, 'in a spirit of solidarity, which, in

[194] See Wendel (n 185) 1020 ff, with further references.

[195] For a prominent example, see U Di Fabio, *Migrationskrise Als Föderales Verfassungsproblem: Gutachten Im Auftrag Des Freistaates Bayern* (2015) 81 ff, www.welt.de/bin/di-fabio-gutachten-150937063.pdf.

[196] Although, terminologically, this does decidedly not amount to a 'suspension' of the Dublin system, see Wendel (n 185) 1021.

[197] ECJ, Case C-578/16 PPU *C. K. and Others v Republika Slovenija* ECLI:EU:C:2017:108, [2017], para 53.

[198] Case C-646/16 *Khadija Jafari and Zainab Jafari* ECLI:EU:C:2017:586, [2017], para 100.

accordance with Article 80 TFEU, underlies the Dublin III Regulation', to exercise the discretionary clause.[199] Whereas the reference to the 'spirit' of solidarity and possible ramifications thereof remain opaque, it constitutes a relatively overt judicial endorsement of the measures taken by the German authorities during crisis. Accordingly, an excessive use of the discretionary clauses does not disactivate the Dublin system but rather fleshes out a mechanism entailed therein that may be utilised, among other things, to cater to a sense of solidarity among the Member States. In this vein, the Court accepts that Member States may, in the implementation of the Dublin III Regulation, aspire to optimise the structural asymmetry of the Dublin system by administrative means.

ii. Ad Hoc Solidarity: The Malta Declaration of 2019

Ideally, mechanisms of fair burden sharing, and, generally, of solidarity, are inherently built into systems of transnational responsibility attribution. As practice in the field of EU migration law demonstrates, this is not always the case.[200] Efforts to strengthen inter-state solidarity in this field are often crisis driven.[201] In the context of the events in 2015 and 2016, this effect was borne out by the unilateral decision to sweepingly activate the discretionary clause by German authorities. The so-called Malta Declaration of 2019[202] adopted a similar approach, albeit one that was negotiated in the context of an intergovernmental forum and involved, at various stages, Union institutions and agencies.[203]

The Malta Declaration was presented as a breakthrough, ending stalemate after Italy had unilaterally closed its ports to persons rescued at sea.[204] This effectively sidestepped responsibilities under the Dublin system, as it prevented the entry of third country nationals, leaving them in a situation of limbo offshore. This untenable situation led to a hastily summoned informal meeting of Justice and Home Affairs ministers in Malta, during which the ministers of interior of Italy, Malta, France and Germany adopted the said declaration. The declaration laid out 'voluntary commitments by Member States for a predictable temporary solidarity

[199] ibid.

[200] See J Bast, 'Solidarität Im Europäischen Einwanderungs- Und Asylrecht' in M Knodt and A Tews (eds), *Solidarität in der EU* (Nomos, 2014) 150 ff, with further references.

[201] See E Tsourdi, 'Solidarity at Work? The Prevalence of Emergency-Driven Solidarity in the Administrative Governance of the Common European Asylum System' (2017) 24 *Maastricht Journal of European and Comparative Law* 667, 675.

[202] This joint declaration of intent should not be mistaken for the 2017 Malta Declaration of the European Council, which drew up certain policy objectives with regard to the external aspects of migration in the Central Mediterranean route; see European Council, *Malta Declaration by the members of the European Council on the external aspects of migration: addressing the Central Mediterranean route* (Press release, 3 February 2017) www.consilium.europa.eu/en/press/press-releases/2017/02/03/malta-declaration/.

[203] See Joint Declaration of Intent on a Controlled Emergency Procedure – Voluntary Commitments by Member States for a Predictable Temporary Solidarity Mechanism (Malta Declaration) (23 September 2019), www.statewatch.org/news/2019/sep/eu-temporary-voluntary-relocation-mechanism-declaration.pdf.

[204] For an overview of these events, see S Carrera and R Cortinovis, 'The Malta Declaration on SAR and Relocation: A Predictable EU Solidarity Mechanism?' (2019) 14 *CEPS Policy Insights* 1, 3.

mechanism'. The Declaration was open for other governments to join, even though enthusiasm remained limited and the initiative comprised no more than a small group of the willing.

The Malta Declaration constitutes a non-binding 'joint declaration of intent'.[205] The Declaration stipulates that its signatory Member States establish a fast-track system of relocation based on pre-declared pledges before disembarkation.[206] The allocation of responsibility for examining applications for international protection therefore sticks to a ship-by-ship approach but aims at accelerated procedures. This solidarity mechanism operates against the background of the Dublin system and must therefore be considered in the light thereof. In legal terms, the mechanism was operationalised through the discretionary clauses in Article 17 of the Dublin III Regulation, even though the declaration does not specify which legal basis is used to that end – the sovereignty clause in Article 17(1) or the humanitarian clause in Article 17(2) thereof.[207] Either way, in this ad hoc framework, some Member States have asserted their willingness to invoke the discretionary clauses with a view to persons rescued at high seas.[208]

One of the central elements of that mechanism concerns rapid processing and smooth operational cooperation, to respect the time limits foreseen in the Malta Declaration.[209] In this regard, the activities of EU agencies are of particular significance.[210] Although reliable and detailed information surrounding these ad hoc arrangements is difficult to come by,[211] EASO and Frontex ensure its effectiveness in practice.[212] Frontex, for its part, has assumed tasks connected to the hotspots in Italy, including identification and nationality determination, registration

[205] On this point, see J van Berckel Smit, 'Taking Onboard the Issue of Disembarkation: The Mediterranean Need for Responsibility-Sharing after the Malta Declaration' (2020) 22 *European Journal of Migration and Law* 492, 514.

[206] See Joint Declaration of Intent on a Controlled Emergency Procedure – Voluntary Commitments by Member States for a Predictable Temporary Solidarity Mechanism (Malta Declaration) (23 September 2019), www.statewatch.org/news/2019/sep/eu-temporary-voluntary-relocation-mechanism-declaration.pdf, para 4.

[207] See Carrera and Cortinovis (n 204) 5, who merely refer to art 17 (2) of the Dublin III Regulation, ie, the humanitarian clause.

[208] This interpretation of the Malta declaration is shared by the European Asylum Support Office (EASO), which is nowadays renamed to the European Union Agency for Asylum (EUAA). The Agency reiterated that this model of relocation 'requires and foresees that the legal basis of the intervention should be art 17 of the Dublin Regulation'. EASO, 'Note on the 'Messina Model' applied in the context of ad hoc relocation arrangements following disembarkation', 12 September 2019, EASO/ED/2019/403, at 1.

[209] Joint Declaration of Intent on a Controlled Emergency Procedure – Voluntary Commitments by Member States for a Predictable Temporary Solidarity Mechanism (Malta Declaration) (23 September 2019), www.statewatch.org/news/2019/sep/eu-temporary-voluntary-relocation-mechanism-declaration.pdf, para 2, explicates that 'swift relocation . . . should not take longer than 4 weeks'.

[210] See already Tsourdi (n 201) 676.

[211] This secrecy may be deliberate, see S Carrera and R Cortinovis, 'Search and Rescue, Disembarkation and Relocation Arrangements in the Mediterranean: Sailing Away from Responsibility?' (2019) 10 *CEPS Papers in Liberty and Security in Europe* 1, 24.

[212] Council of the European Union, 'Working Paper 7219/2019 INIT' (12 June 2019) <www.statewatch.org/media/documents/news/2019/jun/eu-council-wk-guidelines-on-temporary-arrangement-disembarkation.pdf>.

of disembarked individuals through entries into Eurodac and the Schengen Information System II. The involvement of EASO pertained to Malta and Italy alike and aimed at 'matching' an applicant with a Member State willing to assume responsibility for examining her or his application for international protection.[213] To this end, EASO's support included the registration of an applicant, an examination of vulnerability, possible family or cultural links to a person residing in another Member State and consideration with a view to a subsequent fair and proportional allocation system among participating Member States.[214]

This suggests that the Dublin criteria still exerted influence in this respect, despite the fact that this relocation arrangement was operationalised by virtue of Member States' discretion in Article 17 of the Dublin III Regulation. EASO's guidelines suggest that, in practice, the voluntary relocation of responsibility will first run through the Dublin criteria to verify whether one of the participating Member States may be formally responsible for examining the claim. Subsequently, EASO considers other aspects, such as family links that are not covered by the Dublin criteria or cultural ties. Last, the agency is encouraged to pursue a fair and proportionate allocation system among the participating Member States.

This links to the question whether such an ad hoc relocation mechanism may be viewed as an attempt to overhaul the attribution of responsibility enshrined in the Dublin system by administrative means. Unlike the events in 2015 and 2016 that came to be known as the refugee crisis, and where national migration authorities excessively exercised the discretionary clause in the Dublin III Regulation,[215] the administrative authority taking action to bring about a higher degree of perceived solidarity and burden sharing among the Member States in this respect is an EU agency. The declaration required EASO to strive for a fair and proportional allocation system, which should have originally been brought about by the EU legislature. However, such a view is not warranted with a view to the relocation mechanism that was put in place in the context of disembarkation. In the first place, the ship-by-ship approach – in relative terms – concerns a very small group of persons, which gets lost in the great shuffle of the Dublin system more generally. In the second place, the practical implementation of this voluntary mechanism still centres on the upstream application of the Dublin criteria. This suggests that EASO will, whenever possible, give effect to the attribution of responsibility in line with Article 3 (1) of the Dublin III Regulation, that is, based on the list of objective criteria.

At an analytical level, this ad hoc response illustrates how the discretionary clauses can be used to compensate for dysfunctionalities in the Dublin system. Unlike the activation thereof by German authorities in 2015/2016, the Malta declaration followed a coordinated approach. In cooperation with EU agencies,

[213] See Carrera and Cortinovis (n 211) 26.

[214] See EASO, 'Note on the "Messina Model" applied in the context of ad hoc relocation arrangements following disembarkation', 12 September 2019, EASO/ED/2019/403, at 1.

[215] See above at ch 3, s III.B.i.

national migration authorities were able to put into effect a ship-by-ship approach of relocation that was put into practice, legally, through a coordinated activation of the Dublin discretionary clauses. In this sense, the existence of these clauses allowed migration authorities to find a political solution to Italy's refusal to disembark persons at Italian ports, thereby effectively sidestepping responsibilities under EU migration law.

IV. European Standards Precluding Discretionary Power

As the preceding sections indicate, influences of European law incentivise national legal systems to keep or introduce instances of discretionary decision-making in several situations. In this respect, migration law follows a trend observed in relation to European legal trends on national administrative systems more generally, namely that the interactions unfolding within a multi-levelled legal system necessitate the existence of spheres of administrative autonomy on several occasions.[216] These avenues of administrative autonomy will often be fleshed out through legal arrangements that are viewed, for the purposes of this investigation, as discretion. Nonetheless, on other occasions, influences of European law explicitly or implicitly preclude national legal systems from adopting legal arrangements that provide for discretion. Specifically, this is the case in the context of decision-making in matters of asylum law and return detention.

In relation to asylum decision-making, European law includes standards that afford national asylum authorities' administrative autonomy but appears to explicitly preclude legal arrangements that would coincide with limited judicial review, and thus, discretion (subsection A). While this should repress the existence of discretion in these instances of decision-making, it should be noted that some Member States have attempted to introduce discretionary decision-making in the field of asylum law, nonetheless. This prompted the Court of Justice to explicitly reject the notion that EU migration law instruments in these areas could be given effect through legal frameworks involving discretion in these areas of law (subsection B).

A. Discretion and Asylum Decision-making: A Mismatch?

In the context of asylum examinations, the influence that European law exerts on national legal systems follows two rather contradictory impulses. On the one hand, it ensures that administrative decision-making is impartial and objective, thereby safeguarding a rather high degree of administrative autonomy. On the other hand, autonomy is not fleshed out through legal arrangements that qualify

[216] See Mattarella (n 109) 33; Weiß (n 139) 22 ff.

as discretion as understood in this investigation. In fact, by prescribing on national courts to carry out full and *ex nunc* review of administrative decisions, European legal influences preclude the existence in this field. In this sense, it may be argued that discretion and asylum decision-making in European migration law are a mismatch – as a legal phenomenon, the former does not exist in the latter.

In the following, these influences of international and European law on asylum decision-making will be presented. This analysis will focus on standards in EU secondary law that safeguard administrative autonomy (subsection i). While this autonomy could be viewed as speaking to one of the properties of the framework definition of discretion applied in this investigation, standards of European asylum law explicitly bar legal systems from relying on another property thereof, namely limited judicial review. By imposing a standard of full judicial review of asylum decision-making, these influences seek to explicitly rule out that national legal systems may utilise discretion in the context of asylum examinations (subsection ii).

i. Safeguards of Administrative Autonomy in Asylum Law: Impartiality and Objectivity

The key instruments of international refugee protection, the 1951 Geneva Refugee Convention, premises on the notion that asylum authorities should assess asylum claims in an objective fashion.[217] It draws up a list of constellations in which an individual, owing to a 'well-founded fear' of persecution, will qualify as a refugee. Once a person qualifies as a refugee, the Convention presumes that State parties cannot refuse to recognise her or him as such, except where one of the exhaustively listed grounds for exclusion applies. Although research illustrates that decision-making practices can differ strongly from one legal system to another,[218] and even within legal systems,[219] formally, the legal regime established by the Refugee Convention is based on the idea that protection needs are assessed objectively by national asylum authorities.

In EU law, the idea of objectivity in asylum examinations is explicitly linked to a standard of administrative impartiality. Not unlike its predecessor, the Asylum Procedures Regulation tasks national authorities to examine asylum applications 'objectively, impartially and on an individual basis'.[220] That requirement is

[217] This nowadays constitutes the prevalent view in the literature, even though a competing approach features in judicial practice and earlier writings, which presume that asylum examination process would include objective and subjective elements. For an overview of the literature on this point, see A Zimmermann and C Mahler, 'Article 1A, Para 2 1951 Convention' in A Zimmermann, J Dörschner and F Machts (eds), *The 1951 Convention Relating to the Status of Refugees and its 1967 Protocol: A Commentary* (Oxford University Press, 2011) 338 ff, with further references.

[218] See TG Eule et al, *Migrants Before the Law. Contested Migration Control in Europe* (Palgrave Macmillan, 2019) 46, with further references.

[219] See L Riedel and G Schneider, 'Dezentraler Asylvollzug Diskriminiert: Anerkennungsquoten von Flüchtlingen Im Bundesdeutschen Vergleich, 2010–2015' (2017) 58 *Politische Vierteljahresschrift* 23.

[220] Regulation (EU) 2024/1348 of the European Parliament and of the Council of 14 May 2024 establishing a common procedure for international protection in the Union and repealing Directive 2013/32/EU (Asylum Procedures Regulation) [2024] OJ L 2024/1348, art 34 (2).

a codification of the general principle of good administration, which requires administrators to adjudicate without any interest in the outcome of the case apart from the strict application of the rule of law.[221] Accordingly, the objective determination of a person's protection needs precludes the administrative decision-maker to display an attitude that is biased against the protection seeker.[222]

On the one hand, it should be noted that the impartiality of administrative decision-makers does not require the same level of independence as that of judicial authorities.[223] On the other hand, it presupposes – in line with a Weberian understanding of administrative ethos – a sense of neutrality and objectivity in performing administrative tasks.[224] In the context of EU asylum law, such a development is reiterated in the recitals of the Asylum Procedures Regulation, which stipulate that asylum authorities should 'perform their activities with due respect for the applicable ethical principles'.[225] While Member States may adopt organisational frameworks that subject national asylum authorities to varying degrees of organisational dependence, these standards of objectivity and impartially may be said to safeguard a degree of administrative autonomy in relation to national lawmakers.[226]

Empirically, this autonomy may explain the divergent recognition rates in practice.[227] It may be assumed that, as a matter of fact, migration authorities oftentimes have some degree of autonomy in decision-making, thus explaining divergent patterns of conduct.[228] This latitude follows from the specificities of decision-making in asylum law, especially the intricacy in settling the facts of the case and to obtain reliable information about the situation of the individual concerned. In this regard, Mitsch has illustrated how asylum examinations routinely operate against the backdrop of epistemological incompleteness.[229] This follows particularly from the inchoate determination of facts that relate to extraterritorial constellations or prognostic outlooks which draw a line to any inquisitional effort of national asylum authorities. To be sure, factual intricacies of this nature may be reduced, for instance through generalised classifications of certain regions as 'safe'

[221] See P van Reenen, 'Impartiality in the EU Asylum Procedure' (2018) 20 *European Journal of Migration and Law* 338, 344.

[222] This is implied also by the UNHCR, 'Handbook on Procedures and Criteria for Determining Refugee Status and Guidelines on International Protection: Under The 1951 Convention and the 1967 Protocol Relating to the Status of Refugees, 2019, Geneva' (2019) 196 ff.

[223] See van Reenen (n 221) 345.

[224] See M Ruffert, 'National Executives and Bureaucracies' in P Cane et al (eds), *The Oxford Handbook of Comparative Administrative Law* (Oxford University Press, 2020) 507.

[225] Regulation (EU) 2024/1348 of the European Parliament and of the Council of 14 May 2024 establishing a common procedure for international protection in the Union and repealing Directive 2013/32/EU (Asylum Procedures Regulation) [2024] OJ L 2024/1348, Recital 42.

[226] See similarly van Reenen (n 221) 346.

[227] On this phenomenon, see TM Liodden, 'Who Is a Refugee? Uncertainty and Discretion in Asylum Decisions' (2020) 32 *International Journal of Refugee Law* 645, 646, with further references.

[228] See S Rehaag, 'Troubling Patterns in Canadian Refugee Adjudication' (2008) 39 *Ottawa Law Review* 335, 359, with further references.

[229] See L Mitsch, *Das Wissensproblem Im Asylrecht: Zwischen Materiellen Steuerungsdefiziten Und Europäisierung* (Nomos, 2020) 144 ff who speaks of 'Unvollständigkeit der Entscheidungsgrundlage'.

or general reports on the security situation in a certain region in country-of-origin reports.[230] However, such generalised means to remedy epistemological difficulties may not eliminate administrative intricacies in asylum examinations entirely.

On a conceptual level, the question may be raised whether such a measure of administrative latitude may be viewed as a form of administrative self-programming power, and thus, as a parameter of discretion. With a view to the framework definition of discretion applied in this investigation, this question should be answered in the negative. It would be inaccurate to label cognitive intricacy in the settling of facts in terms of discretionary power.[231] Conventional understandings of administrative power tend to construe the establishment of fact as an objective undertaking, and this presumed objectivity is doctrinally ferried over into the field of asylum law. Accordingly, from the conceptual perspective applied in this investigation, administrative freedom that results from epistemological intricacies does not qualify as a property of discretion.

ii. Full and Ex Nunc Review

Administrative systems in Europe tend to agree that discretionary power coincides with forms of limited judicial review. In the context of European asylum law, judicial review of asylum decision-making may be one of the most visible characteristics rallying against the existence of discretion.[232] In this context, European legal influences establish a relatively intensive mode of judicial review, and these standards strongly rally against the presumption that asylum decision-making may involve discretion.

First, in relation to the ECHR, the Strasbourg court has clarified that any arguable violation of the principle of non-refoulement should be subject to an effective remedy pursuant under Article 13 ECHR, and that this implied 'rigorous scrutiny' by the reviewing authority.[233] This may be read, prima facie, as an instruction for the reviewing authority – judicial or executive – to supersede the initial decision in substance, or, in other words, to carry out 'full review'.[234] Such a conclusion, however, should be treated with caution. In the Convention context, 'rigorous' review need not imply the substitution of the initial decision in substance. Rather, the ECtHR explicates that such a method of review presumes that the competent

[230] See ibid 167.

[231] See above at ch 2, s III.

[232] It can even be argued that the gradual invigoration of judicial control in the field of asylum law may have underpinned the expansion of substantive review in the administrative state in Europe more broadly, see E Hirsch Ballin, 'Constitutional Genealogy of Judicial Review in the Administrative State' in J Poorter, E Hirsch Ballin and S Lavrijssen (eds), *Judicial Review of Administrative Discretion in the Administrative State* (Asser; Springer, 2019) 32.

[233] *M.S.S. v Belgium and Greece* ECHR 2011-I, para 293.

[234] This interpretation may be informed by the ECtHR's interpretation of art 6 ECHR, even though the latter provision itself does not apply to asylum cases; on this point, see D Baldinger, *Rigorous Scrutiny versus Marginal Review: Standards on Judicial Scrutiny and Evidence in International and European Asylum Law* (Wolf Legal Publishers, 2013) 224.

national body examines 'the substance of the complaint and afford[s] proper reparation'.[235] To be sure, this requirement may impel national legal systems to provide for full judicial review, enabling judges to supersede the initial decision. However, with respect to the diverse traditions of judicial review in Europe, and the ECtHR's jurisprudence in this regard, such a legal design may not be a matter of course.

The standard imposed by the ECHR is strongly influenced by the Strasbourg court's description of the Convention system as a subsidiary protection regime.[236] Against this backdrop, the ECtHR may be relatively tolerant with respect to different national traditions of limited judicial review. This effect can be illustrated in relation to English courts' review of asylum decisions premised on the Wednesbury unreasonableness test.[237] The ECtHR appeared to accept, in principle, such a marginal standard of review due to the English courts, prior to the adoption of the Human Rights Act 1998.[238] A similar argument may be put forward in relation to a cassation model of judicial review.[239] Such a model evades the rather clear-cut dichotomy of full or limited review and endorses, instead, a method of judicial review that allows judges to quash an initial decision but not to decide *en lieu* of the initial decision-maker. It is not inconceivable that such a model of judicial review could satisfy the requirement of 'rigorous' review as defined by the ECtHR, since it enables the reviewing judge to examine the substance of the complaint and may afford 'proper reparation', namely by referring the matter back to the initial decision-maker without ruling out the existence of discretion.

In the context of EU secondary law, Article 67 (3) of the Asylum Procedures Regulation codifies a standard that reflects, in essence, the jurisprudence of the ECtHR. The Regulation, like its predecessor, requires Member States to provide for a full and *ex nunc* examination of both facts and points of law. The Regulation extends this safeguard beyond cases concerning Article 3 ECHR, that is, arguable claims of inhuman or degrading treatment. It establishes full and *ex nunc* judicial control as a general standard of review in the Common European Asylum System (CEAS).[240] This requirement presupposes that national courts can fully review points of fact and law and, if need be, quash an initial decision.[241]

Characteristically, this introduces a relatively strict standard of judicial review, which may routinely motivate legal systems in Europe to provide for an intensity of judicial review that conceptually precludes the existence of discretionary power. The notion of 'full' review in the CEAS may thus be translated in national legal systems as a mode of control that allows judges to supersede the initial decision

[235] *M.S.S.* (n 233), para 387.
[236] On this point, see T Spijkerboer, 'Subsidiarity and "Arguability": The European Court of Human Rights' Case Law on Judicial Review in Asylum Cases' (2009) 21 *International Journal of Refugee Law* 48, 68.
[237] See above at ch 2, s II.C.i.
[238] See Spijkerboer (n 236) 66 ff, with further references.
[239] Explored in detail above at ch 2, s II.C.ii.
[240] In this sense, Case C-69/10 *Brahim Samba Diouf v Ministre du Travail, de l'Emploi et de l'Immigration* ECLI:EU:C:2011:524, [2011], ECR I-07151, paras 41 ff.
[241] See M Reneman, *EU Asylum Procedures and the Right to an Effective Remedy* (Hart, 2014) 257 ff.

in substance. As such, that avenue of influence appears to rule out the existence of discretionary power from the perspective of an abstract definition thereof.[242] The diversity of national legal arrangements that exist in Europe in this regard, however, should not be ignored. Particularly, some national legal systems maintain arrangements of judicial review may be compatible with the requirement to provide for full and *ex nunc* control but likewise preclude courts to supersede an initial decision in substance. Specifically, this relates to a cassation model of review.[243]

Even though differences exist between national legal systems in this regard, a cassation model of judicial review presumes that courts are generally authorised to annul and remit, but not to review the facts of the case or to supersede an administrative decision in substance.[244] After questions of compatibility of this model of review with the requirement to provide for full and *ex nunc* control arose in several Member States,[245] the issue was finally resolved by the Court of Justice in *Alheto* – a judgment that was awaited with bated breath by some commentators.[246] The case concerned an applicant for international protection from Gaza whose application was rejected by Bulgarian migration authorities.[247] On appeal, the reviewing administrative court raised the question whether the requirement to carry out a full and *ex nunc* examination would oblige the reviewing court to rule itself on the application for international protection where it annuls the initial administrative decision, hence, to effectively supersede the latter. The ECJ answered in the negative, ruling that the Procedures Directive – the predecessor of the Asylum Procedures Regulation – does not specify 'what happens after any annulment of the decision under appeal'. Rather, Member States remain free to provide that national courts would be compelled to refer the file back to the initial decision-maker for the purpose of adopting a new decision.[248] The Asylum Procedures Regulation appears to keep this legal arrangement intact. Not unlike its predecessor, it does not spell out what should happen after the annulment of a decision.

The Court's judgment in *Alheto* affords Member States a degree of latitude in deciding the form of judicial control that should be used in asylum cases. In this regard, the Court appears to accept, in principle, the use of a cassation model of review. This model of judicial review consolidates a situation in which judges do

[242] See above at ch 2, s III.

[243] See above at ch 2, s II.C.ii.

[244] In the context of Czech law, see for instance P Černý, 'Asylum Proceedings in the Czech Republic during the Migration Crisis' (2020) 25 *Journal of Legal Studies* 44, 48.

[245] See Piątek (n 154) 169 ff.; A Králová, 'Legal Remedies in Asylum and Immigration Law: The Balance Between Effectiveness and Procedural Autonomy?' (2018) 16 *Central European Public Administration Review* 67, 73 ff.

[246] Case C-585/16 *Serin Alheto v Zamestnik-predsedatel na Darzhavna agentsia za bezhantsite* ECLI:EU:C:2018:584, [2018], paras 57 ff; for a cursory analysis of the judgment's repercussions for several aspects of asylum law, see G Fernández Arribas, 'The Alheto Judgement: UNRWA Protection as Grounds for Exclusion from Refugee Status and Inadmissibility of an Application for International Protection' (2019) 4 *European Papers Insight* 417.

[247] *Alheto* (n 246), paras 57 ff.

[248] ibid, para 146.

not supersede the decision of the initial decision-maker in substance.[249] From the perspective of an abstract definition of discretionary power, it could therefore be contended that Member States may maintain legal arrangements that could be viewed, from a conceptual perspective adopted in this investigation, as a parameter for discretionary power. Nonetheless, it should be noted that, even if this would be qualified as a form of limited judicial review, at least insofar as the decision-making autonomy that asylum authorities have results from the intricacy of establishing of facts, this should not qualify as discretion.

B. The Preclusion of Discretion as a Judicial Strategy?

Although the Court of Justice is generally reluctant to disrupt traditioned arrangements within national legal systems, EU migration law is one of the fields of law where this reluctance increasingly gives way to targeted judicial interventions. This is particularly evident with regard to the intensity of judicial review carried out by national courts. As has been argued, the Court has expressly limited the scope of review in some contexts, thereby contributing to a partial proliferation of discretion.[250] In other instances, however, it requires national courts to exercise full review, to the effect that administrative discretion is effectively precluded.

It may be difficult to second-guess the reasons why the Court prescribes a specific intensity of judicial control in some instances and refrains from doing so in others. In relation to requirements prescribing a high intensity of control, however, its principal motive appears to be rather evident. It seems to be driven by the desire to ensure that safeguards of migrant protection are effectively protected. Such a strategy ensures that Member States keep from introducing discretionary power where this would conflict with standards of EU law (subsection i) or from undermining core fundamental rights guarantees (subsection ii).

i. Judicial Refutation of Deliberate Misconstructions of Discretion in Asylum Law

The existence or absence of discretionary power in national asylum law is not just a technicality. Rather, it goes to the heart of authority that the executive exerts in relation to the judiciary. Against this backdrop, it may perhaps not be surprising that some Member States have attempted to introduce discretion as a legal phenomenon in the field of EU asylum law, despite standards in the EU asylum acquis that would preclude the existence of discretion. This is perhaps most aptly illustrated by the legal amendments put into practice by Hungary in the aftermath of the so-called refugee crisis. Hungarian lawmakers skilfully relied on a tradition

[249] See Černý (n 244) 48 ff.
[250] See above at ch 3, s II.C.

of discretionary power to advocate for a standard of limited judicial control in the review of asylum examinations.

These reforms may be said to be specifically designed to weaken the position of national courts *vis-á-vis* administrative decision-makers. Although the judiciary in Hungary was previously competent to alter and replace an administrative asylum decision, the then-introduced legislative framework merely provided for a judicial competence to annul and remit.[251] Accordingly, the reform effectively introduced a cassation model of judicial review in asylum decision-making. Even though such a tradition of limited judicial review exists in several Member State legal systems including in Hungary itself, in the context of asylum law, that reform effectively reduced the intensity of judicial review in the context of international protection. This 'shrewd exploitation of comparative reasoning'[252] is an apt embodiment of the legalism characteristic for illiberal policymaking in Europe. Reforms are drafted with the intention to undermine safeguards of Union law, whilst purporting conformity with the latter.[253]

Although the Court in *Alheto* had accepted that a cassation model of judicial review may, in principle, conform with the requirement to provide for full and *ex nunc* control, the specific implementation of that model in Hungary gave rise to the legal equivalent of a game of ping-pong.[254] In the case of *Torubarov*, the application for international protection of Mr Torubarov was rejected twice by the Hungarian administrative authorities and was consequently annulled by the domestic court. After the administrative authority rejected his claim the third time around, the reviewing court sent a preliminary reference to the ECJ to clarify its competence under the Procedures Directive. Specifically, it raised the question whether a practice of referring a case back and forth between an administrative authority and the competent court may be in conformity with the requirement to carry out full and *ex nunc* review, read in the light of Article 47 of the Charter of Fundamental Rights.

The introduction of a cassation model of judicial review in asylum matters effectively removed the power of national courts to vary an initial administrative decision. Judges are thus precluded from prescribing to national administrative authorities a specific course of action, *in casu* to recognise the protection needs of

[251] Act No LXXX of 2007, Act on Asylum, art 68 (HU); for an overview of the applicable case law in Hungarian law prior and subsequent to the 15 September 2015, Case C-556/17 *Alekszij Torubarov v Bevándorlási és Menekültügyi Hivatal* ECLI:EU:C:2019:626, [2019], paras 17 ff; for a genealogy of the reforms more generally, see I Hoffman, 'Application of Administrative Law in the Time of Reforms in the Light of the Scope of Judicial Review in Hungary' (2020) *Studia Iuridica Lublinensia* 101, 106 ff.

[252] A Vincze, 'Talking Past Each Other: On Common Misperceptions in the Rule of Law Debate' in A Lorenz and L Anders (eds), *Illiberal Trends and Anti-EU Politics in East Central Europe* (Palgrave Macmillan, 2021) 218.

[253] For this method of drafting legislations, see KL Scheppele, 'Autocratic Legalism' (2018) 85 *The University of Chicago Law Review* 544, 547.

[254] For that apt depiction, see Case C-556/17 *Alekszij Torubarov v Bevándorlási és Menekültügyi Hivatal* EU:C:2019:339, [2019], Opinion of AG Bobek, paras 1 ff, 79.

Mr. Torubarov, or, alternatively, to assume the power to substitute its own decision on this matter for that of the administration.[255] Against that backdrop, the ECJ repeated, on the one hand, its jurisprudence in *Alheto*, essentially confirming that the Procedures Directive does not determine what should happen after annulment of an administrative decision. In *Torubarov*, on the other hand, the Court added that Member States must, despite this flexibility, comply with Article 47 of the Charter of Fundamental Rights.[256] Accordingly, it would render the right to an effective remedy illusory could a Member State provide for a legal framework that would make a final binding judicial decision inoperative to the detriment of one party.[257] This would go against the *effet utile* of Article 46 (3) of the Procedures Directive (nowadays Article 67 (3) of the Asylum Procedures Regulation), since the administrative body could adopt a decisions that ran counter to the previous full and *ex nunc* assessment by the reviewing court. Against this background, the ECJ confirmed that Member States are obliged to structure their national laws in such a way as to ensure that applicants have at their disposal an effective remedy, which presupposes that the administrative authorities are obliged to comply with the judicial assessment.[258]

In *Torubarov*, the ECJ recounted the intention of the EU legislature to highlight that national courts should be vested with the power to give a binding ruling on the international protection needs of an applicant. Accordingly, where a court has carried out a full and *ex nunc* examination to that end and remits the case to the administrative decision-maker pursuant to the cassation model of judicial review, the administrative authority is bound by the court's assessment. Against this backdrop, the Court explicitly stresses that such a requirement precludes any 'discretionary power' on the side of the administrative authority.[259] As regards the power of national courts to vary an initial administrative decision, however, the Court stuck to the principled pluralism of traditions spelled out in *Alheto*. It corroborated that Member States are free to adopt a legal framework that does not vest national courts with the power to vary an initial administrative decision. Member States may accordingly, in principle, maintain a cassation model of judicial review that requires national judges to refer the case back to the administrative decision-maker.[260]

Despite this principled pluralist stance, the ECJ explicitly highlighted in *Torubarov* that, where Member States oblige courts to remit the case to the administrative decision-maker, the latter may be bound by the preceding full and *ex nunc* examination of the former.[261] Member States must respect Article 47 of the Charter, which acts as a corrective to their flexibility under the Directive.

[255] *Torubarov* (n 251), paras 33 ff.
[256] ibid, para 55.
[257] ibid, para 57.
[258] ibid, paras 58 ff.
[259] ibid, paras 65 ff.
[260] ibid, para 67.
[261] ibid, para 66.

A national legal arrangement that renders a judicial remedy ineffective in practice, for instance due to the administrator's power to adopt a decision converting the former, conflicts with Article 47 of the Charter.[262] Accordingly, the ECJ stipulated that a national court must be empowered to vary an administrative decision in the case that an administrative authority had previously disregarded the courts' full and *ex nunc* assessment of the application for international protection. In keeping with the ping-pong metaphor, this interpretation of Union law puts a halt to the game. Where a national court carries out a full and *ex nunc* assessment to annul and remit an initial administrative decision and the latter than adopts a decision contrary to that judicial assessment where no new elements of examination arise, the national court is empowered to vary the second administrative decision.[263]

The relatively complicated solution endorsed in *Torubarov* appears to be motivated inter alia by the ECJ's understanding that the determination of protection needs should not be conceptualised as involving 'discretion'.[264] In essence, the Court thus explicitly rejected a conception of administrative discretion proposed by the Hungarian government. The latter had argued in *Torubarov* that the national legal framework was justified by the level of complexity that asylum cases entail. According to the government's submission, this complexity could only be mastered by virtue of expertise which may exclusively be found in highly specialised administrative migration authorities.[265] This argument appears to be put forward on false pretences, effectively aiming at ousting national courts' powers in the field of asylum law.[266] However, it suggests that the Hungarian government, in defence of its national policy, relied on a tradition of discretion that puts courts at a relative disadvantage to administrative decision-makers. The Court's explicit rejection of discretionary power in such a situation may be read as a firm response to the autocratic legalism displayed by Hungary's reasoning in this case.

ii. Precluding Discretion in the Name of Migrants' Fundamental Rights: The Case of Return Detention

In *Torubarov*, the Court's explicit refutation of discretion seems to be motivated primarily by the autocratic intentions transpiring in the Hungarian governments' submissions to the case. On a more general note, however, it may be observed that the Court develops standards that explicitly preclude discretionary power in fields of EU migration law where particularly weighty fundamental rights are at stake.[267] In addition to the standards that follow from European human rights

[262] ibid, paras 72 ff.
[263] ibid, para 74.
[264] Explicitly in this regard, ibid, para 75.
[265] See Opinion of AG Bobek, *Torubarov* (n 254), para 79.
[266] See J Bornemann, 'Discretionary Powers: an (Often Overlooked) Focalization Point of the Rule of Law Crisis' (2023) 4 *Revue des Affaires Européennes* 963.
[267] Similarly, see E Tsourdi, 'Asylum in the EU: One of the Many Faces of Rule of Law Backsliding?' (2021) 17 *European Constitutional Law Review* 471, 493.

safeguards in the field of asylum law, this effect can be aptly illustrated in relation to decision-making on return detention.

One of the most controversial aspects of decision-making governed by the Return Directive concerns the detention of third country nationals for the purpose of facilitating return.[268] The Return Directive allows Member States to order detention 'in particular' where there is a 'risk of absconding' or the third country national concerned 'avoids or hampers the preparation of return or the removal process'.[269] Institutionally, the Return Directive leaves Member States the choice whether to assign decision-making in this context to administrative or judicial authorities. Where such a decision is initially taken by an administrative authority, however, the Court has ruled that the national court is 'to substitute its own decision for that of the administrative authority that ordered the detention'.[270] Analytically, this qualifies as an instance in which the ECJ obliges national courts to carry out 'full review'.

At least from the conceptual perspective applied in the present investigation, this squarely precludes the existence of discretionary powers. Seeing that the prescription of full judicial review marks a departure from the principled pluralism in the Courts' approach to national procedural rules, the Court's assertiveness may be puzzling. In relation to Return Directive specifically, the Court departs from a specific instruction in the recitals that authorises Member States to 'decide whether or not the review of decisions related to return implies the power for the reviewing authority or body to substitute its own decision . . . for the earlier decision'.[271] While 'decisions related to return' may not, in substance, extend to decision-making on return detention, it is nonetheless curious to note the Court's willingness to prescribe full judicial review in the context of a legislative instrument that explicitly mentions Member States' autonomy in this regard. The ECJ's approach furthermore cannot be explained by international human rights standards. As the Strasbourg court has emphasised, Article 5 (4) ECHR 'does not guarantee a right to judicial review of such a scope as to empower the court, on all aspects of the case including questions of pure expediency, to substitute its own discretion for that of the decision-making authority'.[272]

Against this backdrop, the Court's explicit prescription of a high-intensity review of national courts appears to be deliberate. Be it in response to autocratic

[268] See I Majcher, 'The European Union Returns Directive: Does It Prevent Arbitrary Detention?' (2013) 3 *Oxford Monitory of Forced Migration* 23.

[269] Directive 2008/115/EC of the European Parliament and of the Council of 16 December 2008 on common standards and procedures in Member States for returning illegally staying third-country nationals (Return Directive) [2008] OJ L348/98, art 15(1).

[270] Cases C-924/19 PPU and C-925/19 PPU *FMS and Others v Országos Idegenrendészeti Főigazgatóság Dél-alföldi Regionális Igazgatóság and Országos Idegenrendészeti Főigazgatóság* ECLI:EU:C:2020:367, [2020], para 293.

[271] Directive 2008/115/EC of the European Parliament and of the Council of 16 December 2008 on common standards and procedures in Member States for returning illegally staying third-country nationals (Return Directive) [2008] OJ L348/98, Recital 15.

[272] *Ermakov v Russia* App 43165/10 (ECtHR, 7 November 2013), para 264.

reforms seeking to undermine the authority of courts in the context of asylum law, or in relation to decisions that interfere with migrants' right to liberty: the ECJ's rejection of discretionary power serves a broader constitutional function. It illustrates that the Court is willing to curtail Member States' procedural autonomy where fundamental rights risk is particularly acute. In both areas of decision-making, the explicit preclusion of discretion reflects not just a technical interpretation of EU secondary law, but also a sensitivity to the volatility of the safeguards that migrants' may infer from European fundamental rights instruments.

V. Interim Conclusion: A Targeted Consolidation of Discretion

Historically, migration decision-making in Europe included vast and virtually unchecked discretionary powers on multiple occasions. While these instances of discretion have gradually been rolled back and subjected to judicial review, discretion has not disappeared from the field of European migration law altogether. Rather, contemporary migration laws in Europe continue to rely heavily on discretion as a legal phenomenon. In the preceding chapter, several mechanisms have been identified that explain the persistence and targeted proliferation of discretionary decision-making as an element of European migration law.

First, discretion has emerged as an epiphenomenon of the requirement to accommodate individualised decision-making. Following notably from the growing importance of fundamental rights safeguards, migration authorities are nowadays increasingly obliged to focus on the specificities of each individual case before them. National legal framework must put decision-makers in the position to duly consider individual circumstances, and to adjust their decision if need be. It is in this vein that the requirement to provide for individualised decision-making safeguards a degree of autonomy of the competent migration authority. While, technically, national lawmakers may provide for such autonomy through a variety of different legal arrangements, the preceding analysis has illustrated that they frequently consider discretion as the most viable tool for doing so. From their perspective, discretion presents itself as the preferred option to ensure that various influences of European law are duly processed at national level.[273]

Individualisation requirements contribute to the persistence and proliferation of discretion in a rather incidental fashion. Occasionally, however, European legal influences may aim ensuring the existence of discretion as a phenomenon in its own right. Particularly, this effect has been illustrated in relation to the case law of the Court of Justice. On multiple occasions, the Court has explicitly confirmed that national legal systems should provide for a measure of 'discretion' in their national legal systems. To be sure, such a reference does not, in and of itself, premeditate

[273] See similarly Wendel (n 3) 205.

the intensity of judicial control, and therefore, the existence of discretion as understood in this investigation. Exceptionally, however, the Court has confirmed that its reference to 'discretion' should coincide with a form of limited review,[274] to the effect that it effectively compelled national legal systems to resort to discretion. In such a situation, the Court appears to have a vested interest in the existence of national administrative discretion as a phenomenon in its own right.

In addition to instances in which European law contributes to the consolidation or proliferation of discretion in pre-existing instances of decision-making, discretion has equally emerged as an element of transnational administrative systems. In European migration law, this applies above all to the discretionary clauses in the Dublin system. Although formally designed as latitude afforded to Member States, in practice, the application of these clauses is frequently delegated to executive actors, and most particularly to administrators deciding in individual cases. These instances of discretionary power have played a central role in the legal response to the so-called migration crisis and its aftermath, allowing for ad hoc crisis policies that operate through an (uncoordinated or coordinated) activation of the Dublin discretionary clause. In effect, this has turned the discretion of migration authorities in this regard to an indispensable regulatory tool for stabilising an otherwise stuttering system of transnational cooperation.

While European legal influences consolidate and occasionally contribute to the proliferation of discretion in several instances, the persistence of discretion in contemporary migration law is targeted and confined to specific decision-making contexts. Discretion is not a pervasive feature of European migration law. Rather, as the preceding section has argued, the persistence of discretion is linked to specific decision-making instances and may, moreover, be explicitly precluded by standards of European law on several other occasions. Above all, this applies to asylum decision-making, where national decision-makers benefit from significant deliberative freedom but not, legally speaking, discretion. Specifically, this conclusion follows from the fact that European law prescribes 'full and *ex nunc*' review, thereby effectively ruling out the existence of discretion, at least as understood here.

In summary, the picture that emerges is one of targeted consolidation rather than gradual repression of discretion. Discretionary decision-making persists as a prominent trait of European migration law, but one that is linked to specific decision-making instances. These instances may be of great practical importance: in relation to security considerations, for instance, discretion has emerged as an expedient tool to ensure a measure of decision-making autonomy while, at the same time, tempering practices that would negate relevant and legitimate interests of migrants.[275] The discretionary clauses in the Dublin system owe much of their prominence to the ad hoc crisis responses that were designed to keep this transnational system of responsibility attribution formally intact. What results is

[274] *Fahimian* (n 96), para 46.
[275] For a detailed analysis on the repercussions of the persistence of discretion for the legal position of migrants, see below at ch 5.

not a field that is pervaded entirely by discretion, but rather a landscape where its existence and scope are selectively consolidated by an interplay of European legal influences and national lawmakers' decisions in accommodating these influences. In this sense, discretion survives as a purposefully deployed instance of administrative autonomy – one that, to borrow from Brand, 'has a useful role to play' within European migration law.[276]

[276] M Brand, 'Discretion, Divergence, and Unity' in S Prechal and B van Roermund (eds), *The Coherence of EU Law: The Search for Unity in Divergent Concepts* (Oxford University Press, 2008) 218.

4

The Transformation of the Exercise of Discretion

Discretion remains a central feature of administrative power in European migration law. It affords migration authorities a measure of autonomy to assess the circumstances of the individual case and, where deemed appropriate, to adjust their decision accordingly. Yet, this raises a fundamental question: to what extent should such discretionary power be instructed by legal standards? Theoretical debates on discretion typically provide two opposing answers to this question. According to an influential understanding, discretionary decision-making involves choosing between several – legally equivalent – options, with no strings attached as to how for why preference is given to one solution or another.[1] In contrast, scholars such as Galligan have argued that discretion is not a matter of free choice but of choosing 'for good reasons'.[2] On this latter view, the exercise of discretion is best understood as a form of deliberation that is instructed, in one way or the other, by standards of legality.[3]

The evolution of discretionary power in European migration law mirrors this debate. While the exercise of discretion in earlier legal arrangements may have been closer to a form of choice between several equivalent options, the nature of exercising discretionary power in this field of law has changed significantly. Contemporary legal frameworks impose a mode of deliberative freedom on migration authorities that is firmly instructed by standards of legality. As this chapter sets out to illustrate, this transformation of the exercise of discretion is driven, in large part, by European legal influences. First, European law has kept instances of wide discretion intact but largely refutes the idea of discretion as an embodiment of sovereign choice (Section I). Second, the way discretion is exercised has been fundamentally reshaped by the applicability of legal principles (Section II). Third, in exercising discretion, national migration authorities must increasingly appraise the transnational implications that their decision may create (Section III). In summary, European legal influences establish the exercise of discretion as a particularly demanding and sophisticated mode of deliberation.

[1] Akin to the whimsical choice between a Martini or a Sherry, as famously put by HLA Hart, 'Discretion' (1956) 127 *Harvard Law Review* 652, 657.

[2] D Galligan, *Discretionary Powers: A Legal Study of Official Discretion* (Oxford University Press, 1986) 7.

[3] These standards can include codified standards of expedience, see insightfully M Jestaedt, 'Maßstäbe Des Verwaltungshandelns' in D Ehlers and H Pünder (eds), *Allgemeines Verwaltungsrecht* 15th edn (De Gruyter, 2016) 328.

It requires decision-makers to appraise and apply the relevant set of norms in a relatively autonomous fashion, subject however to standards of legality instructing this autonomy (Section IV).

I. From Sovereign Power to Limited Administrative Autonomy and Back: Coming Full Circle?

In the early days of migration laws in Europe, the existence of broad discretionary power was linked to the idea that migration control should largely be the prerogative of sovereign states. In this sense, discretion served the function of concentrating this sovereign power in the hands of executives.[4] As a corollary, early legal frameworks regulating migration often included avenues of discretionary power that were subjected to virtually no legal limits or, where such limits existed, no effective judicial enforcement thereof. Gradually, however, these instances of unfettered executive power have been circumscribed by standards of legality and subjected to judicial control, to the effect that discretion may no longer be presumed to give rise to practically unfettered executive power.

Still, it may be noted that particularly far-reaching discretionary powers continue to exist in European migration law, and sovereignty claims by national executive actors have never entirely disappeared in this regard.[5] Crisis discourse and the case law of European courts may have even abetted arguments of that nature in recent years.[6] Against this backdrop, it may be asked in how far European migration law tempers executive power in relation to particularly far-reaching discretionary power. After successively circumscribing executive decision-making to standards of legality, has European migration law come full circle by reintroducing or, at least, tolerating instances of unfettered executive power?

The following sections will highlight that instances of virtually unfettered discretion have lingered on some instances, but that such instances should best be viewed as an administrative anomaly in European migration law (subsection A). As a matter of principle, discretion – even very broad instances thereof – are constraint by limits of legality and provide for some form of (limited) judicial review (subsection B).

A. Unfettered Discretion as an Administrative Anomality

The case for unfettered executive choice is perhaps most cogent in relation to decision-making in the field of migration control. Unlike situations in which third

[4] See C Dauvergne, 'Sovereignty, Migration and the Rule of Law in Global Times' (2004) 67 *The Modern Law Review* 588, 592.

[5] See J Bornemann, 'The Role of Member State Governments in Migration Litigation before the ECJ' (2020) 22 *European Journal of Migration and Law* 541, 544 ff.

[6] See A Desmond, 'From Migration Crisis to Migrants' Rights Crisis: The Centrality of Sovereignty in the EU Approach to the Protection of Migrants' Rights' (2023) 36 *Leiden Journal of International Law* 313.

country nationals already find themselves in the territory of a State, the decision of who may be authorised entry is often associated with vast discretionary power. This effect is exemplified in relation to EU visa law. As has been explored, the Court of Justice has highlighted that national migration authorities should have 'wide discretion' in this regard.[7] This discretion pertains to the verification whether one of the grounds to refuse the issuing of a visa applies, which equally includes the verification 'whether the applicant presents a risk of illegal immigration'.[8] Notwithstanding this wide discretionary power, however, the Court of Justice insists that this power is subject to limits of legality. The case of *Ben Alaya* can serve as a good illustration of this effect.

The judgment concerned a Tunisian national who wished to enrol in a study programme in Germany but whose application for a study visa was repeatedly rejected.[9] Although the Court confirmed that the national migration authority should have 'a measure of discretion',[10] it added that its assessment must be restricted to the conditions for admission laid down in the Students Directive. Accordingly, national authorities were precluded from unilaterally adding conditions other than the ones mentioned in the Directive.[11] This imposes a limit on the exercise of national migration authorities' discretion, namely that national migration authorities must base their decision on one of the grounds for refusal listed in the Directive.

This line of reasoning was later picked up on in *Fahimian*. In this case, the Court ruled that national authorities were allowed to exercise discretion in the application of grounds of refusal that were laid down in the Researchers Directive, but that they were precluded from introducing additional conditions for rejecting an application.[12] In *Fahimian*, the Court further specified that the exercise of discretion relates to the assessment of the relevant facts of the situation and the verification that these facts correspond with one of the grounds relating to the existence of a threat to public security.[13] Again, this significantly limits national authorities' discretion. It does not allow them to justify a negative decision as they deem fit. Instead, a refusal to issue a study or work visa must be based on one of the grounds spelled out in the Directive. All of this suggests that the discretion of migration authorities in refusing to issue a visa remains wide but not unlimited.

A different conclusion may be warranted in relation to resettlement policies. Resettlement refers to the selection and transfer of refugees from one State in which they have sought protection to another State that agrees to admit them as refugees with permanent residence status.[14] In principle, there is nothing to prevent national lawmakers from adopting a legal arrangement imposing an obligation on national

[7] See above at ch 3, s II.A.i.
[8] Case C-84/12 *Koushkaki v Bundesrepublik Deutschland* ECLI:EU:C:2013:862, [2013], para 61.
[9] Case C-491/13 *Ben Alaya v Bundesrepublik Deutschland* ECLI:EU:C:2014:2187, [2014], paras 14 ff.
[10] ibid, para 33.
[11] ibid, paras 29 ff.
[12] Case C-544/15 *Fahimian v Bundesrepublik Deutschland* ECLI:EU:C:2017:255, [2017], paras 36 ff.
[13] ibid, para 41.
[14] UNHCR, 'Resettlement Handbook: Division of International Protection' (2011) 9.

migration authorities to resettle certain (categories of) persons or to provide for judicial control. Empirically, however, European States remain extremely reluctant to authorise resettlement and cling to legal arrangements that enable them to selectively choose who gets to enter their territories. Frequently, this selectivity is facilitated by vast or, in fact, unfettered discretionary powers.[15]

French asylum law, for instance, recognises the Directorate-General for Foreign National's power to organise resettlement but does not spell out any additional indications as to how this should be done.[16] In Sweden, the Ministry of Justice develops general guidelines on the State's resettlement policy, which is subject to parliamentary approval, but leaves the final decision whether a person is resettled to the case officer with the Swedish Migration Agency.[17] Similarly, in Germany, the Residence Act authorises the Minister of Interior to adopt a directive to spell out the State's resettlement policy. By virtue of the most recent directive, for instance, the Bundesamt für Migration und Flüchtlinge (BAMF) is authorised to resettle up to 6350 persons, by focusing particularly on persons who are currently staying in Egypt, Jordan, Kenya, Lebanon or Pakistan.[18]

This suggests that national legal frameworks on resettlement – where they exist – stay clear of any strict legal imperatives for decision-makers on when and how to exercise their power in this regard. Curiously, this legal situation is not principally reversed by the adoption of the Union Resettlement Framework which was adopted as part of the New Pact on Migration and Asylum.[19] The instrument aims at streamlining Member States' practices by laying down the factors to be taken into consideration, such as the eligibility criteria, including – in mandatory terms – the grounds for exclusion, without however affording a subjective right to be resettled.[20] Moreover, the Regulation does not mention the possibility of individuals to appeal a negative decision.[21]

[15] Several Member States provide updated Country Chapters outlining their resettlement policies; which are available via: www.unhcr.org/protection/resettlement/4a2ccf4c6/unhcr-resettlement-handbook-country-chapters.html.

[16] Code de l'entrée et du séjour des étrangers et du droit d'asile, art L714-1 (France) stipulates that the competent authorities 'can organise' resettlement ('peuvent organiser'); the Directorate-General constitutes a sub-unit of the Ministry of the Interior.

[17] See UNHCR (n 14) Country Chapter Sweden, 4.

[18] Aufenthaltsgesetz (AufenthG), art 23(4) (Germany) in conjunction with Bundesministerium des Innern und für Heimat, (Federal Ministry of the Interior and for Homeland), 'Anordnung des Bundesministeriums des Innern und für Heimat für das Resettlement-Verfahren 2024/2025 gemäß § 23 Abs. 4 des Aufenthaltsgesetzes (AufenthG) zur Aufnahme besonders schutzbedürftiger Flüchtlinge unterschiedlicher Staatsangehörigkeit oder staatenloser Flüchtlinge insbesondere aus Ägypten, Jordanien, Kenia, Libanon, Libyen und Pakistan vom 10. April 2024' (Germany).

[19] Regulation (EU) 2024/1350 of the European Parliament and of the Council of May 14 2024 establishing a Union Resettlement and Humanitarian Admission Framework, and amending Regulation (EU) 2021/1147 (Resettlement and Humanitarian Admission Framework Regulation) [2024] OJ L2024/1350.

[20] Explicitly, in this regard, Resettlement and Humanitarian Admission Framework Regulation (n 19), Rec 25.

[21] Equally on the non-availability of judicial review, see T de Boer and M Zieck, 'The Legal Abyss of Discretion in the Resettlement of Refugees: Cherry-Picking and the Lack of Due Process in the EU' (2020) 32 *International Journal of Refugee Law* 54, 67 ff.

In contrast to decision-making in the field of visa law, where standards of legality and judicial review have increasingly delimited executive decision-making freedom, resettlement appears to stick to an understanding of executive power as sovereign choice. On the one hand, this may be explained by the specific characteristics of resettlement as a form of humanitarian admission. Individuals apply for resettlement from outside the territory of the prospective receiving State, and participation in resettlement schemes is largely considered an act of voluntary commitment, embodying States' sovereign choice.[22] On the other hand, such instances of unfettered executive power have been gradually repressed in legal systems in Europe. In this sense, resettlement – and the virtually unfettered executive power that it entails – should best be viewed as an administrative anomaly in European migration law.[23]

B. Sovereign Choice and Absolute Discretion: Walking a Thin Line

The Dublin discretionary clause is closely linked to the idea that Member States should be able to 'sovereignly' decide whether and when to voluntarily assume responsibility for an asylum examination. This is prominently reflected in the fact that the discretionary clause habitually goes by its previous name – the 'sovereignty' clause.[24] Member States are often more than willing to rely on this terminology to argue that Article 35(1) Asylum and Migration Management Regulation (AMMR)[25] (or its predecessor, Article 17(1) of the Dublin III Regulation) would afford them a mode of unfettered executive power. It is worth noting that the ECJ abets such an interpretation when it holds that the provision allows each Member State to decide 'in the exercise of its sovereignty'[26] whether to assume responsibility by virtue of the discretionary clause or not. This encourages arguments that conflate the concepts of discretion and sovereignty, to the effect that Member

[22] See C Ziebritzki, 'The Objective of Resettlement in an EU Constitutional Perspective' in M Foblets and L Leboeuf (eds), *Humanitarian Admission to Europe: The Law between Promises and Constraints* (Nomos, 2020) 291, with further references.

[23] It may be noted that most national legal systems do not consider resettlement as an administrative procedure in the first place, see de Boer and Zieck (n 21) 83.

[24] See S Morgades-Gil, 'The Discretion of States in the Dublin III System for Determining Responsibility for Examining Applications for Asylum: What Remains of the Sovereignty and Humanitarian Clauses After the Interpretations of the ECtHR and the CJEU?' (2015) 27 *International Journal of Refugee Law* 433, 441. In the case law of the ECJ, inter alia Case C-394/12 *Abdullahi v Bundesasylamt* ECLI:EU:C:2013:813, [2013], para 57; Case C-578/16 PPU *C.K., H.F., A.S. v Republika Slovenija* ECLI:EU:C:2017:127, [2017], para 53.

[25] Regulation (EU) 2024/1351 of the European Parliament and of the Council of 14 May 2024 on asylum and migration management, amending Regulations (EU) 2021/1147 and (EU) 2021/1060 and repealing Regulation (EU) No 604/2013 [2024] OJ L2024/1351.

[26] Case C-56/17 *Fathi v Predsedatel na Darzhavna agentsia za bezhantsite* ECLI:EU:C:2018:803, [2018], para 53.

States may rely on the discretionary clause to claim a virtually unfettered freedom to decide when to assume responsibility for asylum examinations themselves.[27]

In *Halaf*, the Court explicitly endorsed an interpretation of the discretionary clause focused on the sovereign nature thereof.[28] The case arose against the background of an application for international protection by an Iraqi national in Bulgaria who had previously applied for international protection in Greece. Based on an entry in the Eurodac system, the Bulgarian authority decided to transfer him back.[29] Mr Halaf brought an action against that decision, holding inter alia that UNHCR had urged European governments not to send asylum seekers back to Greece at that time.[30] On that note, the referring Bulgarian administrative court asked the ECJ to clarify the conditions pursuant to which Bulgaria may assume responsibility for the application of Mr Halaf, regardless of the fact that, according to the list of criteria, it was not responsible in this regard. The ECJ responded by stressing that the exercise of Article 3(2) of the Dublin II Regulation, the predecessor of the discretionary clause nowadays enshrined in Article 35 (1) AMMR, is 'not subject to any particular condition'.[31] Accordingly, this avenue of discretion does not premise on any substantive condition to be met before it may be exercised. The Court acknowledged that this corresponds to the clause's principal objective, namely, to put each Member State in a position to decide 'sovereignly, for political, humanitarian or practical considerations' to assume responsibility for an asylum application.[32]

More recently, the Court demonstrated its alertness to the ramifications and potential misinterpretations that the term sovereignty evokes. Without changing its interpretation of the discretionary clause in substance, it interpreted it to offer Member States what could be viewed as the next best thing to sovereignty, namely 'absolute discretion'.[33] Whereas criticism may be levelled at that terminology as well, it avoids the pitfalls of framing Member States' wide faculty in terms of sovereignty. Since the provision does not rest on any conditions to be applied, it is true that it can be used in a variety of situations, subject largely to the judgment of national decision-makers.

While all of this suggests that the Dublin discretionary clause would not require the fulfilment of any preconditions for its activation, in *X*, the Court clarified that Member States are prevented from using the discretionary clause in relation to applications that have not been filed with them.[34] This followed from the wording of the provision, which insists that a Member State may decide to examine 'an application for international protection ... registered with it'. Accordingly, the

[27] See M Baumgärtel, '"Part of the Game": Government Strategies against European Litigation Concerning Migrant Rights' in T Aalberts and T Gammeltoft-Hansen (eds), *The Changing Practices of International Law* (Cambridge University Press, 2018) 110 ff.

[28] Case C-528/11 *Halaf v Darzhavna agentsia za bezhantsite pri Ministerskia savet* ECLI:EU:C:2013:342, [2013].

[29] ibid, paras 18 ff.

[30] ibid, paras 22 ff.

[31] ibid, para 36.

[32] ibid, para 37.

[33] Case C-661/17 *M.A., S.A., A.Z v International Protection Appeals Tribunal, Minister for Justice and Equality, Attorney General, Ireland* ECLI:EU:C:2019:53, [2019], para 58.

[34] Case C-213/17 *X v Staatssecretaris van Veiligheid en Justitie* ECLI:EU:C:2018:538, [2018], para 60.

discretionary clause in Article 35 (1) of the AMMR is subject to this limit of legality, even though this may not translate to a standard circumscribing discretionary conduct that will gain much relevance in practice.

The fact that this limit of legality circumscribes the application of the Dublin discretionary clause aligns with the findings of national courts. The English Court of Appeal, for instance, overruled the decision of the UK Upper Tribunal in a case concerning the transfer to Italy of an unaccompanied minor who suffered from post-traumatic stress, inter alia after being told that his mother and brother died during the passage across the Mediterranean.[35] Since the applicant's aunt lived in the UK, the Upper Tribunal held that the exercise of the discretionary clause was mandatory in this situation, emphasising that the exercise of the discretionary clause may be mandatory where one of the overarching values of the Dublin system could thereby be fulfilled.[36] Given that government's own policy was aimed at the expedition of procedures, the Upper Tribunal ruled that the individual decision-maker was obliged to exercise the discretionary clause to that end. However, on appeal, Lady Justice Arden highlighted that the wording of the discretionary clause requires an application for international protection to be lodged with a Member State.[37] The applicant in the case at hand stayed in Italy and had, at no point in time, filed an application with the competent English authorities.[38] Accordingly, the discretionary clause was not applicable to that situation. Instead of awarding Member States an unfettered – as in: 'a sovereign' – right to unilaterally assume responsibility for an application, the discretionary clause is limited at least in so far as the application must have been lodged with it.

Of greater practical relevance, however, is the fact that the competent national authorities may be compelled to activate the discretionary clause in certain situations. This effect emerged from fundamental rights enshrined at European level,[39] but likewise in national law.[40] Illustrating this point, an administrative court in Germany considered that the application of the humanitarian clause in Article 17(2) of the Dublin III Regulation would be mandatory with a view to uniting a Syrian family in Germany.[41] The situation concerned a family staying in a Greek refugee camp, despite the adult daughter's vulnerability on account of the sexualised violence and torture she had experienced in Syrian prisons. Since the family's son and, respectively, brother lived in Germany as a beneficiary of subsidiary

[35] *R (on the application of RSM and Another) v Secretary of State for the Home Department* [2017] UKUT 124 (IAC) (12 April 2017).

[36] ibid, para 43.

[37] ibid, para 125.

[38] This textual interpretation of what is nowadays Art 35 (1) AMMR was later confirmed in *X* (n 34), para 60.

[39] For a discussion of the relevant case law, see Morgades-Gil (n 24) 437 ff.

[40] See C Hruschka and F Maiani, 'Regulation (EU) No 604/2013 of the European Parliament and of the Council of 26 June 2013 Establishing the Criteria and Mechanisms for Determining the Member State Responsible for Examining an Application for International Protection Lodged in One of the Member States by a Third-Country National or a Stateless Person (Recast)' in K Hailbronner and D Thym (eds), *EU Immigration and Asylum Law. A Commentary* 2nd edn (Beck; Nomos; Hart, 2016) 1694.

[41] *Verwaltungsgericht Berlin* (Administrative Court Berlin), 15 March 2019, VG 23 L 706.18 A, para 11 ff.

protection, the national administrative court held that the legal asset of family unity transforms the discretionary power that the humanitarian clause affords into a legal obligation to assume responsibility in such a situation. A similar argument has been put forward by the High Administrative Court of Bavaria. The national court acknowledged that the situation of the applicant may substantiate an entitlement ('Anspruch') to exercise the discretionary clause, where any other course of action would be indefensible, inter alia for severe health reasons.[42]

In *R (BAA & Anor)*, the UK Upper Tribunal had to assess the refusal to activate the Dublin discretionary clause in the light of the right to respect for family life under Article 8 ECHR.[43] Based on the finding that a refusal to assume responsibility for an asylum application in this case would violate this fundamental right, Lord Justice Lane acknowledged that the influence of human rights may 'turn the [Secretary of State]'s discretionary power into a duty', even though *in casu*, it remained subject to the assessment of the competent local authorities that the cousin living in the UK was indeed able to care for his relative.[44]

Analytically, this form of influence could best be described as 'nullified' discretion.[45] While decision-makers genuinely benefit from a vast discretion, exceptional circumstances may render all but one option unlawful, *in casu* owing to the respect for fundamental rights. Where this is the case, the deliberative freedom otherwise vested in national migration authorities is turned into an obligation to act in a certain way. This suggests that, notwithstanding the rhetoric of sovereign decision-making surrounding the Dublin discretionary clauses, some limits of legality apply in this regard. While these limits will not frequently compel national authorities to act in one way or another, they still indicate that the Dublin discretionary clause does not give rise to a legally unfettered decision-making power.

II. The Exercise of Discretion as Legally Instructed Decision-Making Freedom

Discretion is often presented as a mode of deliberation that enables administrators to choose between several, legally equivalent outcomes. Such a view is widely held both in legal theory and colloquial discussions. It implies that, within the margins of discretion afforded to them, decision-makers are free to opt for the outcome they prefer, without any instructions as to how this outcome should be reached or which aspects should receive particular attention.[46] In European migration law, however, such an aleatory understanding of the exercise of discretion is largely

[42] *Bayerischer Verwaltungsgerichtshof* (High Administrative Court of Bavaria), 3 December 2015, 13a B 15.50124, para 30.
[43] *R (BAA & Anor) v Secretary of State for the Home Department* [2020] UKUT 227 (IAC), para 173.
[44] ibid, paras 179 ff.
[45] For this effect, see above at ch 2, s I.A.i.
[46] See above at ch 2, s I.A.

precluded. As will be argued in the following, the exercise of discretionary power is instructed, with some detail, by legal principles.[47]

Legal principles do not ultimately call into question the freedom that administrators have in exercising discretion. Instead, these standards of legality instruct the way that decision-makers exercise this freedom.[48] In European migration law, legal principles serve as a corrective to the otherwise rather wide scope of discretion granted to administrators. Against this backdrop, the argument will be put forward that it would be misplaced to consider the exercise of discretion as a sphere of legally unstructured choice. By contrast, discretionary decision-making emerges as a relatively arduous mode of deliberation that compels administrators to autonomously compile and appraise all relevant factors underpinning their decision (subsection A) and to weigh competing interests (subsection B).

A. The Duty of Care and the Autonomous Appraisal of Relevance and Fact

The exercise of discretion characteristically implies a degree of freedom. In exercising this freedom, however, decision-makers are bound to respect certain standards that do not preclude their freedom but instruct the way it should be exercised. What distinguishes the exercise of discretion from non-discretionary conduct, however, is that national migration authorities must apply these legal principles in a relatively autonomous fashion. In this sense, the exercise of discretion goes beyond the mere application of norms to a specific case. It establishes a rather arduous mode of decision-making that is aggravated, in European migration law, by the fact that standards instructing the exercise of national authorities are often spelled out at different levels of a multi-levelled legal system.[49]

Specifically, national migration authorities are required to settle, in a relatively autonomous manner, which aspects are relevant for their decision. While legal frameworks may mention factors that should be considered relevant, the exercise of discretion implies that national administrators are either authorised to consider additional criteria or to weigh these factors in the light of a specific case.[50] In the context of EU migration law, this form of administrative autonomy featured inter alia in *Koushkaki*, where the Court emphasised that the exercise of wide discretion must rest on an individualised examination that 'takes into account the general situation in the applicant's country of residence and . . . individual characteristics, inter alia his family, social and economic situation' and a potential history of illegal

[47] Similarly, see E Brouwer, 'Challenges to EU Legality in the Field of Asylum and Migration Law' in C Kilpatrick and J Scott (eds), *Contemporary Challenges to EU Legality* (Oxford University Press, 2021) 69.

[48] See above at ch 2, s II.B.

[49] See similarly M Wendel, *Verwaltungsermessen Als Mehrebenenproblem: Zur Verbundstruktur Administrativer Entscheidungsspielräume Am Beispiel Des Migrations- Und Regulierungsrechts* (Mohr Siebeck, 2019) 207.

[50] See above at ch 3, s I.B.

stays in one of the Member States.[51] The Court did not, however, exhaustively list the aspects that may be relevant to the individual situation of the applicant, thereby leaving this appraisal of relevance to the competent administrative authority.

While the exercise of discretion implies a degree of freedom, European legal influences tend to compensate for this deliberative freedom through a strict application of procedural safeguards. This compensatory effect has been identified in relation to the discretion of the EU legislature,[52] in EU direct administration,[53] and may likewise be witnessed in relation to national administrative authorities exercising discretion.[54] These procedural requirements include the obligation to examine carefully and impartially all the relevant elements of the situation in question and a duty to state reasons.[55]

One of the requirements that can be linked to the duty of care is the obligation of administrators to duly appraise the facts of the case. In this regard, Mendes has insightfully observed that the standard imposed by the Court of Justice in this regard varies from one context to another.[56] In relation to EU migration law, *Fahimian* is one of the isolated instances in which the Court had explicitly clarified the standard applicable to the appraisal of facts, ruling that the discretionary decision of the competent authority would have to be based 'on a sufficiently solid factual basis'.[57] While this has been interpreted as implying some measure of 'fact-finding discretion',[58] it may nonetheless allow the Court to elaborate, in future judgments, on the degree of factual basis required by the duty of care.

B. The Exercise of Discretion as Weighing of Competing Interests

Legal principles instruct discretionary decision-making, and one way they do is through substantive instructions. One of the most prominent legal principles instructing the substance of the exercise of discretionary power is the principle of proportionality. The principle of proportionality applies to administrative decision-making more generally, not just in the context of instances of deliberation defined, for the purposes

[51] *Koushkaki* (n 8), para 69.

[52] See K Lenaerts, 'The European Court of Justice and Process-Oriented Review' (2012) 31 *Yearbook of European Law* 3, 5 ff.

[53] Seminally, see Case C-269/90 *Technische Universität München v Hauptzollamt München-Mitte* ECLI:EU:C:1991:438, [1991], para 14.

[54] See R Widdershoven, 'The European Court of Justice and the Standard of Judicial Review' in J Poorter, E Hirsch Ballin and S Lavrijssen (eds), *Judicial Review of Administrative Discretion in the Administrative State* (Asser; Springer, 2019) 57.

[55] *Fahimian* (n 12), para 46.

[56] See J Mendes, 'Discretion, Care and Public Interest in the EU Administration: Probing the Limits of Law' (2016) 53 *Common Market Law Review* 419, 431.

[57] *Fahimian* (n 12), para 45.

[58] R Lehner and S Gies, 'Students and Researchers Directive (EU) 2016/801' in D Thym and K Hailbronner (eds), *EU Immigration and Asylum Law: Article-by-Article Commentary* 3rd edn (Beck; Hart; Nomos, 2022) 1071.

of this investigation, as discretion.[59] In relation to discretion, however, proportionality assumes particular importance.[60] It requires decision-makers to weigh competing interests. This may not ultimately transform discretionary conduct into bounded decision-making, but forces migration authorities to attach legal weight to certain factors and relating competing interests to one another.

In European migration law, the significance of the principle of proportionality is derived notably from European fundamental rights guarantees. Especially following the case law of the European Court of Human Rights, restrictions to the entry or stay of non-nationals may interfere with the right to respect for family[61] and private life[62] and would therefore be subject to a proportionality caveat.[63] These fundamental rights considerations were later reproduced in EU legislative instruments and represent one of the core impulses for legal systems to provide for individualised assessments in the field of migration law.[64]

The principle of proportionality requires decision-makers to balance competing interests in the exercise of discretion. In EU migration law, this effect is prominently illustrated by the requirements that the Court of Justice imposes on national decision-makers in the field of restrictions to entry or stay based on public order considerations. In *E.P.*, for instance, the Court confirmed that national authorities may have 'wide discretion' to combat threats to public policy.[65] However, the Court added that the administrative conduct must respect the principle of proportionality. Effectively, this served as a corrective to the wide nature of discretion granted to authorities. The principle of proportionality requires migration authorities inter alia to ascertain whether the infringement allegedly committed is 'sufficiently serious' to justify the immediate termination of the third country national's stay.[66]

Analytically, this confirms that national migration authorities may have 'wide discretion' to determine whether a third country national poses a threat to public policy, but that the legal consequence of such a finding must be assessed in the light of the principle of proportionality. Accordingly, by requiring national migration authorities to assess whether the criminal activity is 'sufficiently serious' to justify the immediate termination of legal stay, the Court insists that migration authorities put their mind to the type of offence (allegedly) committed and the implications that the termination of stay may have for the individual concerned.

The Court adopted a similar approach in relation to decisions negatively affecting family unity. In *G.S. & V.G.*, it highlighted that national migration authorities,

[59] In this sense, proportionality will equally instruct non-discretionary decision-making marked by administrative autonomy, such as in the context of EU asylum law, see E Gökşen, 'Proportionality in Refugee Exclusion: An Underestimated Analysis' (2020) 18 *Journal of International Criminal Justice* 1131.

[60] See Wendel (n 49) 198.

[61] *Berrehab v The Netherlands* Series A no 138 (1988) 11 EHRR 322, paras 22 ff; *Moustaquim v Belgium* Series A no 193 (1991) 13 EHRR 802, paras 34 ff.

[62] *Slivenko v Latvia* App no 48321/99 (ECtHR, 09 October 2003), paras 94 ff.

[63] See Brouwer (n 47) 59.

[64] See above at ch 3, s I.B.

[65] Case C-380/18 *Staatssecretaris van Justitie en Veiligheid v E.P.* ECLI:EU:C:2019:1071, [2019], paras 37, 45.

[66] ibid, paras 47 ff.

in withdrawing or refusing to renew a residence permit on the grounds of public policy, public security or public health, must respect the principle of proportionality.[67] As a corrective, proportionality precludes automatic inferences from the fact that a person has been convicted of a criminal offence. Rather, national migration authorities are required to weigh competing interests. Very severe criminal offences may, in the light of a proportionality assessment, justify the immediate termination of a third country national's stay in a Member State, even if other factors of family life may rally against such a conclusion. Other offences must be weighed against interests of the individual to ascertain whether a negative decision may be warranted.

III. Transnational Effects of the Exercise of Discretion

In European migration law, national authorities are often tasked to consider the ramifications that their actions may create beyond their domestic legal system, that is, the transnational effects of their conduct.[68] The decisions of migration authorities in one legal system may engender effects beyond the legal system in which they operate. Where national migration authorities exercise discretion, they may have to take these transnational effects into account. Unlike in situations of bounded decision-making, however, discretion implies that decision-makers appraise these transnational repercussions in relative autonomy.[69]

Against this backdrop, the question may be raised which legal rules or principles govern migration authorities' exercise of discretion in the light of these transnational effects. With a special focus on EU migration instruments, the following sections will first discuss in how far the principle of transnational solidarity may serve as a standard guiding the exercise of discretion by migration authorities (subsection A). Second, different mechanisms that seek to avoid potential adverse transnational effects of discretionary decision-making will be explored (subsection B). Last, it will be argued that the Court's emphasis on administrative discretion in transnational administrative systems may have contributed to a significant politicisation of administrative power in EU migration law (subsection C).

A. Solidarity and the Exercise of Discretion in Make-Shift Crisis Responses?

In EU migration law, the exercise of discretion can alter the way burdens are allocated between the Member States. This effect is visibly exemplified in the Dublin system, where the activation of the discretionary clause would shift responsibility

[67] Joined Cases C-381/18 and C-382/18 *G.S. and V.G. v Staatssecretaris van Justitie en Veiligheid* ECLI:EU:C:2019:1072, [2019], para 64.

[68] For an early account of that phenomenon, see J Bast, 'Transnationale Verwaltung Des Europäischen Migrationsraums: Zur Horizontalen Öffnung Der EU-Mitgliedstaaten' (2007) 46 *Der Staat* 1, 9.

[69] See Wendel (n 49) 235.

for an asylum application to the Member State of the authority exercising discretion. Against this backdrop, the question may be raised whether national authorities are free – subject to some marginal limits of legality[70] – to exercise their discretion as they deem fit, regardless of the transnational implications of their action, or whether certain transnational legal limits may be identified that constrain the exercise of discretion.

One of the key provisions that may be of relevance in this regard is Article 80 TFEU. It commands that the principle of solidarity and fair sharing of responsibility should govern the relationship between the Member States in the Area of Freedom, Security and Justice.[71] The wording of this provision clarifies that the principle relates to solidarity 'between the Member States' and not in relation to individuals. Accordingly, the question may be raised whether the exercise of discretion by the authorities of one Member State could upset the notion of transnational solidarity between the Member States. If that was the case, solidarity would emerge as a transnational limit to the exercise of discretion.

The ability of the principle of solidarity to act as a limit to the exercise of discretion has been prominently discussed in relation to events during the so-called refugee crisis.[72] In this context, fierce criticism had been levelled at German authorities' large-scale activation of the Dublin discretionary clause. While this exercise of discretion may have kept a sputtering transnational administrative systems intact,[73] it altered the default responsibility allocation otherwise established by the Dublin system. By assuming responsibility in a rather far-reaching way, German authorities may not just have set in motion factual developments outside German territory, which led to a sharp increase of migration towards Europe,[74] they likewise effectively altered the system of burden allocation between the Member States.[75]

The Court of Justice ultimately found the activation of the Dublin discretionary clause by German authorities to serve the idea of transnational solidarity. In *Jafari*, it highlighted that the Dublin system was underpinned by this legal principle and that, accordingly, Member State authorities may unilaterally assume responsibility through the activation of the discretionary clause, even in relation to an 'unusually large number of third country nationals'.[76]

[70] See above at ch 4, s I.B.

[71] See D Thym and E Tsourdi 'Searching for Solidarity in the EU Asylum and Border Policies: Constitutional and Operational Dimensions' (2017) 24 *Maastricht Journal of European and Comparative Law* 605, 609 ff.

[72] See E Küçük, 'The Principle of Solidarity and Fairness in Sharing Responsibility: More than Window Dressing?' (2016) 22 *European Law Journal* 448, 464.

[73] See aptly D Thym, 'Judicial Maintenance of the Sputtering Dublin System on Asylum Jurisdiction: Jafari, A.S., Mengesteab and Shiri' (2018) 55 *Common Market Law Review* 549.

[74] In this sense, the legal phenomenon of transnationality is largely inspired by the sociological conception thereof, see Bast (n 68) 10.

[75] For an analysis of that claim, see L Pries, '"We Will Manage It" - Did Chancellor Merkel's Dictum Increase or Even Cause the Refugee Movement in 2015?' (2019) 58 *International Migration* 18, 24 ff.

[76] Case C-646/16 *Jafari* ECLI:EU:C:2017:586, [2017], para 100.

B. Mechanisms to Mitigate Adverse Transnational Effects

The exercise of discretion by migration authorities in one national system may create effects beyond that national domain. To avoid the occurrence of such negative effects in the first place, EU migration instruments include different mechanisms that allow national migration authorities to cooperate or at least coordinate the exercise of their discretion (subsection i). Moreover, following the attempt of some Member States to rely on an overblown understanding of discretion to undermine the effectiveness of the so-called refugee relocation mechanism, the Court developed a standard of care that may be particularly relevant to ensure the smooth function of transnational administrative systems that entail administrative discretion (subsection ii).

i. Transnational Cooperation Mechanisms: A Practical Necessity of Coordinated Exercise of Discretion?

Instruments of EU migration law have developed procedures to facilitate cooperation between administrative authorities in different Member States. Some legal instruments merely entail a duty of migration authorities to notify their counterparts in other Member States. When exercising the Dublin discretionary clause, for instance, national authorities are under an obligation to enter their decision in the data systems that Union law provides, such as Eurodac.[77] Other sub-fields of EU migration law, however, include more sophisticated systems of transnational cooperation to mitigate potentially adverse transnational effects. The cooperation procedure established in the context of refusing to issue Schengen visas is a prominent case in point.

Schengen visas are a prime example of a legal regime that creates tangible effects between administrations of several, formally distinct, legal systems.[78] While such visas are issued by the authorities of one Member State, they principally authorise the stay in the Schengen area in its entirety.[79] The decision-making of one national migration authority may thus genuinely affect other Member States. Against this backdrop, a degree of administrative uniformity among the Schengen States is necessary, which the Visa Code seeks to establish. In *Koushkaki*, this was the Court's principal motive to reject the argument that national migration authorities may unilaterally introduce grounds for refusing to issue a visa other than the ones

[77] Art 37 (1), third subparagraph AMMR. In the context of the so-called refugee crisis, this may be an obligation that German authorities failed to respect, see M Wendel, 'The Refugee Crisis and the Executive: On the Limits of Administrative Discretion in the Common European Asylum System' (2016) 17 *German Law Journal* 1005, 1021.

[78] See Bast (n 68) 8 ff.

[79] Regulation 810/2009 establishing a Community Code on Visas (Visa Code), Art 2 (2) (a); in exceptional cases, Member States may issue a visa with limited territorial validity, pursuant to Art 25 of the Visa Code.

mentioned in the Visa Code.[80] National visa authorities' wide discretion, however, may cater to a situation where the migration authorities of one Member State issue a visa to a third country national which may, in the view of the competent authority of another Member State, not be warranted by the harmonised conditions enshrined in the Visa Code. In such a situation, the Code permits the latter authority to revoke the visa if it considers that the conditions for its issuance are no longer met.[81]

Avenues of transnational cooperation are geared towards consistent application of the rules spelled out in the Visa Code, particularly in the context of thwarting security threats in the Schengen area. Since national visa authorities have wide discretion in this regard, respect for the procedures envisaged for the purpose of cooperation in the Visa Code are of particular importance.[82] To avoid a situation in which one Member States' migration authority issues a visa to a third country national who is considered a threat by another Member State in the first place, practices of transnational administrative cooperation have emerged in the fairway of Schengen integration.

These practices are particularly relevant in situations in which national migration authorities' exercise discretion. Should a national visa authority utilise its discretion to find that a third country national does not pose a threat to public order and internal security, its decision to issue a visa equally takes effect *vis-á-vis* the competent authorities of other Member States.[83] In this context, visa authorities must be aware of the implications their decisions may have on other Member States and the Schengen area in its entirety,[84] to avoid a situation in which its exercise of discretion could imperil the security or public order of another Member State. This has led to a paradigm change, whereby national migration authorities do not merely focus on the perils to which their respective Member State may be exposed but rather extend their focus to the Schengen area in its entirety.[85]

Against this background, the Visa Code counterbalances the substantive deliberative freedom that the exercise of wide discretion implies, on the one hand, with procedural mechanisms aimed at facilitating transnational cooperation, on the other hand. Especially by allowing for prior consultation, this procedure enables the authorities of one Member State to consult with the central authorities of other Member States in the context of the examination of an application.[86] In addition,

[80] See Wendel (n 49) 302; *Koushkaki* (n 8), paras 45 ff.

[81] Art 34 (2) Visa Code, subject to an obligation to notify the issuing Member State. In this important respect, the transnational effect of Schengen visas differ from the principles applicable in free movement law, see L Lucia, 'Administrative Pluralism, Horizontal Cooperation and Transnational Administrative Acts' (2012) 5 *Review of European Administrative Law* 17, 26.

[82] On the specific importance of procedural requirements, see above at ch 4, s II.A.

[83] On this effect, see Bast (n 68) 27.

[84] See A Meloni, 'EU Visa Policy: What Kind of Solidarity?' (2017) 24 *Maastricht Journal of European and Comparative Law* 646, 661.

[85] On this phenomenon, see W Weiß, *Der Europäische Verwaltungsverbund: Grundfragen, Kennzeichen, Herausforderungen* (Duncker & Humblot, 2010) 34 ff.

[86] This procedure can be found in Art 22 of the Visa Code.

the so-called local Schengen cooperation establishes procedures for cooperation that are aimed at inter-administrative knowledge exchange.[87]

Through these mechanisms of cooperation, some of the adverse effects that the exercise of discretion may create can be mitigated. A mechanism of transnational consultation may prevent conflicts between the administrations of different Member States from the outset. However, these mechanisms elucidate, once more, the particular importance of procedural safeguards in instructing the exercise of discretion.[88] This may be even more relevant where the exercise of discretion creates repercussions beyond the legal system in which the respective authority operates. These transnational effects are one of the central reasons why respect for procedural standards is paramount in the exercise of discretionary decision-making in EU migration law instruments.

Still, transnational cooperation of migration authorities must not compromise the fundamental rights of third country nationals, specifically the right to an effective remedy in Article 47 of the Charter. It may be noted that the Court of Justice highlights a rights-based approach in this regard.[89] As the judgment in *R.N.N.S.* illustrates, the right to an effective remedy must be guaranteed even where national migration authorities have 'wide discretion', and where that discretion is exercised in accordance with procedures of transnational cooperation.[90]

The litigation in *R.N.N.S.* concerned two third country nationals who appealed against a negative visa decision where another Member State had, during the prior-consultation procedure, raised opposition to the issuing of a visa. Besides a ticked box in the standard form indicating that 'one or more Member State(s) consider you to be a threat to public policy, internal security, public health . . . or the international relations of one or more of the Member States', no reasons were communicated to the persons concerned for the refusal of their application.[91] After learning the identity of that Member State in the context of the appeals procedure, the first applicant requested information from the Hungarian authority,[92] and the second applicant pressed the national authority to obtain the respective information from the German authorities; both unsuccessfully though.[93] Against this background, the referring court asked whether a decision to refuse a visa on the ground that another Member State may consider her or him a threat was subject to judicial review in the first place, and if so, how that review would have to be carried out in the light of Article 47 of the Charter of Fundamental Rights.[94]

[87] See Wendel (n 49) 304.
[88] See above at ch 4, s II.A.
[89] See Meloni (n 84) 649.
[90] Joined Cases C-225/19 and C-226/19 *R.N.N.S v Minister van Buitenlandse Zaken* ECLI:EU:C:2020:951, [2020], paras 42 ff.
[91] ibid, paras 15, 22.
[92] ibid, para 18.
[93] ibid, para 24.
[94] ibid, paras 27 ff.

In its response, the ECJ acknowledged the transnational ramifications of visa decisions. With a view to threats to public order or internal security, it noted that it was irrelevant whether these threats affected the Member State issuing the visa or another Member State.[95] Accordingly, the notion of a threat may in this regard not be conceptualised through a self-centred lens, where national decision-makers merely consider the situation of their respective Member State. Rather, the Court's judgment proffered a balanced solution that accommodated, on the one hand, national administrations' transnational cooperation to tackle threats to public order or internal security, ensuring, on the other hand, the applicants' right to an effective remedy. In this regard, its reasoning rested on three related aspects: the duty to state reasons for the refusal, the effectiveness of judicial review and the scope thereof.

The Court clarified, in the first place, that national authorities are under an obligation to state the reasons that motivated their decision. This holds true even where a refusal to issue a visa resulted from an objection during the prior consultation-procedure. In the cases at hand, the applicants were informed of the refusal of their application by means of the standard form. The Court noted in this regard that the standard form included a section for 'remarks', whereby the national authority may provide said information.[96] This constitutes, second, a precondition for effective judicial review. The Court held that the individual concerned must be able to ascertain the reasons motivating the decision taken to defend her or his rights under the best possible conditions, that is, with the full knowledge of the facts.[97]

In the third place, the ECJ considered the scope of judicial review in the light of Article 47 of the Charter of Fundamental Rights, holding that judicial review of a refusal decision 'cannot be limited to a formal examination of the grounds [of refusal]'. Rather, it reiterated that review must cover the legality of the decision, taking into account all of the elements of the file, both factual and legal, on which the competent national authority based its decision. Whereas decision-making in this regard is subject to 'broad discretion' and review thereof must be limited, the ECJ held that national courts are nonetheless tasked to ascertain whether the contested decision is based on a sufficiently solid factual basis and not vitiated by manifest errors.[98]

The obligation to carry out limited judicial review in this regard affects the court of the Member State that adopted the final decision refusing to issue a visa – *in casu* the Dutch court. In the context of transnational administrative cooperation, however, the ECJ was asked to clarify the manner of review regarding the merits of the objection to issue a visa that was raised by another Member State. In its response, the Court obliged the courts of the Member State which adopted the final decision to verify that the prior consultation-procedure has been applied

[95] ibid, para 36.
[96] ibid, paras 38 ff.
[97] ibid, para 43.
[98] ibid, paras 48 ff.

correctly, which includes the assertion that the applicant was correctly identified as the subject of the objection at issue and that procedural guarantees, such as the duty to state reasons, were respected.[99] Nonetheless, it is an inevitable feature of transnational administrative cooperation that the substantive legality of the decision to file an objection by another Member States' authorities cannot be reviewed by the courts of the Member State that adopted the final decision refusing a visa. In the light of Article 47 of the Charter, such a transnational arrangement must be accommodated by virtue of an indication as to which authority may be contacted to invoke the remedies available to ensure effective judicial review.[100] Thus, the national migration authority is under an obligation to communicate which authority of another Member State had objected the issuing of a visa.

Regarding the ECJ's acknowledgement of 'wide discretion' and its transnational repercussions, this judgment illustrates two aspects: first, it suggests once again that the ECJ's occasional imposition of a method of 'limited review' should not be mistaken for a neutralisation of judicial control.[101] Second, it exemplifies why the exercise of 'wide discretion' necessitates a particularly vigorous application of procedural safeguards. On the one hand, the Visa Code does not provide for a full-fledged mechanism of judicial review whereby the court of one Member State could establish the legality of the decision of another Member States' migration authorities. On the other hand, the Court imposes an obligation to procedurally safeguard the right to an effective remedy of the third country national concerned, including the duty to state reasons. By virtue of this procedural safeguard, the Court effectively puts the applicant in a situation to file a complaint in the Member State that had raised the objection against the visa being issued. This procedural solution demonstrates the Court's awareness of the problems that are inherently linked to transnational repercussions of national authorities' discretion. National migration authorities' 'wide discretion' must be exercised in a manner that simultaneously safeguards public order and internal security of other Member States as well as the (fundamental) rights of the third country national. The Court's solution in this regard attempts to get a grip on these matters through strengthened procedural rights of the applicant, particularly the right to an effective remedy, which must not effectively be negated by a transnational cooperation mechanism.

ii. Duty of Care in the Exercise of Discretion in Transnational Administrative Systems

A particularly contentious example of discretion in transnational administrative systems concerns the so-called refugee relocation mechanism. This mechanism was established as an ad hoc crisis measure intended to respond to mounting asylum

[99] ibid, paras 51.
[100] ibid, para 52.
[101] For that effect, see above ch 3, s II.C.i.

applications in some Member States. While the scheme envisioned certain quotas of persons to be relocated, it equally vested national migration authorities with discretion to decide whether to refuse or accept the relocation of asylum applicants in individual cases. By insisting that such discretion may exclusively be based on reliable information in relation to individual third country nationals, the Court's jurisprudence clarified that Member States could not use this discretion to deny relocations in a generalised fashion. As will be argued in the following, this points to a growing awareness on the side of the Court of Justice that instances of discretion in transnational administrative systems must be strictly subjected to a standard of care.

The refugee relocation mechanism had been laid down in two Council Decisions, envisioning the relocation of 160,000 third country nationals from Greece and Italy, the bottlenecks of European refugee movements at the time, to other Member States by virtue of a mandatory quota system.[102] The system considered applicants for international protection to be eligible for relocation only under the condition that the rates of recognition of international protection for persons fleeing her or his country of origin exceeded 75 per cent. Accordingly, the term 'refugee' relocation mechanism may be misleading, as it jumps to conclusions. Rather, relocation should serve as an instrument to redistribute the burden for assessing whether a person may qualify as such (or, alternatively, as a beneficiary of other forms of protection). This arrangement nonetheless hints at one of the fallacies of this quota system; on the one hand, it allowed the Commission to conclude that 96 per cent of all persons registered to that end had been relocated;[103] on the other hand, the actual number of 34,000 persons pales in comparison to the initial quota of 160,000 persons to be relocated.[104] In quantitative terms, the relocation mechanism therefore fell short of expectations.

Despite its relatively small quantitative impact, the mandatory nature of relocation caused a stir in legal debates across the EU and its Member States, provoking fundamental opposition among some national governments.[105] Since the Council Decisions were adopted by a majority in the Council, some Member State governments' contestations were voted down. Among the four governments opposing the mandatory relocation of applicants for international protection, Hungary and Slovakia mounted a legal challenge against the mandatory relocation mechanism (and the second Council Decision specifically)[106] whereas other Member States plainly refused to implement it.

[102] Council Decision (EU) 2015/1523 of 14 September 2015 establishing provisional measures in the area of international protection for the benefit of Italy and Greece [2015] OJ L239/146; and Council Decision (EU) 2015/1601 of 22 September 2015 establishing provisional measures in the area of international protection for the benefit of Italy and Greece (Decision 2015/1601) [2015] OJ L248/80.

[103] European Commission, 'European Agenda on Migration: Continuous efforts needed to sustain progress' [Press Release IP/18/1763, 14 March 2018].

[104] See R Byrne, G Noll and J Vedsted-Hansen, 'Understanding the Crisis of Refugee Law: Legal Scholarship and the EU Asylum System' (2020) 33 *Leiden Journal of International Law* 1, 9.

[105] See M Duszczyk, K Podgórska and D Pszczółkowska, 'From Mandatory to Voluntary: Impact of V4 on the EU Relocation Scheme' (2020) 21 *European Politics and Society* 470, 472 ff.

[106] Decision 2015/1601 (n 102).

The Court of Justice's response to governmental opposition in this context has been resolute. It firmly rejected governmental arguments challenging the mandatory quota system in the relocation system. In the first of two rulings, it upheld the legality of the Council Decisions, highlighting the fact that Member States may refuse relocation of an applicant for international protection where that person can reasonably be considered a danger to national security or public order or where one of the exclusion grounds in the Qualification Directive applies.[107] This broadly precludes refusal on other grounds, such as a person's religious background or cultural ties.[108] In addition, the Court equally rejected the Polish government's claim, as an intervening party, that the Council Decisions themselves may frustrate public order by virtue of giving rise to significant secondary movement, meaning that relocated applicants for international protection leave the assigned Member State before their claim is effectively examined. Should Member States experience practical difficulties of such nature, the Court highlighted that these issues would have to be resolved in a spirit of cooperation between the authorities of the Member States involved.[109]

After the Court's 2017 judgment, the fundamental opposition to mandatory relocation of applicants for international protection did not subside. To the contrary, opposing Member States opted for strategies of non-implementation of the relocation mechanism that tapped into a broader trend of autocratic backsliding.[110] The constitutional transformations in Hungary may serve as a case in point. The firm refusal to implement the relocation mechanism inspired efforts of constitutional reform, to the end that national lawmakers argued they would be under an obligation to protect the constitutional identity of Hungary. When a first attempt to change the constitution accordingly failed by a narrow margin, the Constitutional Court rushed to the aid of the government, holding that, in principle, it would accept arguments of constitutional identity to defy the implementation of the relocation mechanisms.[111] Eventually, the governing coalition re-gained a sufficient majority to amend the Hungarian constitution in 2018, introducing a passage stipulating that '[t]he protection of the constitutional identity and Christian culture of Hungary shall be an obligation of every organ of the State'.[112] This may vest national lawmakers with a splendid constitutional

[107] Joined Cases C-643/15 and C-647/15 *Slovak Republic and Hungary v Council of the European Union* ECLI:EU:C:2017:631, [2017], para 308.

[108] ibid, para 304.

[109] ibid, para 306.

[110] See T Drinóczi and A Bień-Kacała, 'Illiberal Constitutionalism: The Case of Hungary and Poland' (2019) 20 *German Law Journal* 1140, 1158 ff.

[111] See D Kelemen and L Pech, 'The Uses and Abuses of Constitutional Pluralism: Undermining the Rule of Law in the Name of Constitutional Identity in Hungary and Poland' (2019) *Cambridge Yearbook of European Legal Studies* 59, 67 with further references.

[112] The unofficial translation of Art R) of the Fundamental Law which entered into force on 29 June 2018; for an overview of events, see R Uitz, 'National Constitutional Identity in the European Constitutional Project: A Recipe for Exposing Cover Ups and Masquerades' (11 November 2016) https://verfassungsblog.de/national-constitutional-identity-in-the-european-constitutional-project-a-recipe-for-exposing-cover-ups-and-masquerades/.

argument to refuse implementation of binding Union law, namely the Council Decisions establishing a mandatory relocation scheme.

Unsurprisingly, efforts of this nature exacerbated tensions between EU institutions and the respective Member States. The Commission's monitoring of the relocation process repeatedly showed the non-implementation thereof by some Member States, which eventually motivated the initiation of infringement procedures against Hungary, Poland and the Czech Republic. Due to the continuous resistance of these three Member States to effectuate the relocation mechanism, the procedure reached its judicial phase in 2020.[113] In its response, the ECJ broadly rejected the arguments of the defending governments, nevertheless exploring in detail the scope of administrative power afforded to national migration authorities by virtue of the Council Decisions to refuse relocation under certain circumstances in detail.

Member States may prove the necessity of refusing relocation by way of reference to the respective provisions in the Council Decisions, particularly Article 5.[114] Article 5(7) of each Council Decisions authorises Member State migration authorities to refuse relocation either where there are 'serious reasons for applying the exclusion provisions [in the Qualification Directive]' or where there are 'reasonable grounds for regarding him or her as a danger to their national security or public order'. With a view to the first ground for refusing relocation, national migration authorities must establish that the applicant for international protection has committed a 'serious crime', based on a full investigation into all the circumstances of the individual case. Regarding the second ground for refusal, the Court acknowledged that national migration authorities are tasked to establish 'reasonable' grounds to consider an applicant for international protection a danger to national security or public order, which need not necessarily relate to a serious crime.[115]

In this regard, the Court confirmed that national migration authorities would have 'wide discretion' whether a third country national to be relocated may pose a threat to national security or public order.[116] In the exercise of that discretion, however, the Court clarified that national authorities are obliged to base their assessment on 'consistent, objective and specific evidence', underscoring the suspicion that the applicant 'actually or potentially' presents a danger to national security or public order. This implies that the competent authorities are at any rate required to carry out an overall examination of the circumstances of the individual case, based on all the facts within their knowledge.[117]

[113] Joined Cases C-715/17, C-718/17 and C-719/17 *European Commission v Poland, Hungary and Czech Republic* ECLI:EU:C:2020:257, [2020].
[114] ibid, para 152.
[115] ibid, para 156.
[116] ibid, para 158, with reference to *E.P.* (n 65), para 49.
[117] See M Savino, 'On Failed Relocation and Would-Be Leviathans: Towards the New Pact on Migration and Asylum', ADiM Blog (1 July 2020) 6.

These safeguards may be linked to the duty of care in exercising discretion,[118] as these standards instruct national migration authorities' exercise of discretion. Especially in the context of a transnational administrative system like the one established by the relocation mechanism, the duty of care may be of paramount importance. Disrespect for such standards would allow migration authorities to undermine the effectiveness of the relocation mechanism altogether. It is only in situations where reliable information exists that a person may be viewed as posing a threat to national security or public order and that migration authorities can legitimately exercise their discretion to refuse relocation. This precludes practices that refuse relocation in a sweeping fashion, based on the understanding that any third country national may pose a danger. Instead, national migration authorities' discretion may be exercised exclusively in relation to facts concerning the individual case.

It is interesting to note that this approach contrasts notably with the Court's jurisprudence on the activation of the discretionary clause in the Dublin system. Unlike the latter, the Court's case law on the refugee relocation goes to great lengths to preclude a sweeping exercise of discretionary power which would allow national administrations to render the relocation system moot. These divergent approaches can be explained by the fact that the exercise of discretion serves different purposes. In relation to the Dublin system, it follows from the case law of the Court of Justice that the unilateral assumption of responsibility through the activation of the discretionary clause may further the objective of transnational solidarity, whereas the exercise of discretion in the refugee relocation mechanism would lead to the refusal of relocation in an individual case. Had the Court ruled differently in the latter context, national migration authorities could have opted for practices that would have ultimately undermined the relocation system at large.

C. Politicisation of the Exercise of Discretion in European Migration Law

The ECJ's acknowledgement of 'wide discretion' constitutes a peculiar form of European legal influence. By ensuring that national migration authorities have a degree of autonomy, it interferes with the relative authority traditionally attributed to administrative actors in national systems.[119] Accordingly, where administrations previously did not have such a measure of autonomy, the Court's affirmation of their 'wide discretion' may be seen as effectively empowering administrators in relation other national actors.[120]

Once national migration authorities find their relative authority elevated or at least consolidated on account of the 'wide discretion' vested in them *qua* Union

[118] See above at ch 4, s II.A.

[119] For this phenomenon, see above at ch 3, s I.B.i.

[120] See M Ruffert, 'National Executives and Bureaucracies' in P Cane et al (eds), *The Oxford Handbook of Comparative Administrative Law* (Oxford University Press, 2020) 522.

law, this detaches them to some extent from national lawmakers. In effect, this may be said to cut them off from one of the prime sources of legitimacy of administrative actors.[121] As a corollary, Union law elevates the relative authority of national administrations by virtue of 'wide discretion' while stripping them, at the same time, of a significant legitimacy asset.[122] This effect may be less pronounced where the executive itself benefits from relatively direct democratic legitimacy, as for instance in the context of presidential systems.[123] Where national administrations derive their authority by and large from the democratic accountability of the legislature, and Union law bars the latter from interfering with administrative power, this may invite criticism – at least from the perspective of national law.

On an intermediate level of abstraction, this suggests that the exercise of 'wide discretion' may not merely constitute a technicality, with no political ramifications whatsoever.[124] By contrast, the Court's jurisprudence in this regard may have catered to a politicisation of administrative power. To be sure, the preceding analysis does not produce quantifiable empirical evidence to that effect. Nonetheless, it illustrates how supranational affirmations of 'wide discretion' may charge administrative decision-making with significant political weight.

This is specifically the case for decision-making in an area of law that is highly politicised such as the refugee relocation mechanism. The Court's reasoning in this context can be viewed as a judicial strategy of conflict resolution.[125] On the one hand, the Court firmly opposes arguments that would impair the uniform application and binding nature of Union law. On the other hand, it affords 'wide discretion' to decision-makers in the context of a case-by-case investigation.[126] This effectively channels the principled dissent of some Member States into a question of diligent administrative deliberation. Where national migration authorities gather consistent, objective, and specific evidence to support the suspicion that an applicant for international protection poses a danger to national security or public order, relocation of that person may be refused.

Accordingly, the Court emphasises that the relocation mechanism duly accounts for 'reasonable' security concerns. Such a reasoning disregards the high politics surrounding the relocation mechanism. Rather, the Court considers the powers vested in national migration authorities, focusing on the nitty-gritty of the relocation procedure instead. Where practical difficulties arise in the context of that procedure, they must be resolved in a 'spirit of cooperation and mutual trust

[121] On this point, see BG Mattarella, 'Law and Discretion. A Public Law Perspective on the EU' in J Mendes (ed), *EU Executive Discretion and the Limits of Law* (Oxford University Press, 2019) 37.

[122] See C Möllers, 'Verwaltungsrecht Und Politik' in A Bogdandy, S Cassese and PM Huber (eds), *Handbuch Ius Publicum Europaeum: Band V: Verwaltungsrecht in Europa: Grundzüge* (CF Müller, 2014) 1218.

[123] For that phenomenon, see ch 2, s I.B.

[124] See similarly E Chiti, 'Is EU Administrative Law Failing in Some of Its Crucial Tasks?' (2016) 22 *European Law Journal* 576, 585.

[125] See J Bornemann, 'Judicial Responses to Autocratic Legalism: The European Court of Justice in a Cleft Stick?' (2022) 7 *European Papers* 651, 667 ff.

[126] *Poland, Hungary and Czech Republic* (n 113), para 160.

between the authorities of the Member States'.[127] In practice, initial difficulties of the relocation process were subsequently mitigated, inter alia through the involvement of Europol, to reduce potential threats to public order or national security.[128] By virtue of their refusal to implement all the relocation obligations imposed upon them, the Court therefore highlighted that the defendant Member States did not just violate EU law but equally missed out on an opportunity of practical cooperation established with a view to ensuring public order and security in the Member States.

In this vein, the Court's response may be understood as an effort of de-politicisation of the refugee relocation mechanism. By acknowledging the possibility of Member States to refuse relocation of individual applicants on security grounds, the Court may have cooled heated tempers, while still rejecting lavish sovereignty claims. This method of de-politicisation, however, may have catered to the politicisation of the exercise of administrative discretion.[129] Although the Court appears eager to distance its reasoning from arguments of principled opposition, its acknowledgement of national migration authorities' wide discretion vests the latter with significant responsibility in the light of the political salience surrounding refugee relocation. Accordingly, the decision whether to relocate a third country national to the respective national territory ultimately rests with the national migration authorities, subject to significant autonomy that the qualifier of 'wide discretion' implies. Where fundamental opposition against refugee relocation lingers amongst national actors, this criticism would technically have to be levelled at national administrators.[130]

Analytically speaking, politicisation does not operate as a legal limit to the exercise of discretionary power. However, the Court's approach to respond to national security concerns by affording national migration administrations 'wide discretion' may undermine the ability of administrations to operate impartially and carefully. Given the fierce opposition of some national government, it may be presumed that governmental actors attempt to exert influence on national migration authorities, to the effect that the latter's exercise of discretion would be (mis) used to undermine the effects of the relocation scheme.[131] In this vein, the political pressure may be high to disregard the limits of legality and the standard of care reiterated by the Court's case law.[132]

[127] ibid, para 164.

[128] ibid, para 166.

[129] See generally on this phenomenon, Möllers (n 122) 1211.

[130] Although it can be questionable whether national governments would rhetorically bother with such technicalities of responsibility attribution.

[131] For a similar finding, see A Zhelyazkova, 'Do EU Policies Constrain Government Autonomy? Insights from the Implementation of EU Migration Policies' (2024) 47 *West European Politics* 595, 600.

[132] In this sense, the Court's approach may undermine national migration officers' ability to depoliticise their work through references to professionalism, see LM Borrelli and A Lindberg, 'The Creativity of Coping: Alternative Tales of Moral Dilemmas among Migration Control Officers' (2018) 4 *International Journal of Migration and Border Studies* 163, 171.

IV. Interim Conclusion: Discretion as a Sophisticated Mode of Decision-Making

A conventional understanding of discretion suggests that the exercise thereof would coincide with relaxed standards of deliberation. This is not unreasonable. After all, discretion implies a degree of decision-making freedom, and to some extent, it allows decision-makers to choose between one option or another. As the preceding section illustrates, however, the exercise of discretion in European migration law does not conform with such an understanding. Despite the degree of deliberative freedom that it implies, the exercise of discretion finds itself circumscribed and instructed by standards of legality in this field of law.

In European migration law, the standards that instruct and limit administrative conduct originate from different levels of a multi-levelled legal system.[133] National migration authorities are subjected to standards of international, supranational and national law, and the exercise of discretion implies that administrators collect the relevant normative programme in this regard in a relatively autonomous fashion.[134] From the perspective of administrators, this interaction of standards of legality with the exercise of discretion establishes the latter as a particularly sophisticated mode of decision-making. National migration authorities are afforded a degree of autonomy but must – in exercising it – appraise independently the norms and factors that may be relevant in an individual case. Failure to fully appraise all relevant elements of deliberation or failure to respect procedural requirements may flaw the exercise of their discretion.

Ultimately, from the perspective of administrators, this establishes discretion as a particularly demanding mode of deliberation: the relative autonomy that the exercise of discretion implies runs up against multiple standards of legality that must be strictly followed, deliberative freedom notwithstanding. Unlike a mode of decision-making that allows administrators to opt for one of several, equivalent options, this confirms that, in European migration law, discretionary conduct has emerged as a particularly sophisticated mode of decision-making that requires migration authorities to exercise their autonomy in a way that respects the limits and instructions derived from standards of legality originating from different layers of a multi-levelled legal system.

[133] See already Jestaedt (n 3) 351.
[134] See Wendel (n 49) 207.

5

Discretion and the Legal Position of Migrants

As a phenomenon, discretion is usually discussed in relation to administrative decision-makers. This is not surprising, given that street-level bureaucrats are the actors that exercise such powers, and the ability of law to draw limits to that exercise has attracted the better part of academic attention.[1] Still, the existence, scope and nature of discretionary power affect the way individuals experience and interact with public power. Accordingly, the following section will shift the focus of analysis to the position of individuals affected by the exercise of discretionary power. Such a 'user perspective'[2] allows for an exploration of how migrants, as principal subjects of European migration law, experience discretionary decision-making and how they may utilise the law as a means of protection against administrative practices.

One of the pronounced criticisms levelled at broad discretionary powers relates to the fact that it makes it difficult, if not impossible, for individuals to effectively challenge administrative decision-making. This may reasonably be criticised for exposing migrants to a risk of being confronted with arbitrariness.[3] More narrowly designed and legally instructed discretion, by contrast, may coincide with safeguards and avenues of redress that offer protection to the individuals concerned. Against this backdrop, it will be argued in the following section that discretion, as a targeted and legally instructed phenomenon of European migration law, offers several avenues of migrant protection. The relative improvements and opportunities that discretion offers migrants in contemporary European migration law may significantly reduce the risk of arbitrariness to which individuals are exposed.

By focusing on the legal position of migrants, the following section analyses the guarantees and mechanisms that individuals have at their disposal to protect their interests in relation to discretionary decision-making. In this regard, it sets out to highlight that European migration law vests migrants with options to counter discretionary practices. To be sure, this is not to suggest that migrants would

[1] See above at ch 4.

[2] See insightfully E Desmet, 'Analysing Users' Trajectories in Human Rights: A Conceptual Exploration and Research Agenda' (2014) 8 *Human Rights & International Legal Discourse* 121, 123 ff.

[3] See P Mindus, 'Justice of Others: Arbitrary Law-Making in Contemporary Migration Policy' (2020) 14 *Etikk i praksis. Nordic Journal of Applied Ethics* 1, 2.

not be exposed to arbitrariness on (multiple) other accounts.[4] Rather, the argument that standards of legality circumscribing and instructing administrative decision-making guard against arbitrary practices and occasionally improve the legal position of migrants is limited to the analysis of discretion as a contemporary feature of European migration law.

The degree of discretion vested in migration officials is constitutive of a highly hierarchical power relationship between administrators and migrants. Following the transformation of discretionary power, however, this relationship may be recalibrated (Section I). Even where migration authorities exercise discretion, migrants can rely on guarantees derived from individual rights (Section II). Moreover, on several occasions, discretion has come to replace instances of decision-making that would have affected individuals unfavourably by default, thus allowing individuals to draw migration authorities' attention to the specificities of their individual case (Section III). In addition, a growing set of standards of legality enables individuals to challenge the substance of discretionary conduct (Section IV) and to challenge discretionary decision-making before courts (Section V).

I. Between Executive Domination and Individual Protection

The relationship between migrants and administrations is often described as a highly hierarchical one.[5] To some extent, the broad scope and prevalence of discretion in European migration law mirrors this understanding. Discretionary decision-making tends to subjugate migrants to outcomes that are difficult to counter or challenge in court. In this sense, discretion can be singled out as an element underpinning the domination that executives exercise over individuals: when faced with decision-making based on broad discretionary power, individuals will find themselves largely at the mercy of migration authorities, without any meaningful options of redress.[6]

While discretionary powers have been gradually circumscribed and narrowed down by standards of legality, the volatility and unpredictability to which migrants are subjected have not entirely disappeared.[7] In this sense, it should be acknowledged that the persistence of discretion, even as a targeted and legally instructed

[4] See only J Bornemann and F Maiani, 'Temporal Governance, Precarity in the New Pact on Migration and Asylum' (2025) 31 *European Public Law* 371.

[5] See TG Eule et al, *Migrants Before the Law. Contested Migration Control in Europe* (Palgrave Macmillan, 2019) 235.

[6] See I Honohan, 'Domination and Migration: An Alternative Approach to the Legitimacy of Migration Controls' (2014) 17 *Critical Review of International Social and Political Philosophy* 31, 40; A Sager, 'Immigration Enforcement and Domination: An Indirect Argument for Much More Open Borders' (2017) 70 *Political Research Quarterly* 42.

[7] See Eule et al (n 5) 140.

phenomenon, may taint the lived experiences of migrants.[8] In European migration law, this volatility may be particularly pronounced in two constellations: first, the scope of discretion may be broader in relation to individuals who are considered outsiders, either because they apply from outside the state territory or because they reside on a short-term basis (subsection A). Second, migration authorities continue to have discretion to terminate the legal stay of migrants who are considered to pose a security threat. In this context, discretion may be singled out as one of the key elements underpinning the general conditionality of migrants' stay in the host state, which may be reduced over time but never fully repressed (subsection B).

A. Of Outsiders and Insiders: Discretion as a Mediator for Belonging

The existence and scope of discretion can be linked to the way that legal systems mediate migrants' belonging in European societies.[9] Particularly, wide discretionary powers persist in European migration law mainly in relation to individuals who seek entry into the territory of their prospective host state but do so from abroad.[10] This is aptly illustrated by the wide discretion that EU law affords Member States' visa authorities.[11] Visas are routinely issued prior to departure, and the handling of visa claims falls, as a rule, onto consulates abroad. In this sense, the wide discretion that EU migration law affords visa authorities is a prerequisite for a form of 'pre-border control' that facilitates legal access for some, while seeking to repress entry for others.[12] Discretion is the key legal component allowing for this selectivity. It enables migration authorities to decide in relative freedom whose entry into state territory is authorised. Were it not for this wide discretion, the limits of legality that EU migration law impose on national migration authorities' deliberation would strip State authorities of the opportunity to issue visas in a selective fashion.

The selectivity underpinning visa policies resonates with the conventional idea that migrants should not have a strong legal position or claim-right to seek entry to another country.[13] In this sense, it may be argued that discretion is instrumental in governing the legal position of migrants as that of 'outsiders' – individuals in

[8] See L Goldring, 'Precarious Legal Status Trajectories as Method, and the Work of Legal Status' (2022) 26 *Citizenship Studies* 460, 465.

[9] On this point, see D Thym, 'Deciphering the Role of (Migration) Law in the Social Construction of "Otherness"' in M Jesse (ed), *European Societies, Migration, and the Law. The 'Others' amongst 'Us'* (Cambridge University Press, 2020) 349.

[10] See for instance MJ Alpes and A Spire, 'Dealing with Law in Migration Control: The Powers of Street-Level Bureaucrats at French Consulates' (2013) 23 *Social & Legal Studies* 261.

[11] See above at ch 3, s II.

[12] See V Moreno-Lax, *Accessing Asylum in Europe: Extraterritorial Border Controls and Refugee Rights under EU Law* (Oxford University Press, 2017) 81.

[13] See C Grey, 'The Rights Of Migration' (2014) 20 *Legal Theory* 25, 26.

respect of whom the exposure to a degree of arbitrariness may be more acceptable than for persons belonging to the society of the receiving state.[14] However, besides the fact that European migration law may provide safeguards against such arbitrariness, the differentiation between out- and insiders is notoriously nebulous,[15] and individuals may turn from an 'immigrating subject' to a 'transitory' subject whose legal position should be gradually approximated and aligned with that of non-migrants.[16] This may explain why migration authorities have wide discretion to terminate legal stay on the basis of a short-term visa, but instances of discretion are subject to stricter constraints with respect to more permanent stay.[17]

The width of discretion of migration authorities to terminate stay on public order grounds will largely depend on the time a person has lawfully resided in the territory of the host state.[18] In this context, the power of migration authorities is strongly influenced by the interpretation of European courts.[19] The European Court of Human Rights (ECtHR) has expanded the scope of the right to the protection of family and private life to the situation of migrants.[20] Likewise, the European Court of Justice (ECJ) has interpreted EU secondary law instruments to include safeguards compelling national decision-makers to duly consider the specificities of the individual case before adopting a decision interfering with long-term residence or residence for reasons of family reunification.[21]

B. Discretion and the Termination of Stay: Security and Securitisation

It is no coincidence that many instances of discretionary power in European migration law relate to administrative assessment of threats to public order and security. Security threats are often unpredictable and dynamic in nature, to the effect that decision-makers may need to have a measure of discretion to duly respond to such threats.[22] Since national authorities are frequently authorised to

[14] For such a view in relation to US and Canadian visa law, see F Mégret, 'The Travel Visa as the Ubiquitous Legal Infrastructure of Everyday Global Mobility Arbitrariness' (2024) 25 *German Law Journal* 1265, 1280 ff.

[15] See B Anderson et al, 'Insider/Outsider: Categorical Rivalries?' in S Seubert et al (eds), *Moving Beyond Barriers. Prospects for EU Citizenship* (Edward Elgar, 2018).

[16] SB Coutin et al, 'Deferred Action and the Discretionary State: Migration, Precarity and Resistance' (2017) 21 *Citizenship Studies* 951, 954.

[17] See C Costello, *The Human Rights of Migrants and Refugees in European Law* (Oxford University Press, 2016) 67.

[18] See M Stronks, *Grasping Legal Time. Temporality and European Migration Law* (Cambridge University Press, 2022) 20.

[19] See D Sindbjerg Martinsen, 'Judicial Policy-Making and Europeanization: The Proportionality of National Control and Administrative Discretion' (2011) 18 *Journal of European Public Policy* 944.

[20] See A Desmond, 'The Private Life of Family Matters: Curtailing Human Rights Protection for Migrants under Article 8 of the ECHR?' (2018) 29 *The European Journal of International Law* 261.

[21] See above at ch 3, s I.B.

[22] See BG Mattarella, 'Law and Discretion. A Public Law Perspective on the EU' in J Mendes (ed), *EU Executive Discretion and the Limits of Law* (Oxford University Press, 2019) 35.

consider the security-implications of their migration-related decisions, European migration law tends to afford them a measure of discretion in this regard.[23]

This has significant implications for the legal position of migrants. Security considerations may justify the refusal of entry, the premature termination of or refusal to prolong legal stay of third country nationals.[24] It is in this vein that discretionary power subjects migrants to a significant degree of volatility, materialising particularly in a pervasive fear of loss of status and, possibly, expulsion.[25] Owing to the discretion of migration authorities to adopt measures safeguarding public order and security, migrants' presence in a host state is intrinsically volatile.[26] Unlike other individuals, migrants are subjected to a form of 'precarious presence', whereby loss of legal residence will always be a daunting possibility.[27]

To be sure, the discretion of migration authorities to terminate stay on public order grounds is limited by several safeguards of protection. In relation to migrants that have been convicted of committing a crime, the ECtHR has highlighted that national migration authorities must strike a fair balance between a variety of interests, including the 'nature and seriousness of the offence committed' and the 'length of the applicant's stay in the country from which he or she is to be expelled'.[28] In EU law, strong safeguards against the termination of stay apply to long-term residents and the Court of Justice has confirmed that migration authorities would have to carry out an individualised assessment in such cases.[29] These safeguards reduce the volatility to which migrants are exposed but may not ultimately rule out the possibility that migration authorities exercise their discretion in a way that would unfavourably affect them.

This volatility is exacerbated by measures and practices premised on the view that migration would inherently pose a security threat to the host country. This has been termed 'securitisation' of migration in the literature.[30] While securitisation

[23] For an overview, see V Stehlík, 'Discretion of Member States Vis-à-Vis Public Security: Unveiling the Labyrinth' (2017) 17 *International and Comparative Law Review* 127.

[24] See J Chlebny, 'Public Order, National Security and the Rights of Third-Country Nationals in Immigration Cases' (2018) 20 *European Journal of Migration and Law* 115, 120 ff.

[25] See K Griffith and S Gleeson, 'The Precarity of Temporality: How Law Inhibits Immigrant Worker Claims' (2017) 39 *Comparative Labor Law & Policy Journal* 111, 112.

[26] See I Hasselberg, *Enduring Uncertainty. Deportation, Punishment and Everyday Life* (Berghahn, 2016) 23 ff.

[27] M Griffiths, 'Interrogating Time and Temporality in Migration Governance' in E Carmel, K Lenner and R Paul (eds), *Handbook on the Governance and Politics of Migration* (Edgar Elgar, 2021) 320. This uncertainty may even affect individuals who have naturalised, ie, become citizens of the host state. Under certain – admittedly exceptional – conditions, these persons may be stripped of their acquired nationality and may likewise lose the protection against loss of lawful stay attributed thereto, see seminally C Joppke, 'Terror and the Loss of Citizenship' (2016) 20 *Citizenship Studies* 728.

[28] For instance, *Üner v The Netherlands* App no 46410/99 (ECtHR, 18 October 2006), para 57.

[29] Council Directive 2003/109/EC of 25 November 2003 concerning the status of third-country nationals who are long-term residents (LTRD) [2003], OJ L16/44, arts 9(3), 12(3); see above at ch 3, s I.B.ii.

[30] The term was first coined by J Huysmans, 'The European Union and the Securitization of Migration' (2000) 38 *Journal of Common Market Studies* 751, 756.

tends to result from the interplay of actors operating at different levels of authority,[31] the wide discretion of migration authorities to ward off security threats may be one of the prominent avenues for such a securitisation paradigm to play out at the national administrative level. Unlike situations in which securitisation discourse has explicitly underpinned the adoption of legal frameworks, wide discretion puts administrators in the position to decide whether a security threat persists and how to best respond to it. This may explain why security discourse has become one of the dominant frames through which human mobility and control are treated in European migration law.[32] It allows governments to implement restrictive policies through administrative practice, ordering migration authorities to exercise their wide discretion in security matters in such a way that decision-making will frequently affect migrants unfavourably.

Empirically, one of the most visible instances of securitisation through national migration authorities' wide discretion occurred in relation to the EU's refugee relocation mechanism. National governments have presented the mandatory relocation of asylum seekers as a policy that would inherently imperil national security,[33] to the effect that national administrators were ordered to exercise their discretion in a way that relocation would be refused for virtually every person covered by the scheme.[34] This may be viewed as a form of blame avoidance through discretion. National governments use securitisation discourse to exert influence on the way that street-level bureaucrats exercise discretion.[35] Although the Court of Justice ultimately ruled that such a practice ignored the limits of legality imposed on national migration authorities in this regard,[36] it illustrates how securitisation may lead to an exercise of discretion that would undermine the legal position of migrants.

II. Discretion and Individual Rights of Migrants: An Uneasy Relationship?

According to a widely held view in legal theory, the conferral of individual rights limits, or even excludes the existence of discretionary power.[37] To some extent,

[31] See V Bello, 'The Spiralling of the Securitisation of Migration in the EU: From the Management of a "Crisis" to a Governance of Human Mobility?' (2022) 48 *Journal of Ethnic and Migration Studies* 1327.

[32] Cf on this point, ibid 1330.

[33] See M Kabata and A Jacobs, 'The "Migrant Other" as a Security Threat: The "Migration Crisis" and the Securitising Move of the Polish Ruling Party in Response to the EU Relocation Scheme' (2023) 31 *Journal of Contemporary European Studies* 1223; D Stivas, 'The Art of Securitising: Orbán's Handling of the European Refugee Crisis' (2023) 31 *Journal of Contemporary European Studies* 184.

[34] See above at ch 4, s III.B.ii.

[35] On this point, see insightfully C Hood, 'Discretion and Blame Avoidance' in T Evans and PL Hupe (eds), *Discretion and the Quest for Controlled Freedom* (Palgrave Macmillan, 2020) 30.

[36] Joined Cases C-715/17, C-718/17 and C-719/17 *European Commission v Poland, Hungary and Czech Republic* ECLI:EU:C:2020:257, [2020].

[37] For insightful discussions, see N MacCormick, 'Discretion and Rights' (1989) 8 *Law and Philosophy* 23, 31 ff; in relation to EU migration law C Warin, 'Individual Rights in EU Migration and Asylum Law' (*EU Immigration and Asylum Law and Policy*, 6 January 2020) <https://eumigrationlawblog.eu/individual-rights-in-eu-migration-and-asylum-law/>.

this view is reproduced in the literature on migration law. Against the backdrop of the prominent role that migration systems assign to discretionary decision-making, Coutin et al suggest that such migration regimes should be qualified as 'discretionary state', which – unlike regimes qualified as 'contractual states' – largely operate in the absence of claim-based rights for migrants. In this sense, public officials are said to have 'the power to decide the fate of its noncitizen subjects by awarding, denying, and determining the benefits of deferred action or other forms of liminal legality'.[38] As the analysis of the existence and nature of discretion in European migration law suggests, however, a binary analytical distinction between rights and discretion does not entirely hold water. Rather, migrants may be able to invoke rights vis-à-vis public officials, even if the latter exercise discretion. Empirically, this finding is visible in at least three constellations.

First, the existence of migrant rights does not preclude the possibility that administrators have discretion in assessing whether one of the criteria for accessing those rights are satisfied. In the context of the EU Family Reunification Directive, for instance, the Court of Justice ruled that this instrument imposes on Member States 'precise positive obligations, with corresponding clearly defined individual rights'.[39] However, the Court is quick to add that this right is only afforded where several conditions are satisfied, and one of these requirements compels national migration authorities to ascertain whether the individual conduct of the application represents a genuine, present and sufficiently serious threat affecting the fundamental interests of society.[40] While this does not explicitly confirm that national authorities should have discretion, it has been argued in the preceding sections that Member States will routinely accommodate this requirement through legal frameworks that are viewed, for the purposes of this investigation, as discretion.[41] Similarly, in *Ben Alaya*, the Court highlighted that applicants for student visas 'must . . . be issued with a residence permit' where they 'meet the general and specific conditions exhaustively listed in [the Students and Researchers Directive]'.[42] This establishes the existence of a 'non-discretionary right', as Fernhout puts it,[43] but does not preclude the existence of discretion. Rather, national migration authorities retain discretion when ascertaining whether the conditions for a visa are satisfied, specifically the grounds relating to the existence of a threat to public policy, public security or public health.[44]

A second point of reflection worth pondering when considering the interaction between migrant rights and discretion in European migration law concerns the availability of judicial redress. In Europe, the availability of judicial redress

[38] Coutin et al (n 16) 953.

[39] Joined Cases C-381/18 and C-382/18 *G.S. and V.G. v Staatssecretaris van Justitie en Veiligheid* ECLI:EU:C:2019:1072, [2019], para 61.

[40] ibid, para 63.

[41] See above at ch 3, s I.C.

[42] Case C-491/13 *Ben Alaya v Bundesrepublik Deutschland* ECLI:EU:C:2014:2187, [2014], para 27.

[43] R Fernhout, 'An Analysis of the Ben Alaya Case (C-491/13): When Conditions of the Students Directive Are Met, That Directive Confers Entitlement to a Student Visa, without Leaving the National Authorities Any Discretion in That Regard' (2015) 17 *European Journal of Migration and Law* 147, 149.

[44] *Ben Alaya* (n 42), para 33.

is designed as an individual (fundamental) right to an effective remedy. In the context of EU law, for instance, the fundamental right to an effective remedy interacts with specifications in secondary law instruments, to the effect that national legal systems may have to provide effective avenues for individuals to seek judicial redress.[45] This creates significant consequences, both for the conceptual understanding of discretion in European migration law, but also for the possibility of individuals to challenge discretionary decision-making in court. Conceptually, the existence of some form of judicial review is considered as a formative element distinguishing discretion from uncontrolled freedom.[46] At the same time, the possibility to challenge an administrative decision in court is crucial for allowing individuals to enforce legal safeguards in practice.

Regarding the interaction of discretion and migrant rights, it is therefore important to note that the existence of discretion is not per se called into question by the availability of an individual (fundamental) right to an effective remedy. While secondary law may spell out requirements following from this right that would preclude the existence of discretion, such as the standard of full and *ex nunc* review applied in EU asylum law, a constitutional safeguard in Article 47 of the Charter of Fundamental Rights does not by itself prescribe a specific intensity of judicial review. In this sense, it can be highlighted that an individual fundamental right such as the one enshrined in Article 47 of the Charter of Fundamental Rights, does not rule out the existence of discretion.

Third, a prominent view in the literature suggests that the existence and scope of discretion should be reduced to the bare minimum when fundamental individual rights are at stake.[47] This notion is equally reflected in European migration law. While the existence of discretion and individual rights are not necessarily mutually exclusive, the case for limiting discretion is certainly stronger in situations in which decision-making interferes with such individual rights.[48] In European migration law, this effect is visible in relation to decision-making that restricts core guarantees of migrant protection. In relation to asylum decision-making or the ordering of detention, the respective legal frameworks even explicitly preclude discretionary power.[49] Regarding other individual rights, migration authorities may retain a measure of discretion, but this is certainly more constrained than decision-making in areas not underpinned by weighty individual rights.

On an intermediate level of abstraction, this illustrates that the case for more narrowly circumscribed discretionary power is stronger in relation to

[45] Charter of Fundamental Rights of the European Union [2012] OJ C362/391, art 47, see also A Słowik, 'Multiple Sources of Right to an Effective Remedy in EU Migration and Asylum Law: Towards Common Standards on Judicial Protection?' (2024) 31 *Maastricht Journal of European and Comparative Law* 27.

[46] See above at ch 2, s III.

[47] See for instance P Mindus, 'Towards a Theory of Arbitrary Law-Making in Migration Policy' (2020) 14 *Etikk i praksis. Nordic Journal of Applied Ethics* 9, 15.

[48] See B Jordan, B Stråth and A Triandafyllidou, 'Comparing Cultures of Discretion' (2003) 29 *Journal of Ethnic and Migration Studies* 373, 393.

[49] See above at ch 3, s IV.

decision-making affecting individuals unfavourably.[50] Specifically, measures restricting migrants' fundamental rights, such as the right to non-refoulement, the right to liberty or the right to family reunification, will frequently be strictly circumscribed by detailed standards of legality and therefore will not entail broad discretionary powers. Conversely, the scope of discretion will often be much broader where the exercise of discretion may affect migrants favourably. This is the case where migration authorities have the power to depart from a negative decision on a discretionary basis, for instance, for reasons of individual hardship.

III. Open-Ended Deliberation as Relative Improvement

While discretion is often presented as a source of arbitrariness, some authors have highlighted that the open-ended nature of discretionary decision-making may likewise create positive effects for migrants. The flexibility that discretion entails can be exercised to benefit individuals. This effect was already noted by Jordan et al in relation to decision-making practices in the context of labour migration in Europe,[51] and other authors have detected similar tendencies in other regions of the world.[52] The following section argues that the open-ended nature of administrative assessment may be one of the overlooked virtues of discretion. It suggests that the open-ended deliberation that discretion entails marks a relative improvement in the legal position of migrants, serving as an avenue of individualised justice (subsection A). Unlike previous legal frameworks that would have compelled administrators to automatically decide unfavourably in a migrant's case, discretion enables individuals to try to persuade decision-makers to acknowledge the specificities of their situation and to decide in their favour (subsection B).

A. Discretion as an Avenue of Individualised Justice

Theoretical accounts often acknowledge that discretion may be of a two-faced nature. On the one hand, it is frequently criticised for the risk of arbitrariness and unpredictability it entails. On the other hand, scholars recognise that discretion allows administrators to take account of the specific circumstances of the individual case before them and, if deemed necessary, adjust their decision accordingly.[53] Different traditions emphasise this latter, more considerate, characterisation of

[50] See Mattarella (n 22) 34.
[51] See Jordan, Stråth and Triandafyllidou (n 48) 393.
[52] See GA Abarca and SB Coutin, 'Sovereign Intimacies: The Lives of Documents within US State-Noncitizen Relationships: Sovereign Intimacies' (2018) 45 *American Ethnologist* 7.
[53] See LM Borrelli, L Johannesson and A Lindberg, 'Predictable Patterns of Unpredictability: A Literature Review of Discretion in Migration Control' (2025) 7 *Political Research Exchange* 1, 4.

discretion[54] – and a similar tendency can be observed in European migration law.[55] By affording migration authorities the ability to adapt decisions to the individual case before them, the existence of discretion can positively influence the legal position of migrants.

At first sight, an individualised assessment may not appear to be a particularly strong safeguard for migrants. Rather, open-ended individualised assessments may affect the person concerned favourably on some occasions, and unfavourably on others. However, in many instances of European migration law, the existence of a genuinely open-ended discretionary power marks a relative improvement when contrasted with previous legal arrangements. By replacing decision-making that would have been unfavourable by default, the selective propagation of discretionary power therefore effectively strengthens the legal position of migrants.[56]

In European migration law, this effect is exemplified by the practice of Spanish authorities refusing to grant long-term residence status to persons with a criminal record. The relevant national legal framework required national migration authorities to ascertain whether the person concerned had any convictions for an offence under Spanish law.[57] The Spanish Supreme Court interpreted this provision to mean that the application for long-term residence status of any person with a criminal record would have to be rejected by default.[58] This interpretation compelled national migration authorities to adopt an unfavourable decision, without any discretion to depart from such a restrictive stance. However, this legal arrangement had to be adjusted when the Court of Justice ruled that national migration authorities would have to be able to carry out an individual assessment that allows them to weigh up 'a certain number of factors'; specifically, the seriousness or nature of the offence committed by the person, the threat that (s)he presents to public policy or security and the length of residence in and ties to the host Member State.[59] Following this judicial intervention, Spanish law had to replace an instance of bounded decision-making, that is, a decision that would have affected the legal position of migrants negatively by default, with a legal arrangement that ensures a measure of administrative flexibility in this regard. As has been argued elsewhere, national legal systems routinely accommodate this flexibility through legal arrangements that qualify as discretion as understood in this investigation.[60] Accordingly, this illustrates how the proliferation of discretion marks a relative improvement of the legal position of migrants.

[54] For instance, the French tradition of the *pouvoir discrétionnaire*, see above at ch 2, s II.A.i.

[55] See M Wendel, *Verwaltungsermessen Als Mehrebenenproblem: Zur Verbundstruktur Administrativer Entscheidungsspielräume Am Beispiel Des Migrations- Und Regulierungsrechts* (Mohr Siebeck, 2019) 193 ff.

[56] See above at ch 3, s I.C.ii.

[57] Real Decreto 557/2011, de 20 de abril, por el que se aprueba el Reglamento de la Ley Orgánica 4/2000, sobre derechos y libertades de los extranjeros en España y su integración social, tras su reforma por Ley Orgánica 2/2009 [derogado], BOE núm 103, 30 April 2011, ref BOE-A-2011-7703, art 149(2)(f).

[58] Joined Cases C-503/19 and C-592/19 *UQ and SI v Subdelegación del Gobierno en Barcelona* ECLI:EU:C:2020:629, [2020], para 20.

[59] ibid, para 38.

[60] See above at ch 3, s I.C.ii.

In this context, individuals may rely on the fact that administrators duly acknowledged that they had discretion in the first place. Were administrators to incorrectly presume that they had no discretion, individuals can challenge this neglect in court. The failure to exercise discretion may thus itself 'come to be seen as a culpable act of discretion', as Hood put it.[61] In European migration law, this effect has been illustrated in the context of the Dublin discretionary clause, where national courts have occasionally considered the application thereof as mandatory in the light of migrants' fundamental rights.[62] While this need not necessarily result in a favourable outcome for individuals, national courts may procedurally oblige administrators to consider whether the exercise of the Dublin discretionary clause would be appropriate in light of the individual situation before them.[63]

B. Swaying Administrators in Their Exercise of Discretion

On the one hand, the obligation of migration authorities to duly consider whether they have a measure of discretion strengthens the legal position of migrants, as it allows administrators to depart from a mode of decision-making that would otherwise affect individuals unfavourably by default. On the other hand, this changes the way that migrants get to interact with migration authorities and, consequently, the law. Unlike legal arrangements that allow individuals to claim certain rights or to invoke safeguards against a specific conduct, this relative improvement tasks individuals to 'sway the state's exercise of discretion', as Coutin et al put it.[64] Individuals may therefore draw the attention of migration authorities to the fact that the legal framework would allow for discretion in the first place and that this discretion should be exercised in her or his favour. While this does not offer the same type of protection that other safeguards against unfavourable decision-making afford, it still marks a relative improvement in the legal position of migrants, as the uncertainty of discretionary conduct replaces the 'hopeless certainty' of a negative decision by default.[65]

One of the practical advantages of this development lies in the fact that individuals may point migration authorities to specificities of their individual case, including specific considerations of hardship.[66] The existence of discretion implies that these considerations may assume legal weight. This relative improvement

[61] Hood (n 35) 29.

[62] See above at ch 4, s I.B.

[63] This approach was exemplified by the Rechtbank Den Haag 9 June 2016, ECLI:NL:RBDHA:2016:6809 (zaak nrs NL 16.1136 and NL 16.1138). Such a notion of a failure to exercise discretion exists in other legal systems in Europe as well, see for an overview C Grabenwarter, '§ 90 Ermessenslehren' in A Bogdandy, S Cassese and PM Huber (eds), *Handbuch Ius Publicum Europaeum.: Band V: Verwaltungsrecht in Europa: Grundzüge* (CF Müller, 2014) 1035.

[64] Coutin et al (n 16) 954.

[65] This phrase has been cited from A Triandafyllidou, 'The Migration Archipelago: Social Navigation and Migrant Agency' (2018) 57 *International Migration* 5, 8.

[66] See Eule et al (n 5) 215.

notwithstanding, it should be noted that opening administrative conduct to the possibility of incorporating considerations of compassion[67] or migrants' deservingness[68] may come at the cost of lack of legal certainty in the long run.[69] While the proliferation of discretion may therefore mark a relative improvement of the legal position of migrants, it likewise runs the risk of eliciting 'a kind of charitable paternalism, that might consist of selective discretionary assistance, or of quite neglectful indifference', as Jordan et al have put it.[70]

IV. Virtues and Potentials of Legally Instructed Choice

In European migration law, the nature and exercise of discretion changed fundamentally following the increased significance of legal principles.[71] While discretion is sometimes viewed as a form of free choice in theoretical discussions – an aleatory decision between several, legally equivalent options – the preceding sections have highlighted that, in European migration law, the exercise of discretion is increasingly instructed and structured by legal principles. This creates significant potentials for migrants. Legal principles serve as standards of legality that migration authorities must respect in their exercise of discretion. While the applicability of legal principles may therefore not necessarily ensure a favourable outcome for individuals, they serve as benchmarks against which the legality of discretionary conduct can be assessed (subsection A). This alters the way that migrants can engage with discretionary decision-making. Legal principles vest migrants with an option to understand the motives underpinning an administrator's exercise of discretion, and to assess whether, in their view, all relevant aspects have been duly considered (subsection B).

A. Towards a Migrant-Focused Exercise of Discretion?

From the perspective of individuals, the fact that legal principles increasingly structure and instruct the exercise of discretion in European migration law creates options to hold migration authorities to account. One of the most significant improvements in the legal position of migrants in this regard derives from

[67] In relation to Canadian immigration law, see for instance on this point L Sossin, 'From Neutrality to Compassion: The Place of Civil Service Values and Legal Norms in the Exercise of Administrative Discretion' (2005) 55 *The University of Toronto Law Journal* 427.

[68] See LM Borrelli, 'Should (S)He Stay or Should (S)He Go? Street-Level Suspicion and the Construction of the "(Un)Deserving Migrant"' (2022) 27 *Geopolitics* 1093.

[69] See B Oomen et al, 'Strategies of Divergence: Local Authorities, Law, and Discretionary Spaces in Migration Governance' (2021) 34 *Journal of Refugee Studies* 3608, 3625.

[70] Jordan, Stråth and Triandafyllidou (n 48) 393.

[71] For the far-reaching effects of EU legal principles for national migration systems, see J Bast, 'Of General Principles and Trojan Horses: Procedural Due Process in Immigration Proceedings under EU Law' (2010) 11 *German Law Journal* 1006.

the growing relevance of the principle of proportionality. As has been argued, this principle is at the heart of a targeted proliferation of discretion, shifting decision-making away from automatic outcomes that would disadvantage individuals, and replacing it with a mode of open-ended deliberation.[72]

At the same time, it has also transformed the way discretion is exercised. Both national and European courts have utilised standards of proportionality to instruct the exercise of discretion, thereby compelling migration authorities to pay greater attention to the specific situation of the individual migrants.[73] It requires decision-makers to appraise all relevant aspects of the individual situation and to strike a fair balance between public and individual interests. This may not guarantee a favourable outcome for individuals in all cases, but it instructs discretionary conduct to fully acknowledge the interests at stake and to put competing interest in relation to each other. In this sense, it caters to a more migrant-focused exercise of discretion.

The principle of proportionality often reveals its positive effects for migrants only 'in tandem' with other safeguards.[74] For migrants, the relative substantive improvements that the principle of proportionality brings about will transpire when migration authorities are likewise compelled to respect complementary, procedural obligations. These safeguards assume a particularly prominent role as standards instructing the exercise of discretionary power.[75] They counterbalance the deliberative freedom that discretion implies. In EU law, this notion of a compensatory relationship originally transpired in the context of direct administration,[76] and was later reproduced in situations of indirect administration.[77] The ECtHR has similarly interpreted Article 8 ECHR to imply that discretionary conduct should be circumscribed by a regulatory framework that includes procedural safeguards to ensure that the individual is duly involved in the decision-making process and that her or his interests are thus safeguarded.[78] Effectively, this approach seeks to strike a balance: on the one hand, seeking to safeguard the room for deliberative freedom that should be left to the administrator, and, on the other hand, the expectation of individuals about improved protection against discretionary decision-making that legal systems should offer.[79]

[72] See above at ch 5, s III.

[73] See BG Mattarella, 'Law and Discretion: A Public Law Perspective on the EU' in J Mendes (ed), *EU Executive Discretion and the Limits of Law* (Oxford University Press, 2019) 25.

[74] J Rochel, 'Working in Tandem: Proportionality and Procedural Guarantees in EU Immigration Law' (2019) 20 *German Law Journal* 89, see particularly 100 ff.

[75] See J Mendes, 'Discretion, Care and Public Interest in the EU Administration: Probing the Limits of Law' (2016) 53 *Common Market Law Review* 419, 430 ff.

[76] Case C-269/90 *Technische Universität München v Hauptzollamt München-Mitte* ECLI:EU:C:1991:438, [1991], para 14.

[77] Case C-89/17 *Secretary of State for the Home Department v Rozanne Banger* ECLI:EU:C:2018:570, [2017], para 51; and Case C-544/15 *Fahimian v Bundesrepublik Deutschland* ECLI:EU:C:2017:255, [2017], para 46.

[78] *Lazoriva v Ukraine* App no 6878/14 (ECtHR, 17 April 2018), para 63.

[79] For this point, see Mendes (n 75) 430 ff.

Several procedural safeguards that instruct the exercise of discretionary power in European migration law can be linked to the duty of care. First, the Court of Justice has noted that administrators are obliged to act impartially when exercising their discretion.[80] While administrators cannot be held to the same level of impartiality that applies to judicial actors, European courts have clarified that such a duty to act impartially should instruct administrative deliberations nonetheless.[81] Furthermore, the Court of Justice has ruled that impartiality should be linked to the idea of a 'level playing field for the parties to the proceedings and their respective interests', suggesting that administrative conduct should be characterised by 'objectivity . . . and the absence of any interest in the outcome of the proceedings apart from the strict application of the rule of law'.[82] Inspired by the case law of the ECtHR, the Court of Justice moreover highlighted that the obligation for administrators to act impartially should include sufficient guarantees to rule out any legitimate doubt as to the bias of the administrative decision-maker.[83]

This resonates with a Weberian understanding of administrative ethos, pursuant to which administrators act with a sense of neutrality and objectivity in the performance of their tasks.[84] With a view to European migration law, this safeguard precludes discretionary practices that would unduly dismiss individual interests in favour of governmental preferences. The duty to act impartially obliges individual decision-makers to exercise their discretion in a manner that fully and fairly appraises the interests of the individual, balancing them against competing public interests. Despite the normative potential of this duty, however, it should be noted that it has so far only occasionally transpired in the case law of European courts. As a safeguard limiting and instructing discretion in European migration law, so far, it has explicitly only been mentioned by the Court of Justice in *Fahimian*, while similar references are missing in relation to other instances of national migration authorities' 'wide discretion'.[85] Still, building on the reasoning in *Fahimian*, impartiality may emerge as one of the procedural safeguards instructing the way that migration authorities should exercise discretion in the future.

In practice, significant improvements for individuals may follow from the fact that migration authorities are obliged to state reasons when exercising discretion. This puts them in the position to ascertain whether the legal and factual preconditions for the exercise of discretion were present,[86] and – if they consider that

[80] *Fahimian* (n 77), para 46. It should be highlighted that these procedural safeguards may also apply to decision-making that does not qualify, for the purposes of this investigation, as discretion; see P van Reenen, 'Impartiality in the EU Asylum Procedure' (2018) 20 *European Journal of Migration and Law* 338.

[81] See ibid 343 ff.

[82] Case C-506/04 *Wilson v Ordre des avocats du barreau de Luxembourg* ECLI:EU:C:2006:587, [2006], para 52.

[83] Case C-439/11 *Ziegler SA v European Commission* ECLI:EU:C:2013:513, [2013], para 155.

[84] See M Ruffert, 'National Executives and Bureaucracies' in Peter Cane et al (eds), *The Oxford Handbook of Comparative Administrative Law* (Oxford University Press, 2020) 507.

[85] *Fahimian* (n 77), para 46.

[86] ibid.

migration authorities would not be able to rely on discretion in a specific case – challenge this decision in court.[87] This is linked to the fact that discretion does not represent a pervasive feature of European migration law, but rather occurs in relation to specific instances of deliberation. By obliging administrators to communicate the reasons why they exercise discretion in one way or another, individuals are enabled to verify whether administrative conduct stayed within the limits of discretion and was not exercised where no such power is conferred by the legal framework.

Connectedly, the obligation to state reasons also enables individuals to revise the factual basis of the decision affecting them.[88] The Court of Justice has ruled, in this regard, that the exercise of wide discretion must be based 'on a sufficiently solid factual basis'.[89] This may be a particularly relevant safeguard of migrant protection, especially in the light of securitisation discourse,[90] which may impel national decision-makers to exercise their discretion in a way that would unduly pursue a security-paradigm in relation to individuals who may not reasonably be linked to any such threat to public order or internal security. The duty to state reasons ensures that measures interfering with the legal position of migrants are only adopted vis-à-vis individuals who genuinely pose a threat to the security of the host society. National migration authorities are obliged, in this regard, to rely on 'consistent, objective and specific evidence that provides grounds' for viewing a third country national as posing a security threat.[91]

In substance, the Court of Justice has held that a statement of reasons 'must disclose in a clear and unequivocable fashion' the reasons for the decision taken.[92] In European migration law, however, the level of detail with which migration authorities must communicate the reasons for their discretionary decisions tends to remain relatively vague. Particularly, several EU migration law instruments require national authorities to communicate the reasons for their decision through a standard form. The Schengen Borders Code, for instance, tasks authorities to fill out such a form if they adopt a decision refusing entry but does not command them to flesh out why they consider an individual to pose a threat to inter alia public policy or internal security.[93]

On the one hand, communication through such a standardised form may be a practical necessity in an area of law that can be characterised as

[87] See on this point below at ch 5, s V.

[88] See generally on this point H Hofmann, 'The Duty of Care in EU Public Law: A Principle Between Discretion and Proportionality' (2020) 13 *Review of European Administrative Law* 87, 98.

[89] *Fahimian* (n 77), para 45; Joined Cases C-225/19 and C-226/19 *R.N.N.S v Minister van Buitenlandse Zaken* ECLI:EU:C:2020:951, [2020], para 49.

[90] See above at ch 5, s I.B.

[91] Case C-380/18 *Staatssecretaris van Justitie en Veiligheid v E.P.* ECLI:EU:C:2019:1071, [2019], para 49; *European Commission* (n 36), para 159.

[92] *Technische Universität München* (n 76), para 26.

[93] Regulation (EU) 2016/399 of the European Parliament and of the Council of 9 March 2016 on a Union Code on the rules governing the movement of persons across borders (Schengen Borders Code) (codification) [2016] OJ L77/1, art 14(2), in conjunction with Annex V, Part B.

'mass administration'.[94] On the other hand, a lack of clear reasons motivating decision-making may compromise the legal position of individuals. In the context of transnational cooperation of visa authorities, for instance, the Court has clarified that insufficient information in this regard may undermine the right to an effective remedy. This right requires national authorities to indicate, in the standard form's 'remarks' section, the Member State that had objected the issuing of a visa and the specific ground for refusal and, where appropriate, the essence of the reasons for that objection.[95] It puts individuals in the position to challenge the authority that had raised objections against the issuing of a visa, but does not necessarily require authorities to specify, in all detail, the reasons motivating their decision.

B. Participatory Elements in the Exercise of Discretion?

Discretionary power is often criticised for exposing individuals to a high degree of unpredictability.[96] This criticism is particularly pronounced in relation to the field of migration law, where the scope of discretion tends to be rather wide.[97] A growing importance of procedural safeguards, however, tends to alter the way that migrants get to interact with public officials exercising discretion.[98] For individuals, it opens up options of participation.[99] Procedural safeguards enable individuals to raise aspects that should guide the administrators' deliberation, thereby mitigating an individual's exposure to highly unpredictable decision-making and attenuating the relational vulnerability that may be said to otherwise characterise discretion.[100]

On several occasions, EU migration law instruments include participatory elements,[101] including in situations that entail wide discretion of national migration authorities. The Students and Researchers Directive, for instance, affords national authorities 'wide discretion' in the assessment whether to authorise or refuse entry of an applicant on public security grounds,[102] but obliges national

[94] D Thym and J Bornemann, 'Migration Policy: Between Crisis Preparedness, Ad Hoc Solutions, and Administrative Capacity-Building' in D Fromage, A Héritier and P Weismann (eds), *EU Regulatory Responses to Crises. Adaptation or Transformation?* (Oxford University Press, 2025) 151.

[95] *R.N.N.S* (n 89), para 46.

[96] See E Chiti, 'Is EU Administrative Law Failing in Some of Its Crucial Tasks?' (2016) 22 *European Law Journal* 576, 594.

[97] See above at ch 4, s I.

[98] See Eule et al (n 5) 215.

[99] See already on this point, D Galligan, *Discretionary Powers: A Legal Study of Official Discretion* (Oxford University Press, 1986) 340 ff.

[100] See K Rundle, 'Administrative Discretion and Governing Relationships: Situating Procedural Fairness' in Denise Meyerson, Catriona Mackenzie and Therese MacDermott (eds), *Procedural Justice and Relational Theory. Empirical, Philosophical, and Legal Perspectives* (Routledge, 2021) 242 ff.

[101] For participatory elements in sub-areas of European migration law that do not entail discretionary decision-making, see for instance M Moraru, 'Judicial Interactions Upholding the Right to Be Heard of Asylum Seekers, Returnees and Immigrants: The Symbiotic Protection of the EU Charter and General Principles of EU Law' in F Casarosa and M Moraru (eds), *The Practice of Judicial Interaction in the Field of Fundamental Rights: The Added Value of the Charter of Fundamental Rights of the EU* (Edward Elgar, 2022) 265 ff.

[102] *Fahimian* (n 77), para 42.

authorities to notify an applicant if information or documentation supplied in support of her or his application is incomplete, thereby allowing the individual to submit additional information within a reasonable timeframe.[103] This procedure requires migration authorities, in the exercise of their discretion, to interact with the individuals concerned.

A similar legal arrangement exists in the EU Visa Code. The Code stipulates that competent visa authorities, in justified cases, may call the applicant for an interview or request additional documentation.[104] Unlike the procedural obligation to request additional information in the Researchers and Students Directive, however, the Visa Code does not oblige migration authorities to allow the individual to submit additional information. Rather, this procedural element operates exclusively at the will of administrative authorities, and individuals cannot rely on this obligation as a safeguard against discretionary decision-making.

On an intermediate level of abstraction, this suggests that procedural elements may facilitate a participatory exercise of discretion, and that EU migration law includes some isolated examples to this effect. Overall, however, European migration law does not subject the exercise of discretionary power to procedural rules that would allow individuals to interact with administrative decision-makers. The main remedy – and the most tangible improvement in the enforcement of standards limiting discretionary conduct – operates not at an administrative but at the judicial level. Effective judicial review is the principal avenue for individuals to counter discretionary decision-making; the extent to which this safeguards the legal position of migrants will be discussed in the following section.

V. Protection Through External Control

In European migration law, the principal mechanism for individuals to resist discretionary decision-making is through challenges before a court. Although the standards of legality that limit and instruct discretionary decision-making may improve the legal position of individuals vis-à-vis administrative authorities, much of the protection that individuals derive from these norms results from the fact that discretionary conduct operates 'within externally controlled limits'.[105] Accordingly, judicial review is paramount in offering protection to migrants affected by discretionary decision-making. As has been argued in the preceding sections, the extent and intensity of judicial review has undergone significant adjustments in the fairway of influences of European law. Chief among those

[103] Directive (EU) 2016/801 of the European Parliament and of the Council of 11 May 2016 on the conditions of entry and residence of third-country nationals for the purposes of research, studies, training, voluntary service, pupil exchange schemes or educational projects and au pairing (recast) (Researchers and Students Directive) [2016] OJ L132/21, art 34(3).

[104] Regulation (EC) 810/2009 of the European Parliament and of the Council of 13 July 2009 establishing a Community Code on Visas (Visa Code) [2009] OJ L243/1, art 21(8).

[105] T Evans and PL Hupe, 'Conceptualizing Discretion' in T Evans and PL Hupe (eds), *Discretion and the Quest for Controlled Freedom* (Palgrave Macmillan, 2020) 7.

influences is the safeguard of an effective remedy – a guarantee that, in European migration law, is conceptualised as a fundamental right.[106]

A. Availability of Judicial Protection

Originally, instances of discretionary decision-making precluding any form of judicial review existed on several occasions in migration laws in Europe. Especially in relation to individuals seeking authorisation to enter from outside the territory of their prospective host state, immigration laws in Europe usually stuck to legal frameworks that precluded the availability of judicial remedies altogether.[107] Compared to other fields of European administrative law, this may raise eyebrows. In relation to most sub-areas of administrative law, discretionary power has been subjugated to forms of external control by courts in legal systems in Europe.[108] Accordingly, it may not be surprising to see that European legal influences increasingly preclude instances of deliberative freedom operating in the absence of any form of external judicial control.[109] Most notably, this form of influence originates from the fundamental right to an effective remedy that nowadays stretches virtually all elements of EU migration law.

Unlike other fields of administrative law, however, this extension of judicial review to instances of discretionary power occurred with a significant delay. Only recently was the Court of Justice asked to confirm that the right to an effective remedy should equally apply to individuals applying for short-term visas and entry authorisations for the purpose of research and studies at Member State consulates.[110] This goes to show that, in relation to some instances of decision-making, European migration law has lagged behind the general trend in European administrative law. However, it should likewise be noted that some instances of discretionary decision-making in European migration law continue to bar individuals from challenging decisions altogether. Most notably, this effect can be witnessed in relation to resettlement policies – a field of European migration law that has been described in the literature as a 'legal abyss of discretion'.[111]

While deliberative freedom in the absence of any form of external control does not qualify as discretion for the purposes of the present investigation,[112]

[106] See above at ch 5, s II.

[107] See E Brouwer, 'Effective Remedies for Third Country Nationals in EU Law: Justice Accessible to All?' (2005) 7 *European Journal of Migration and Law* 219, 228.

[108] See for instance R Caranta, 'On Discretion' in S Prechal and B van Roermund (eds), *The Coherence of EU Law: The Search for Unity in Divergent Concepts* (Oxford University Press, 2008) 186.

[109] For an overview of the case law of the Court of Justice of the EU, see A Słowik, 'Of Roads and Inroads: In Search of Ways for Effective Protection of Fundamental Rights of Migrants and Asylum Seekers in the CJEU's Case Law' (2025) 50 *European Law Review* 310.

[110] Case C-403/16 *El Hassani v Minister Spraw Zagranicznych* ECLI:EU:C:2017:960, [2016], para 41; Case C-949/19 *M.A. v Konsul Rzeczypospolitej Polskiej* ECLI:EU:2021:186, [2020], para 41.

[111] T de Boer and M Zieck, 'The Legal Abyss of Discretion in the Resettlement of Refugees: Cherry-Picking and the Lack of Due Process in the EU' (2020) 32 *International Journal of Refugee Law* 54.

[112] See above at ch 2, s III.

this terminology of discretion as a 'legal abyss' reflects the fact that resettlement schemes in Europe, at least as they currently stand, do not provide for any possibility to challenge decisions before a court.[113] European courts have so far refused to extend fundamental rights safeguards, such as the right to an effective remedy, to decision-making in this regard.[114] While the New Pact on Migration and Asylum includes a Regulation establishing common rules on resettlement and humanitarian admission,[115] it remains to be seen whether the Court of Justice will consider these rules and, by extension, the financing of resettlement through the EU's budget, sufficient to render decision-making in this field of law as falling within the scope of the Charter of Fundamental Rights.[116] In the absence of a clarification on this point, decision-making in the field of resettlement will continue to operate in the absence of a European fundamental rights guarantee to an effective remedy.

Notwithstanding the absence of judicial redress in the field of resettlement, as a rule, contemporary European migration law empowers individuals to challenge discretionary decision-making in court. This largely precludes forms of discretion that operate in the absence of judicial oversight. For migrants, the ability to challenge discretionary decision-making before a court constitutes the most significant avenue for holding administrative actors to account. Through a form of external control, it enables individuals to ensure that standards delimiting and instructing the exercise of discretionary power and thereby safeguarding their legal position are respected by migration authorities.

B. Limited Review and Migrants' Chances of Success

From the outset, it should be noted that individuals challenging discretionary decisions fight an uphill battle. Success in resisting discretionary decisions is far from certain, given that individuals will routinely be required to demonstrate that the action of an administrative authority is vitiated by a particularly evident, manifest error of appraisal.[117] In this vein, limited judicial review of administrative action renders it unlikely that individuals will be successful in challenging administrative action.[118] Still, in contemporary European migration law, the legal position

[113] Most national legal systems do not treat resettlement as an administrative procedure in the first place, see de Boer and Zieck (n 111) 83.

[114] See ibid 68 ff.

[115] Regulation (EU) 2024/1350 of the European Parliament and of the Council of May 14 2024 establishing a Union Resettlement and Humanitarian Admission Framework, and amending Regulation (EU) 2021/1147 (Resettlement and Humanitarian Admission Framework Regulation) [2024] OJ L2024/1350.

[116] For a discussion of arguments regarding the possible applicability of the Charter to Member State actions in this regard, see J Rijpma, 'External Migration and Asylum Management: Accountability for Executive Action Outside EU-Territory' (2017) 2 *European Papers* 571, 585 ff.

[117] See similarly for equal treatment cases, J Gerards, 'Intensity of Judicial Review in Equal Treatment Cases' (2004) *Netherlands International Law Review* 135, 144.

[118] See on this point D Cole, 'Judging the Next Emergency: Judicial Review and Individual Rights in Times of Crisis' (2003) 101 *Michigan Law Review* 2565, 2565 ff.

of migrants is not entirely hopeless. Particularly, European fundamental rights ensure that the reviewing court must, in any case, control the limits of discretion, which includes limits of statutory law and legal principles instructing the exercise thereof, such as considerations of proportionality.[119] As has been argued in the preceding sections, these standards of legality have gained significance in European migration law, since discretion is conceptualised as legally instructed freedom that relates to specific instances of deliberation.[120]

Legal systems in Europe tend to agree that courts should perform limited judicial control when reviewing discretionary decision-making. However, there is no uniform model of judicial review of discretionary power in different legal systems in Europe, and the current state of European migration law reflects this diversity. Both the ECtHR and the Court of Justice of the EU accept, in principle, divergent intensities of judicial review. The way that the intensity of judicial control affects individuals is therefore contingent on these diverse legal contexts: while the extension of judicial review to decisions of consulates creates an avenue of judicial redress that did not exist beforehand, the Court of Justice has occasionally (and exceptionally) prescribed a limited form of review, which – in the German legal context it referred to – effectively reduced the intensity of judicial review.[121]

This goes to show that the chances of individuals to successfully challenge discretionary decision-making are rather slim. Limited forms of judicial review favour the legality of administrative acts. While the odds are therefore principally stacked against the individual when challenging discretionary decision-making, it should be noted that the standards of legality instructing the latter may allow courts to recalibrate and genuinely increase the intensity of their review. Particularly the principle of proportionality, notwithstanding different national traditions and modi,[122] allows courts to probe into the substance of a balance of interests.[123]

VI. Interim Conclusion: Virtues of Diligently Exercised Discretion

The preceding sections examined how discretionary power shapes the legal position of migrants in European migration law. Contrary to the conventional view that discretion necessarily undermines individual protection, it has been argued that discretionary decision-making, when embedded within a framework of legal safeguards and subject to external control, may afford migrants meaningful avenues to challenge and influence administrative outcomes. In this sense, discretion is not

[119] See Wendel (n 55) 392.
[120] See above at ch 4, s II.
[121] See above at ch 3, s II.C.ii.
[122] See J Mathews, 'Proportionality Review in Administrative Law' in S Rose-Ackerman, P Lindseth and B Emerson (eds), *Comparative Administrative Law* 2nd edn (Edgar Elgar, 2019) 416 ff.
[123] See Wendel (n 55) 397.

per se a threat to the legal position of migrants. Rather, the applicability of legal principles such as proportionality, impartiality or the duty to state reasons transform it into a site of both constraint and potential.

Without turning a blind eye to the fact that discretion may be a component element of legal frameworks that expose migrants to volatility and unpredictability, the targeted existence and legally instructed nature of discretion may have brought about a relative improvement in the legal position of migrants. By replacing mandatory decisions that would have otherwise played out to the disadvantage of individuals, discretion opens a space for individualised justice, allowing for specificities of the individual case to gain legal weight. Moreover, through a combination of substantive and procedural safeguards, discretion is reshaped into an instrument of constrained and externally controlled freedom rather than unfettered executive power.

Nonetheless, the effects of discretion in European migration law remain ambivalent. While the proliferation of legal standards has improved the ability of migrants to contest administrative decisions, significant gaps remain – particularly in relation to decision-making in the context of resettlement schemes, where legal oversight continues to be absent. The preceding sections have therefore argued for a continued recalibration of the legal position of migrants vis-à-vis discretionary decision-making: by developing a coherent set of safeguards instructing the exercise of discretion, European lawmakers and courts can contribute to the emergence of discretion as a legal phenomenon that provides for administrative flexibility without unduly undermining the legal position of migrants.

6

Conclusion: The Hidden Virtues of Discretion in European Migration Law

This investigation explored the existence, exercise and effects of discretionary power in European migration law. It examined the reasons underpinning its continued relevance and highlighted the transformation that the exercise of discretion has undergone in the fairway of European legal influences. Ultimately, this investigation focused on the effects that the persistence of substantively transformed discretion creates for migrants. From each of these three angles, discretion may be said to coincide with certain hidden virtues. Unlike the criticism that is often levelled at discretion as a feature of migration laws in Europe, the preceding investigation argues that the functions and beneficial effects of discretion as a contemporary feature of European migration law should not be ignored.

The hidden virtues of discretion transpire in relation to each of the analytical perspectives explored. For national lawmakers, discretion presents itself as an expedient tool to accommodate the variety of influences originating from European legal sources (Section I). From the perspective of administrators, discretion emerges as a 'flexibility reservoir',[1] enabling them to compile and apply standards of legality originating from different levels of European migration law, and to do so in relative autonomy (Section II). Regarding the legal position of migrants, the legally instructed nature of discretionary conduct, coupled with the availability of judicial control, bring about a relative improvement when compared to previous legal arrangements (Section III). Ultimately, this underscores the impression that discretion, as a contemporary legal phenomenon in European migration law, constitutes an expedient tool for national lawmakers and administrators, and one that coincides with certain improvements in the legal position of migrants (Section IV).

I. Discretion as a Tool to Process the Influences of a Multi-Levelled Legal System

At first glance, the enduring prominence of wide discretionary powers in European migration law appears paradoxical. European legal systems have generally worked towards narrowing the space for discretion. Yet, discretion remains a prominent

[1] Aptly, M Wendel, *Verwaltungsermessen Als Mehrebenenproblem: Zur Verbundstruktur Administrativer Entscheidungsspielräume Am Beispiel Des Migrations- Und Regulierungsrechts* (Mohr Siebeck, 2019) 205.

and recurring feature of migration decision-making in Europe. The preceding investigation explored the reasons and mechanisms underpinning this persistence, arguing that discretion presents itself as a particularly expedient tool for national lawmakers to accommodate the versatile influences originating from European law (subsection A). Although national lawmakers frequently have some flexibility as to how these standards are to be incorporated, the preceding investigation illustrates that, in European migration law, European legal influences occasionally insist that national legal systems provide for discretion as a legal phenomenon in its own right (subsection B).

A. Reasons Underpinning the Targeted Consolidation of Discretion

Discretionary power is not a ubiquitous feature of European migration law. Instead, its presence is tied to specific deliberative situations and contexts. This begs the question why discretionary power appears precisely in those instances, while being excluded in others. What are the reasons underlying the targeted consolidation of discretion in European migration law? The preceding investigation shed light on the mechanisms that underpin the persistence of discretion in this field of law. It argues that the targeted consolidation of discretion is largely driven by European legal influences, and that several instances of influence can be identified that condition the persistence of discretion in European migration law.

First, European legal influences have at times fostered the proliferation of discretionary decision-making in European migration law. This dynamic is particularly evident in relation to European individualisation requirements. Such requirements oblige national legal systems to ensure that decision-making adequately reflects the circumstances of the individual case. To comply with such a requirement, national lawmakers must provide space for administrative autonomy – an autonomy that is frequently given effect to through awards of discretionary power.

On other occasions, second, European legal influences reinforce existing instances of discretion. In relation to decision-making assessing potential threats for public order or national security, European legal influences largely accept that national legal systems vest migration authorities with discretion. Although these instances of discretion are nowadays limited to specific instances of decision-making, European legal influences generally keep them intact and reinforce their existence of several occasions. European legal influences likewise accept, in principle, that national lawmakers rely on discretion as a core component facilitating selectivity in migration decision-making. As the preceding analysis illustrates, European legal influences reinforce the discretion of national migration authorities in relation to decision-making governing access to State territory. Discretion operates as the principal legal mechanism enabling this selectivity.

Third, discretion is a defining feature of transnational administrative systems established by EU migration law instruments. The discretionary clauses in the Dublin system are a case in point. These clauses have served as legal justifications for measures designed to preserve the Dublin system in moments of severe crisis. In this sense, discretion equally surfaces as a tool to secure the smooth functioning of transnational administrative systems. When viewed in combination with instances in which European legal safeguards consolidate or proliferate the existence of discretion, this supports the impression that discretion, to borrow Brand's formulation, 'has a useful role to play' within European migration law.[2] From the perspective of national lawmakers, discretion presents itself as a particularly expedient tool to integrate diverse influences of European law.

B. Pluralism and a European Vested Interest in Discretion

European legal influences do not typically instruct national lawmakers, in explicit terms, to provide for discretion. Rather, such influences tend to operate in more subtle ways. European law may require national legal systems to provide for a degree of administrative autonomy, but this does not in itself guarantee the existence of discretion as defined here. A safeguard of administrative autonomy does not necessarily imply limited judicial review, which constitutes a distinct and constitutive element of discretion in this analysis. In practice, however, national lawmakers will often view discretion as the most natural option for ensuring a measure of administrative autonomy.

Still, the preceding analysis revealed that European migration law sometimes departs from this implicit mode of influence. On several occasions, European law has explicitly required national legal systems to provide for 'discretion'. To be sure, such references do not, strictly speaking, coincide with forms of limited judicial review, but merely serve as a shorthand for administrative autonomy. Yet, European migration law may be singled out as one of the fields of law in which these legal influences exceptionally give way to more explicit safeguards of discretion. Specifically, this can be witnessed in relation to the case law of the Court of Justice of the EU, which exceptionally had clarified that acknowledgements of 'discretion' should likewise coincide with a standard of limited judicial review.[3]

It is equally significant that, where national lawmakers sought to introduce discretion in areas where this is precluded by EU law, the Court explicitly rejected the notion that national lawmakers could rely on discretion as an element of national migration law.[4] This suggests that European legal actors, and the Court of Justice specifically, may have a vested interest in the existence (or absence) of discretion. Unlike influences that consolidate or proliferate discretion as a tool to safeguard administrative autonomy or preserve transnational administrative systems, European migration law may be home to legal influences that explicitly insist upon the incorporation of discretion as a legal phenomenon in its own right.

[2] M Brand, 'Discretion, Divergence, and Unity' in Sacha Prechal and Bert van Roermund (eds), *The Coherence of EU Law: The Search for Unity in Divergent Concepts* (Oxford University Press, 2008) 218.

[3] Case C-544/15 *Fahimian v Bundesrepublik Deutschland* ECLI:EU:C:2017:255, [2017], para 46.

[4] Case C-556/17 *Alekszij Torubarov v Bevándorlási és Menekültügyi Hivatal* ECLI:EU:C:2019:626, [2019], para 75.

II. Discretion as a Guarantee of Administrative Flexibility

The exercise of discretion is inextricably linked to a measure of administrative autonomy. In European migration law, instances of virtually unfettered executive powers have largely given way to discretionary powers that are instructed and delimited by standards of legality. Discretion enables migration authorities to compile and apply the normative programme relevant to the case before them, and to do so in relative autonomy. In this sense, discretion may be viewed as a virtuous element of European migration law. It vests national migration authorities with the flexibility to fully consider the specificities of the individual case, thereby producing outcomes that may be viewed as preferential to bounded decision-making.[5]

Yet, on the flipside, it may be noted that the administrative flexibility that discretion implies imposes on administrators a particularly sophisticated and demanding mode of decision-making. It tasks migration authorities to independently appraise the relevant norms, procedural requirements and potential transnational effects of their decision, all while being subject to (at least some degree of) judicial control. As a corollary, the exercise of discretion constitutes a challenging act of both cognition and volition that administrators must perform. In the absence of conclusive legal instructions, the exercise of discretion therefore coincides with a high degree of administrative responsibility for diligent decision-making.

At the same time, in European migration law, this responsibility carries with it a risk of politicising administrative conduct. By deferring responsibility to administrative authorities, wide discretion exposes individual administrators to immense political pressure to exercise discretion in a way that aligns with the preferences of other actors.[6] Although European legal influences impose a duty of care on national migration authorities, it has been argued that this safeguard may not entirely shield administrators from the political weight attached to their decisions.

III. Discretion and Relative Improvements of Migrants' Legal Position

The preceding investigation has explored the effects that discretionary power creates for the legal position of migrants in European migration law. A conventional view in this regard considers discretion as a source of arbitrariness that largely subjects migrants to the whim of executive authorities. Yet, the interaction between discretion and migrants' legal position is more complex than this view would have it. Once the exercise of discretion is subject to instructions and limits that are effectively protected by judicial review, discretion may evolve into a site where migrants can contest and influence administrative decision-making.

[5] See above at ch 5, s III.A.

[6] This has been illustrated in relation to the refugee relocation mechanism, see above at ch 4, s III.C.

From this perspective, discretion can be linked to several aspects that affect migrants favourably. First, instances of instructed discretion require migration authorities to attribute legal weight to the specifics of the individual case. Consequently, discretion enables migrants to draw the attention of decision-makers to specific aspects of their individual case, to the effect that this may ultimately swing the decision in their favour. Second, on several occasions, discretion has come to replace rules that would have otherwise operated to the disadvantage of individuals. By replacing bounded decision-making to the detriment of individuals with genuinely open-ended discretionary power, European legal influences may have effectively improved the legal position of migrants.

Third, these improvements of the legal position of migrants gain practical relevance through the availability of an effective judicial remedy. While European migration law has precluded judicial review on several occasions until rather recently and, occasionally, continues to do so to this date,[7] discretion is nowadays largely conceptualised in this field of law as a power that is subject to judicial review. This enables migrants to challenge discretionary decision-making. Admittedly, their chances of success in this regard will be tarnished by the fact that the reviewing court will carry out a mode of limited judicial review. Against the backdrop of previous legal frameworks in European migration law, however, the existence of limited judicial review may already mark an improvement in the legal position of migrants.

Taken together, these aspects suggest that discretion, as a phenomenon of contemporary European migration law, cannot be reduced to the risk of arbitrariness that inheres in autonomous administrative decision-making. Rather, its effects for migrants remain ambiguous. On the one hand, discretionary power exposes individuals to a mode of decision-making that principally accepts the determinations of public officials. By consolidating and, at times, expanding discretion, European migration law establishes this premise as a dominant mode of interaction between migration authorities and individuals concerned. On the other hand, as a legally instructed and targeted phenomenon, discretion offers migrants a variety of avenues for challenging administrative conduct. Coupled with the availability of judicial review, this transforms discretion into a mode of decision-making that, despite its ambivalent effects on migrants, may coincide with relative improvements of the legal position of migrants.

IV. Discretion and its Hidden Virtues

The preceding investigation has explored the existence, exercise and effects of discretion in European migration law. It has argued that discretion, though often viewed with suspicion, can be linked to certain virtues. From the perspective of national lawmakers, discretion functions as a tool to accommodate the versatile influences of European law. For migration authorities, it provides a means

[7] See above at ch 5, s I.

to adjust decision-making in the light of situations involving complexity or risk. From the perspective of migrants, the effects of discretion should not be reduced to the possible arbitrariness to which it may give rise. Instead, as the preceding investigation suggests, the transformation of discretion from a mode of executive choice to a legally instructed autonomy tends to create relative improvements of migrants' legal position.

The enduring presence of discretion in European migration law, despite its risks and ambiguities, should therefore not be dismissed as a superfluous source of arbitrariness. Despite the persistence of discretion as a prominent element of European migration law, its exercise has undergone substantive transformation: in contemporary European migration laws, discretion rarely denotes unfettered choice but instead requires administrators to autonomously apply a plurality of norms under the guidance of legal principles. This transformed mode of discretion reshapes it into a structured and reviewable practice, offering migrants meaningful avenues to contextualise and influence outcomes. In this sense, discretion has emerged not merely as an unavoidable feature of European migration law, but as a phenomenon that elicits certain virtues: it secures administrative flexibility while providing migrants with meaningful avenues to contest decision-making.

BIBLIOGRAPHY

Abarca, GA and Coutin, SB, 'Sovereign Intimacies: The Lives of Documents within US State-Noncitizen Relationships: Sovereign Intimacies' (2018) 45 *American Ethnologist* 7.

Acosta, D, 'Court of Justice of the European Union (Ninth Chamber), WT v Subdelegacíon Del Gobierno En Guadalajara: Case C-448/19, Judgment of 11 June 2020, EU:C:2020:467' (2020) 22 *European Journal of Migration and Law* 457.

Alexy, R, 'Ermessensfehler' (1986) 41 *Juristen Zeitung* 701.

Alpes, MJ and Spire, A, 'Dealing with Law in Migration Control: The Powers of Street-Level Bureaucrats at French Consulates' (2013) 23 *Social & Legal Studies* 261.

Anderson, B et al, 'Insider/Outsider: Categorical Rivalries?' in S Seubert et al (eds), *Moving Beyond Barriers. Prospects for EU Citizenship* (Edward Elgar, 2018) 242–60.

Aschenbrenner Rodriguez, K, 'Discretionary (In)Justice Continued: Discretion as a Tool to Deny Asylum' (2025) 31 *Washington and Lee Journal of Civil Rights and Social Justice* 1.

Aschke, M, '§ 40 VwVfG' in J Bader and M Ronellenfitsch (eds), *BeckOK VwVfG* (CH Beck, 2019).

Asta, F, 'Arbitrary Decision-Making and the Rule of Law: The Role of the Jurisdiction in Migrants' Detention Proceedings – Between Discretion and Arbitrariness' (2020) 14 *Etikk i praksis Nordic Journal of Applied Ethics* 107.

Auby, J-B, 'The Transformation of the Administrative State and Administrative Law' in S Cassese, A Bogdandy and P Huber (eds), *The Max Planck Handbooks in European Public Law: Volume I: The Administrative State* (Oxford University Press, 2017) 601–30.

Azoulai, L and Clément-Wilz, L, 'Le Principe de Légalité' in J-B Auby and J Dutheil de la Rochère (eds), *Traité de Droit Administratif Européen* 2nd edn (Bruylant, 2014) 543–64.

Baldinger, D, *Rigorous Scrutiny versus Marginal Review: Standards on Judicial Scrutiny and Evidence in International and European Asylum Law* (Wolf Legal Publishers, 2013).

Barak, A, *Proportionality: Constitutional Rights and Their Limitations* (Cambridge University Press, 2012).

Barkhuysen, T and van Emmerik, M, 'Judicial Review in Dutch Environmental Law: General Observations' in J Poorter, E Hirsch Ballin and S Lavrijssen (eds), *Judicial Review of Administrative Discretion in the Administrative State* (Asser; Springer, 2019) 103–20.

Bast, J, 'Transnationale Verwaltung Des Europäischen Migrationsraums: Zur Horizontalen Öffnung Der EU-Mitgliedstaaten' (2007) 46 *Der Staat* 1.

——, 'Of General Principles and Trojan Horses - Procedural Due Process in Immigration Proceedings under EU Law' (2010) 11 *German Law Journal* 1006.

——, 'Solidarität Im Europäischen Einwanderungs- Und Asylrecht' in M Knodt and A Tews (eds), *Solidarität in der EU* (Nomos, 2014) 143–62.

Baumgärtel, M, '"Part of the Game": Government Strategies against European Litigation Concerning Migrant Rights' in T Aalberts and T Gammeltoft-Hansen (eds), *The Changing Practices of International Law* (Cambridge University Press, 2018) 103–28.

Bell, J, 'Judicial Review in the Administrative State' in J de Poorter, E Hirsch Ballin and S Lavrijssen (eds), *Judicial Review of Administrative Discretion in the Administrative State* (TMC Asser Press, 2019) 3–26.

Bello, V, 'The Spiralling of the Securitisation of Migration in the EU: From the Management of a "Crisis" to a Governance of Human Mobility?' (2022) 48 *Journal of Ethnic and Migration Studies* 1327.

Bignami, F, 'Comparative Administrative Law' in M Bussani and U Mattei (eds), *The Cambridge Companion to Comparative Law* (Cambridge University Press, 2012) 145–70.

Bigo, D, 'Security and Immigration: Toward a Critique of the Governmentality of Unease' (2002) 27 *Alternatives* 63.

Blake, M, 'Exclusion, Discretion, and Justice' in A Sager (ed), *The Ethics and Politics of Immigration. Core Issues and Emerging Trends* (Bloomsbury, 2016) 29–44.

Blauberger, M and Schmidt, SK, 'Free Movement, the Welfare State, and the European Union's over-Constitutionalization: Administrating Contradictions' (2017) 95 *Public Administration* 437.

Block, L, 'Regulating Membership: Explaining Restriction and Stratification of Family Migration in Europe' (2015) 36 *Journal of Family Issues* 1433.

Bonjour, S, 'The Power and Morals of Policy Makers: Reassessing the Control Gap Debate' (2011) 45 *International Migration Review* 89.

Bornemann, J, 'The Guises of and Guidance to Administrative Discretion in the European Court of Justice's Interpretation of EU Immigration Law' (2019) 12 *Review of European Administrative Law* 97.

——, 'The Role of Member State Governments in Migration Litigation before the ECJ' (2020) 22 *European Journal of Migration and Law* 541.

——, 'Judicial Responses to Autocratic Legalism: The European Court of Justice in a Cleft Stick?' (2022) 7 *European Papers* 651.

——, 'Discretionary Powers - an (Often Overlooked) Focalization Point of the Rule of Law Crisis' (2023) 4 *Revue des Affaires Européennes* 963.

Bornemann, J and Maiani, F, 'Temporal Governance, Precarity in the New Pact on Migration and Asylum' (2025) 31 *European Public Law* 371.

Borrelli, LM, 'Should (S)He Stay or Should (S)He Go? Street-Level Suspicion and the Construction of the "(Un)Deserving Migrant"' (2022) 27 *Geopolitics* 1093.

Borrelli, LM, Johannesson, L and Lindberg, A, 'Predictable Patterns of Unpredictability: A Literature Review of Discretion in Migration Control' (2025) 7 *Political Research Exchange* 1.

Borrelli, LM and Lindberg, A, 'The Creativity of Coping: Alternative Tales of Moral Dilemmas among Migration Control Officers' (2018) 4 *International Journal of Migration and Border Studies* 163.

Brand, M, 'Discretion, Divergence, and Unity' in S Prechal and B van Roermund (eds), *The Coherence of EU Law: The Search for Unity in Divergent Concepts* (Oxford University Press, 2008) 217–32.

Brinktrine, R, *Verwaltungsermessen in Deutschland Und England: Eine Rechtsvergleichende Untersuchung von Entscheidungsspielräumen Der Verwaltung Im Deutschen Und Englischen Verwaltungsrecht* (CF Müller, 1998).

Brouwer, E, 'Effective Remedies for Third Country Nationals in EU Law: Justice Accessible to All?' (2005) 7 *European Journal of Migration and Law* 219.

——, 'Challenges to EU Legality in the Field of Asylum and Migration Law' in C Kilpatrick and J Scott (eds), *Contemporary Challenges to EU Legality* (Oxford University Press, 2021) 48–70.

Bukve, O, *Designing Social Science Research* (Palgrave Macmillan, 2019).

Bullinger, M, 'Das Ermessen Der Öffentlichen Verwaltung: Entwicklung, Funktionen, Gerichtskontrolle' (1984) 39 *JuristenZeitung* 1001.

Byrne, R, Noll, G and Vedsted-Hansen, J, 'Understanding the Crisis of Refugee Law: Legal Scholarship and the EU Asylum System' (2020) 33 *Leiden Journal of International Law* 1.

Caranta, R, 'On Discretion' in S Prechal and B van Roermund (eds), *The Coherence of EU Law. The Search for Unity in Divergent Concepts* (Oxford University Press, 2008) 183–216.

Carling, J, 'The Phrase "Refugees and Migrants" Undermines Analysis, Policy and Protection' (2023) 61 *International Migration* 399.

Carrera, S and Cortinovis, R, 'Search and Rescue, Disembarkation and Relocation Arrangements in the Mediterranean: Sailing Away from Responsibility?' (2019) 10 *CEPS Papers in Liberty and Security in Europe* 1.

——, 'The Malta Declaration on SAR and Relocation: A Predictable EU Solidarity Mechanism?' (2019) 14 *CEPS Policy Insights* 1.

Carrera, S and Wiesbrock, A, 'Civic Integration of Third-Country Nationals: Nationalism versus Europeanisation in the Common EU Immigration Policy' (2009) *CEPS Papers in Liberty and Security in Europe* 1.

Černý, P, 'Asylum Proceedings in the Czech Republic during the Migration Crisis' (2020) 25 *Journal of Legal Studies* 44.

Chapus, R, *Droit Administratif Général* 15th edn (Montchrestien, 2001).

Chiti, E, 'Is EU Administrative Law Failing in Some of Its Crucial Tasks?' (2016) 22 *European Law Journal* 576.

Chlebny, J, 'Public Order, National Security and the Rights of Third-Country Nationals in Immigration Cases' (2018) 20 *European Journal of Migration and Law* 115.

Chrétien, P, Chifflot, N and Tourbe, M, *Droit Administratif* (Dalloz, 2018).

Coglianese, C and Yoo, CS, 'Introduction: The Bounds of Executive Discretion in the Regulatory State' (2016) 164 *University of Pennsylvania Law Review* 1587.

Cole, D, 'Judging the Next Emergency: Judicial Review and Individual Rights in Times of Crisis' (2003) 101 *Michigan Law Review* 2565.

Cornelisse, G, 'What's Wrong With Schengen? Border Disputes and the Nature of Integration in the Area Without Internal Borders' (2014) 51 *Common Market Law Review* 1.

Costello, C, 'Administrative Governance and the Europeanisation of Asylum and Immigration Policy' in H Hofmann and A Türk (eds), *EU Administrative Governance* (Edward Elgar, 2006) 287–340.

——, *The Human Rights of Migrants and Refugees in European Law* (Oxford University Press, 2016).

Coutin, SB et al, 'Deferred Action and the Discretionary State: Migration, Precarity and Resistance' (2017) 21 *Citizenship Studies* 951.

Craig, P, *UK, EU and Global Administrative Law: Foundations and Challenges* (Cambridge University Press, 2015).

Darling, J, 'The Politics of Discretion: Authority and Influence in Asylum Dispersal' (2022) 94 *Political Geography* 1.

Dauvergne, C, 'Sovereignty, Migration and the Rule of Law in Global Times' (2004) 67 *The Modern Law Review* 588.

Davis, KC, *Discretionary Justice: A Preliminary Inquiry* (Louisiana State University Press, 1969).

de Boer, T and Zieck, M, 'The Legal Abyss of Discretion in the Resettlement of Refugees: Cherry-Picking and the Lack of Due Process in the EU' (2020) 32 *International Journal of Refugee Law* 54.

de Búrca, G, 'Proportionality and Wednesbury Unreasonableness: The Influence of European Legal Concepts on UK Law' (1997) 3 *European Public Law* 561.

de Verdelhan, H, 'Art. 72 TFEU as Seen by the Court of Justice of the EU: Reminder, Exception, or Derogation?' (2024) 9 *European Papers* 1330.

Decker, A, '§ 114' in H Posser, HA Wolff and A Decker (eds), *BeckOK VwGO* (CH Beck, 2025).

Desmet, E, 'Analysing Users' Trajectories in Human Rights: A Conceptual Exploration and Research Agenda' (2014) 8 *Human Rights & International Legal Discourse* 121.

Desmond, A, 'The Private Life of Family Matters: Curtailing Human Rights Protection for Migrants under Article 8 of the ECHR?' (2018) 29 *The European Journal of International Law* 261.

——, 'From Migration Crisis to Migrants' Rights Crisis: The Centrality of Sovereignty in the EU Approach to the Protection of Migrants' Rights' (2023) 36 *Leiden Journal of International Law* 313.

Di Fabio, U, *Migrationskrise Als Föderales Verfassungsproblem: Gutachten Im Auftrag Des Freistaates Bayern* (2015).

Dicey, AV, *Introduction to the Study of the Law of the Constitution* 8th edn (Macmillan, 1908).

Dörrenbächer, N, 'Frontline Uses of European Union (EU) Law: A Parallel Legal Order? How Structural Discretion Conditions Uses of EU Law in Dutch and German Migration Offices' (2018) 38 *Journal of Public Policy* 455.

Dreyer-Plum, D, 'Dublin Revisited: Geographic Asymetry and Corrective Allocation Mechanisms' (2020) 22 *European Journal of Migration and Law* 386.

Drinóczi, T and Bień-Kacała, A, 'Illiberal Constitutionalism: The Case of Hungary and Poland' (2019) 20 *German Law Journal* 1140.

Duszczyk, M, Podgórska, K and Pszczółkowska, D, 'From Mandatory to Voluntary. Impact of V4 on the EU Relocation Scheme' (2020) 21 *European Politics and Society* 470.

Dworkin, R, *Taking Rights Seriously* (Harvard University Press, 1977).

Eliantonio, M, 'Deference to the Administration in Judicial Review: The European Union' in G Zhu (ed), *Deference to the Administration in Judicial Review: Comparative Perspectives* (Springer, 2019) 165–79.
Eule, TG et al, *Migrants Before the Law. Contested Migration Control in Europe* (Palgrave Macmillan, 2019).
Evans, T and Hupe, PL, 'Conceptualizing Discretion' in T Evans and PL Hupe (eds), *Discretion and the quest for controlled freedom* (Palgrave Macmillan, 2020) 1–13.
Farcy, J-B, 'Equality in Immigration Law: An Impossible Quest?' (2020) 20 *Human Rights Law Review* 725.
Fehling, M, 'Rechtsvergleichende Methode Und Europäisches Verwaltungsrecht' (2016) Beiheft 1 *Europarecht* 59.
Fernández Arribas, G, 'The Alheto Judgement: UNRWA Protection as Grounds for Exclusion from Refugee Status and Inadmissibility of an Application for International Protection' (2019) 4 *European Papers Insight* 417.
Fernhout, R, 'An Analysis of the Ben Alaya Case (C-491/13): When Conditions of the Students Directive Are Met, That Directive Confers Entitlement to a Student Visa, without Leaving the National Authorities Any Discretion in That Regard' (2015) 17 *European Journal of Migration and Law* 147.
Fletcher, G, 'Some Unwise Reflections About Discretion' (1984) 47 *Law and Contemporary Problems* 269.
Frankenberg, G, 'Critical Comparisons: Re-Thinking Comparative Law' (1985) 26 *Harvard International Law Journal* 411.
Frier, P-L and Petit, J, *Droit Administratif* 9th edn (Librairie générale de droit et de jurisprudence, 2014).
Galetta, D-U, 'Le Principe de Proportionnalité' in J-B Auby and J Dutheil de la Rochère (eds), *Traité de Droit Administratif Européen* 2nd edn (Bruylant, 2014) 501–26.
Galligan, D, *Discretionary Powers: A Legal Study of Official Discretion* (Oxford University Press, 1986).
Garoupa, N and Mathews, J, 'Strategic Delegation, Discretion, and Deference: Explaining the Comparative Law of Administrative Review' (2014) 62 *The American Journal of Comparative Law* 1.
Gaudemet, Y, *Droit Administratif* 21st edn (Librairie générale de droit et de jurisprudence, 2015).
Gerards, J, 'Intensity of Judicial Review in Equal Treatment Cases' (2004) *Netherlands International Law Review* 135.
Gerbaudo, M, 'The X Case: The Influence of the Resource Requirement on Long Term Residents' Integration and National Authorities' Discretionary Powers' (2019) 4 *European Papers Insight* 801.
Giacomelli, E, 'The Emergence of New Street-Level Bureaucracies in Italy's Asylum Reception System' (2021) 19 *Journal of Immigrant & Refugee Studies* 272.
Giannini, MS, *Il Potere Discrezionale Della Pubblica Amministrazione: Concetto e Problemi* (Giuffrè, 1939).
Gökşen, E, 'Proportionality in Refugee Exclusion: An Underestimated Analysis' (2020) 18 *Journal of International Criminal Justice* 1131.
Goldring, L, 'Precarious Legal Status Trajectories as Method, and the Work of Legal Status' (2022) 26 *Citizenship Studies* 460.
Grabenwarter, C, '§ 90 Ermessenslehren' in A Bogdandy, S Cassese and P M Huber (eds), *Handbuch Ius Publicum Europaeum: Band V: Verwaltungsrecht in Europa: Grundzüge* (CF Müller, 2014) 1017–46.
Grey, C, 'The Rights Of Migration' (2014) 20 *Legal Theory* 25.
Grey, JH, 'Discretion in Administrative Law' (1979) 17 *Osgoode Hall Law Journal* 107.
Griffith, K and Gleeson, S, 'The Precarity of Temporality: How Law Inhibits Immigrant Worker Claims' (2017) 39 *Comparative Labor Law & Policy Journal* 111.
Griffiths, M, 'Interrogating Time and Temporality in Migration Governance' in E Carmel, K Lenner and R Paul (eds), *Handbook on the Governance and Politics of Migration* (Edgar Elgar, 2021) 316–28.
Groenendijk, K and Strik, T, 'Family Reunification in Germany, Netherlands and the EU since 2000: Reciprocal Influence and the Role of National and EU Actors' in S Beichel-Benedetti and C Janda (eds), *Hohenheimer Horizonte: Festschrift für Klaus Barwig* (Nomos, 2018) 355–81.
——, 'Directive 2003/86 on the Right to Family Reunification: A Surprising Anchor in a Sensitive Field' in E (Lilian) Tsourdi and P De Bruycker (eds), *Research Handbook on EU Migration and Asylum Law* (Edward Elgar, 2022) 306–26.
Gross, T, 'Das Ausländerrecht Zwischen Obrigkeitsstaatlicher Tradition Und Menschenrechtlicher Herausforderung' (2014) 139 *Archiv des öffentlichen Rechts* 420.

Grote, R, 'Ermessenslehre Und Ermessenspraxis in Frankreich' [1986] *Neue Zeitschrift für Verwaltungsrecht* 269.

Guild, E, *Security and Migration in the 21st Century* (Polity Press, 2009).

Gusy, C, 'Ermessen Und Ermessensbindung Im Ausländerrecht' (1984) 5 *Verwaltungsblätter für Baden-Württemberg* 393.

Hailbronner, K and Gies, S, 'Council Directive 2004/114/EC of 13 December 2004 on the Conditions of Admission of Third-Country Nationals for the Purposes of Studies, Pupil Exchange, Unremunerated Training or Voluntary Service' in K Hailbronner and D Thym (eds), *EU Immigration and Asylum Law. A Commentary* 2nd edn (CH Beck; Nomos; Hart, 2016) 567–616.

Halleskov, L, 'The Long-Term Residents Directive: A Fulfilment of the Tampere Objective of Near-Equality?' (2005) 7 *European Journal of Migration and Law* 181.

Hart, HLA, 'Discretion' (1956) 127 *Harvard Law Review* 652.

Hasselberg, I, *Enduring Uncertainty. Deportation, Punishment and Everyday Life* (Berghahn, 2016).

Hawkins, K, 'The Use of Legal Discretion: Perspectives from Law and Social Science' in K Hawkins (ed), *The Uses of Discretion* (Oxford University Press, 1992) 11–46.

Hernández-Carretero, M, 'Hope and Uncertainty in Senegalese Migration to Spain: Taking Chances on Emigration but Not upon Return' in N Kleist and D Thorsten (eds), *Hope and Uncertainty in Contemporary African Migration* (Routledge, 2017) 113–33.

Heyer, K, 'Keeping Migrants at the Margins. Governing through Ambiguity and the Politics of Discretion in the Post-2015 EUropean Migration and Border Regime' (2022) 97 *Political Geography* 1.

Hirsch Ballin, E, 'Constitutional Genealogy of Judicial Review in the Administrative State' in J Poorter, E Hirsch Ballin and S Lavrijssen (eds), *Judicial Review of Administrative Discretion in the Administrative State* (Asser; Springer, 2019) 27–38.

Hoffman I, 'Application of Administrative Law in the Time of Reforms in the Light of the Scope of Judicial Review in Hungary' [2020] *Studia Iuridica Lublinensia* 101.

Hofmann, H, 'The Duty of Care in EU Public Law – A Principle Between Discretion and Proportionality' (2020) 13 *Review of European Administrative Law* 87.

Honohan, I, 'Domination and Migration: An Alternative Approach to the Legitimacy of Migration Controls' (2014) 17 *Critical Review of International Social and Political Philosophy* 31.

Hood, C, 'Discretion and Blame Avoidance' in T Evans and PL Hupe (eds), *Discretion and the quest for controlled freedom* (Palgrave Macmillan, 2020) 23–40.

Hruschka, C and Maiani, F, 'Regulation (EU) No 604/2013 of the European Parliament and of the Council of 26 June 2013 Establishing the Criteria and Mechanisms for Determining the Member State Responsible for Examining an Application for International Protection Lodged in One of the Member States by a Third-Country National or a Stateless Person (Recast)' in K Hailbronner and D Thym (eds), *EU Immigration and Asylum Law. A Commentary* 2nd edn (CH Beck; Nomos; Hart, 2016) 1478–604.

Hupe, PL and Evans, T, 'Controlled Freedom: Dealing with Discretion' in T Evans and PL Hupe (eds), *Discretion and the Quest for Controlled Freedom* (Palgrave Macmillan, 2020) 409–28.

——, 'Discretion in Governance: An Introduction' in T Evans and PL Hupe (eds), *Discretion and the Quest for Controlled Freedom* (Palgrave Macmillan, 2020) 213–20.

Hupe, PL and Hill, M, 'Discretion in the Policy Process' in T Evans and PL Hupe (eds), *Discretion and the Quest for Controlled Freedom* (Palgrave Macmillan, 2020) 237–58.

Husa, J, 'The Truth Is Out There? Legal Pluralism and the Language-Game' in SP Donlan and L Heckendorn Urscheler (eds), *Concepts of Law. Comparative, Jurisprudential, and Social Science Perspectives* (Routledge, 2014) 75–90.

Hutchinson, T and Duncan, N, 'Defining and Describing What We Do: Doctrinal Legal Research' (2012) 17 *Deakin Law Review* 83.

Huysmans, J, 'The European Union and the Securitization of Migration' (2000) 38 *Journal of Common Market Studies* 751.

Iglesias Sánchez, S, 'The Constitutional Status of Foreigners and European Union Citizens: Loopholes and Interactions in the Scope of Application of Fundamental Rights' in D Thym (ed), *Questioning EU Citizenship: Judges and the Limits of Free Movement and Solidarity in the EU* (Hart, 2017) 243–66.

International Organization for Migration (ed), *Laws for Legal Immigration in the 27 EU Member States*, vol 16 (International Organization for Migration, 2009).
Jestaedt, M, 'Maßstäbe Des Verwaltungshandelns' in D Ehlers and H Pünder (eds), *Allgemeines Verwaltungsrecht* 15th edn (De Gruyter, 2016) 325–71.
Joppke, C, 'Terror and the Loss of Citizenship' (2016) 20 *Citizenship Studies* 728.
Jordan, B, Stråth, B and Triandafyllidou, A, 'Comparing Cultures of Discretion' (2003) 29 *Journal of Ethnic and Migration Studies* 373.
Kabata, M and Jacobs, A, 'The "Migrant Other" as a Security Threat: The "Migration Crisis" and the Securitising Move of the Polish Ruling Party in Response to the EU Relocation Scheme' (2023) 31 *Journal of Contemporary European Studies* 1223.
Kantstroom, D, 'Surrounding the Hole in the Doughnut: Discretion and Deference in US Immigration Law' (1997) 71 *Tulane Law Review* 703.
Kelemen, D and Pech, L, 'The Uses and Abuses of Constitutional Pluralism: Undermining the Rule of Law in the Name of Constitutional Identity in Hungary and Poland' (2019) *Cambridge Yearbook of European Legal Studies* 59.
Kmieciak, Z, 'The Efficiency of Administrative Courts (in the Light of European and Polish Experiences)' (2013) 15 *Comparative Law Review* 135.
Kmieciak, Z and Wegner, J, 'Deference to the Public Administration in Judicial Review: A Polish Perspective' in G Zhu (ed), *Deference to the Administration in Judicial Review: Comparative Perspectives* (Springer, 2019) 363–77.
Kostakopoulou, T, '"Integrating" Non-EU Migrants in the European Union: Ambivalent Legacies and Mutating Paradigms' (2002) 8 *Columbia Journal of European Law* 181.
Králová, A, 'Legal Remedies in Asylum and Immigration Law: The Balance Between Effectiveness and Procedural Autonomy?' (2018) 16 *Central European Public Administration Review* 67.
Krommendijk, J, 'The Preliminary Reference Dance between the CJEU and Dutch Courts in the Field of Migration' (2018) 10 *European Journal of Legal Studies* 101.
Küçük, E, 'The Principle of Solidarity and Fairness in Sharing Responsibility: More than Window Dressing?' (2016) 22 *European Law Journal* 448.
Lacey, N, 'The Jurisprudence of Discretion: Escaping the Legal Paradigm' in K Hawkins (ed), *The Uses of Discretion* (Oxford University Press, 1992) 361–88.
Lagasse, D, *L'Erreur Manifeste d'Appreciation en Droit Administratif: Essai sur les Limites du Pouvoir Discrétionnaire de l'Administration* (Bruylant, 1986).
Lehner, R and Gies, S, 'Students and Researchers Directive (EU) 2016/801' in D Thym and K Hailbronner (eds), *EU Immigration and Asylum Law: Article-by-Article Commentary* 3rd edn (CH Beck; Hart; Nomos, 2022) 1048–128.
Lenaerts, K, 'The European Court of Justice and Process-Oriented Review' (2012) 31 *Yearbook of European Law* 3.
——, 'The Court's Outer and Inner Selves: Exploring the External and Internal Legitimacy of the European Court of Justice' in M Adams, H Waele, J Meeusen and G Straetmans (eds), *Judging Europe's Judges: The Legitimacy of the Case Law of the European Court of Justice* (Hart, 2013) 13–60.
Liodden, TM, 'Who Is a Refugee? Uncertainty and Discretion in Asylum Decisions' (2020) 32 *International Journal of Refugee Law* 645.
Lipsky, M, *Street-Level Bureaucracy: Dilemmas of the Individual in Public Services* (Russel Sage Foundation, 1980).
Lucia, L, 'Administrative Pluralism, Horizontal Cooperation and Transnational Administrative Acts' (2012) 5 *Review of European Administrative Law* 17.
Luntley, M, 'Expertise and the Space for Discretion' in T Evans and PL Hupe (eds), *Discretion and the Quest for Controlled Freedom* (Palgrave Macmillan, 2020) 339–56.
MacCormick, N, 'Discretion and Rights' (1989) 8 *Law and Philosophy* 23.
Maiani, F, 'The Reform of the Dublin System and the Dystopia of "Sharing People"' (2017) 24 *Maastricht Journal of European and Comparative Law* 622.
Majcher, I, 'The European Union Returns Directive: Does It Prevent Arbitrary Detention?' (2013) 3 *Oxford Monitory of Forced Migration* 23.

Marsch, N and Tünsmeyer, V, 'The Principle of Proportionality in German Administrative Law' in S Ranchordás and B Waard (eds), *The Judge and the Proportionate Use of Discretion: A Comparative Study* (Routledge, 2016) 13–42.
Mascini, P, 'Discretion from a Legal Perspective' in T Evans and PL Hupe (eds), *Discretion and the Quest for Controlled Freedom* (Palgrave Macmillan, 2020) 121–42.
Mathews, J, 'Proportionality Review in Administrative Law' in S Rose-Ackerman, P Lindseth and B Emerson (eds), *Comparative Administrative Law* 2nd edn (Edgar Elgar, 2019) 405–19.
Mattarella, BG, 'Law and Discretion. A Public Law Perspective on the EU' in J Mendes (ed), *EU Executive Discretion and the Limits of Law* (Oxford University Press, 2019) 21–39.
Mégret, F, 'The Travel Visa as the Ubiquitous Legal Infrastructure of Everyday Global Mobility Arbitrariness' (2024) 25 *German Law Journal* 1265.
Meloni, A, 'EU Visa Policy: What Kind of Solidarity?' (2017) 24 *Maastricht Journal of European and Comparative Law* 646.
Mendes, J, 'Discretion, Care and Public Interest in the EU Administration: Probing the Limits of Law' (2016) 53 *Common Market Law Review* 419.
——, 'Administrative Discretion in the EU: Comparative Perspectives' in S Rose-Ackerman and P Lindseth (eds), *Comparative Administrative Law* 2nd edn (Edward Elgar, 2017) 632–49.
——, 'Bounded Discretion in EU Law: A Limited Judicial Paradigm in a Changing EU' (2017) 80 *The Modern Law Review* 443.
Mendes, J and Venzke, I, 'Introducing the Idea of Relative Authority' in J Mendes and I Venzke (eds), *Allocating Authority: Who Should Do What in European and International Law?* (Hart, 2018) 1–25.
Miaz, J, 'Asylum Adjudication and Street-Level Discretion: Negotiating Practice Rules' (2024) 26 *Journal of Comparative Policy Analysis* 25.
Mincer M, *Uznanie Administracyjne* (Uniwersytet Mikołaja Kopernika, 1983).
Mindus, P, 'Justice of Others: Arbitrary Law-Making in Contemporary Migration Policy' (2020) 14 *Etikk i praksis Nordic Journal of Applied Ethics* 1.
——, 'Towards a Theory of Arbitrary Law-Making in Migration Policy' (2020) 14 *Etikk i praksis Nordic Journal of Applied Ethics* 9.
Mitsch, L, *Das Wissensproblem Im Asylrecht: Zwischen Materiellen Steuerungsdefiziten Und Europäisierung* (Nomos, 2020).
Möllers, C, *The Three Branches: A Comparative Model of Separation of Powers* (Oxford University Press, 2013).
——, 'Verwaltungsrecht Und Politik' in A Bogdandy, S Cassese and PM Huber (eds), *Handbuch Ius Publicum Europaeum: Band V: Verwaltungsrecht in Europa: Grundzüge* (CF Müller, 2014) 1175–220.
Moraru, M, 'Judicial Interactions Upholding the Right to Be Heard of Asylum Seekers, Returnees and Immigrants: The Symbiotic Protection of the EU Charter and General Principles of EU Law' in F Casarosa and M Moraru (eds), *The Practice of Judicial Interaction in the Field of Fundamental Rights. The Added Value of the Charter of Fundamental Rights of the EU* (Edward Elgar, 2022) 264–89.
Moreno-Lax, V, *Accessing Asylum in Europe: Extraterritorial Border Controls and Refugee Rights under EU Law* (Oxford University Press, 2017).
Morgades-Gil, S, 'The Discretion of States in the Dublin III System for Determining Responsibility for Examining Applications for Asylum: What Remains of the Sovereignty and Humanitarian Clauses After the Interpretations of the ECtHR and the CJEU?' (2015) 27 *International Journal of Refugee Law* 433.
Mouzourakis, M and Costello, C, 'The Common European Asylum System: Where Did It All Go Wrong?' in M Fletcher, E Herlin-Karnell and C Matera (eds), *The European Union as an Area of Freedom, Security and Justice* (Routledge, 2017) 263–99.
Müller-Graff, P-C, 'Modern Comparative Law: The Forces behind and the Challenges Ahead in the Age of Transnational Harmonisation' in A B Engelbrekt and J Nergelius (eds), *New Directions in Comparative Law* (Edward Elgar, 2009) 255–70.
Nickels, E, 'A Note on the Status of Discretion in Police Research' (2007) 35 *Journal of Criminal Justice* 570.

Oomen et al, 'Strategies of Divergence: Local Authorities, Law, and Discretionary Spaces in Migration Governance' (2021) 34 *Journal of Refugee Studies* 3608.

Pache, E, *Tatbestandliche Abwägung Und Beurteilungsspielräume* (Mohr Siebeck, 2001).

Parchomiuk, J, 'Abuse of Discretionary Powers in Administrative Law. Evolution of the Judicial Review Models: From "Administrative Morality" to the Principle of Proportionality' (2018) 26 *Časopis pro právní vědu a praxi* 453.

Peers, S, *EU Justice and Home Affairs Law: Volume I: EU Immigration and Asylum Law* 4th edn (Oxford University Press, 2016).

Piątek, W, 'The Right to an Effective Remedy in European Law: Significance, Content and Interaction' (2019) 6 *China-EU Law Journal* 163.

Pottie, L and Sossin, L, 'Demystifying the Boundaries of Public Law: Policy, Discretion, and Social Welfare' (2005) 28 *University of Columbia Law Review* 147.

Pratt, A, 'Dunking the Doughnut: Discretionary Power, Law and the Administration of the Canadian Immigration Act' (1999) 8 *Social & Legal Studies* 199.

Pratt, A and Sossin, L, 'A Brief Introduction of the Puzzle of Discretion' (2009) 24 *Canadian Journal of Law and Society* 301.

Prek, M and Lefèvre, S, '"Administrative Discretion", "Power of Appraisal" and "Margin of Appraisal" in Judicial Review Proceedings before the General Court' (2019) 56 *Common Market Law Review* 339.

Pretis, D, 'Grundzüge Des Verwaltungsrechts in Gemeineuropäischer Perspektive: Italien' in A Bogdandy, S Cassese and PM Huber (eds), *Handbuch Ius Publicum Europaeum: Band V: Verwaltungsrecht in Europa: Grundzüge* (CF Müller, 2014) 371–434.

Pries, L, '"We Will Manage It" - Did Chancellor Merkel's Dictum Increase of Even Cause the Refugee Movement in 2015?' (2019) 58 *International Migration* 18.

Ranchordás, S and Waard, B, 'Concluding Remarks' in S Ranchordás and B Waard (eds), *The Judge and the Proportionate Use of Discretion: A Comparative Study* (Routledge, 2016) 191–204.

Raz, J, 'Legal Principles and the Limits of Law' (1972) 81 *The Yale Law Journal* 823.

Rehaag, S, 'Troubling Patterns in Canadian Refugee Adjudication' (2008) 39 *Ottawa Law Review* 335.

Reneman, M, *EU Asylum Procedures and the Right to an Effective Remedy* (Hart, 2014).

Rennert, K, '§ 114' in E Eyermann (ed), *VwGO* (CH Beck, 2019).

Riedel, L and Schneider, G, 'Dezentraler Asylvollzug Diskriminiert: Anerkennungsquoten von Flüchtlingen Im Bundesdeutschen Vergleich, 2010–2015' (2017) 58 *Politische Vierteljahresschrift* 23.

Rijpma, J, 'External Migration and Asylum Management: Accountability for Executive Action Outside EU-Territory' (2017) 2 *European Papers* 571.

Ritleng, D, 'Judicial Review of EU Administrative Discretion: How Far Does the Separation of Powers Matter?' in J Mendes and I Venzke (eds), *Allocating Authority: Who Should Do What in European and International Law?* (Hart, 2018) 183–216.

Rochel, J, 'Working in Tandem: Proportionality and Procedural Guarantees in EU Immigration Law' (2019) 20 *German Law Journal* 89.

Rode, L-H, *§ 40 VwVfG Und Die Deutsche Ermessenslehre* (Peter Lang, 2003).

Roughan, N, 'Polities and Relative Authorities' (2018) 16 *International Journal of Constitutional Law* 1215.

Rubin, E, 'Discretion and Its Discontent' (1997) 72 *Chicago-Kent Law Review* 1299.

Ruffert, M, 'Europäisierung Des Verwaltungsrechts' in A Bogdandy, S Cassese and PM Huber (eds), *Handbuch Ius Publicum Europaeum: Band V: Verwaltungsrecht in Europa: Grundzüge* (CF Müller, 2014) 1221–51.

——, 'National Executives and Bureaucracies' in P Cane et al (eds), *The Oxford Handbook of Comparative Administrative Law* (Oxford University Press, 2020) 505–25.

Rundle, K, 'Administrative Discretion and Governing Relationships: Situating Procedural Fairness' in D Meyerson, C Mackenzie and T MacDermott (eds), *Procedural Justice and Relational Theory. Empirical, Philosophical, and Legal Perspectives* (Routledge, 2021) 232–51.

Sachs, M, '§ 40 Ermessen' in P Stelkens, H J Bonk and M Sachs (eds), *VwVfG Verwaltungsverfahrensgesetz: Kommentar* 8th edn (CH Beck, 2014).

Sager, A, 'Immigration Enforcement and Domination: An Indirect Argument for Much More Open Borders' (2017) 70 *Political Research Quarterly* 42.

Savino, M, 'On Failed Relocation and Would-Be Leviathans: Towards the New Pact on Migration and Asylum', ADiM Blog (1 July 2020).
Scheppele, KL, 'Autocratic Legalism' (2018) 8 *The University of Chicago Law Review* 544.
Schmidt-Aßmann, E, *Das Allgemeine Verwaltungsrecht Als Ordnungsidee: Grundlagen Und Aufgaben Der Verwaltungsrechtlichen Systembildung* 2nd edn (Springer, 2006).
——, 'GG Art. 19 Abs. 4' in R Herzog, M Herdegen, R Scholz and H Klein (eds), *Grundgesetz: Kommentar*, vol 88 (CH Beck, 2019).
Schönberger, C, 'Verwaltungsrechtsvergleichung: Eigenheiten, Methoden Und Geschichte' in A Bogdandy, S Cassese and P M Huber (eds), *Handbuch Ius Publicum Europaeum: Band IV: Verwaltungsrecht in Europa: Wissenschaft* (CF Müller, 2014) 493–540.
Schwarze, J, *European Administrative Law* (Sweet & Maxwell, 1992).
Shiner, R, 'Precedent, Discretion and Fairness' in MA Stewart (ed), *Law, Morality and Rights* (Springer Science, 1983).
Sindbjerg Martinsen, D, 'Judicial Policy-Making and Europeanization: The Proportionality of National Control and Administrative Discretion' (2011) 18 *Journal of European Public Policy* 944.
Słowik, A, 'Multiple Sources of Right to an Effective Remedy in EU Migration and Asylum Law: Towards Common Standards on Judicial Protection?' (2024) 31 *Maastricht Journal of European and Comparative Law* 27.
——, 'Of Roads and Inroads: In Search of Ways for Effective Protection of Fundamental Rights of Migrants and Asylum Seekers in the CJEU's Case Law' (2025) 50 *European Law Review* 310.
Sossin, L, 'From Neutrality to Compassion: The Place of Civil Service Values and Legal Norms in the Exercise of Administrative Discretion' (2005) 55 *The University of Toronto Law Journal* 427.
Spijkerboer, T, 'Subsidiarity and "Arguability": The European Court of Human Rights' Case Law on Judicial Review in Asylum Cases' (2009) 21 *International Journal of Refugee Law* 48.
Spirig, J, *Like Cases Alike or Asylum Lottery: Inconsistency in Judicial Decision Making at the Swiss Federal Administrative Court* (Zurich Open Repository and Archive, 2018).
Starck, C, 'Rechtsvergleichender Generalbericht' in M Bullinger (ed), *Verwaltungsermessen im modernen Staat* (Nomos, 1986) 17–52.
Stehlík, V, 'Discretion of Member States Vis-à-Vis Public Security: Unveiling the Labyrinth' (2017) 17 *International and Comparative Law Review* 127.
Stern K, *Ermessen Und Unzulässige Ermessensausübung: Eine Analyse Der Subjektiven Und Objektiven Elemente* (Duncker & Humblot 1964).
Stivas, D, 'The Art of Securitising. Orbán's Handling of the European Refugee Crisis' (2023) 31 *Journal of Contemporary European Studies* 184.
Stronks, M, *Grasping Legal Time. Temporality and European Migration Law* (Cambridge University Press, 2022).
Strumia, F, 'European Citizenship and EU Immigration: A Demoi-Cratic Bridge between the Third Country Nationals' Right to Belong and the Member States' Power to Exclude' (2016) 22 *European Law Journal* 417.
Thym, D, 'Respect for Private and Family Life under Article 8 ECHR in Immigration Cases: A Human Right to Regularize Illegal Stay?' (2008) 57 *International and Comparative Law Quarterly* 87.
——, 'Residence as de Facto Citizenship? Protection of Long-Term Residence under Article 8 ECHR' in R Rubio-Marín (ed), *Human Rights and Immigration* (Oxford University Press, 2014) 106–44.
——, 'Judicial Maintenance of the Sputtering Dublin System on Asylum Jurisdiction: Jafari, A.S., Mengesteab and Shiri' (2018) 55 *Common Market Law Review* 549.
——, 'Deciphering the Role of (Migration) Law in the Social Construction of "Otherness"' in M Jesse (ed), *European Societies, Migration, and the Law. The 'Others' amongst 'Us'* (Cambridge University Press, 2020) 323–55.
——, 'Legal Framework for EU Immigration Policy' in D Thym and K Hailbronner (eds), *EU Immigration and Asylum Law: Article-by-Article Commentary* 3rd edn (CH Beck; Hart; Nomos, 2022) 383–431.
——, '"Public Policy" as a Chameleonlike Concept: The Quest for Coherence in the CJEU Case Law On Migration and Union Citizenship' (2024) 9 *European Papers* 1366.

——, *European Migration Law* (Oxford University Press, 2023).
Thym, D and Bornemann, J, 'Migration Policy: Between Crisis Preparedness, Ad Hoc Solutions, and Administrative Capacity-Building' in D Fromage, A Héritier and P Weismann (eds), *EU Regulatory Responses to Crises. Adaptation or Transformation?* (Oxford University Press, 2025) 133–55.
Thym, D and Tsourdi, E, 'Searching for Solidarity in the EU Asylum and Border Policies: Constitutional and Operational Dimensions' (2017) 24 *Maastricht Journal of European and Comparative Law* 605.
Triandafyllidou, A, 'The Migration Archipelago: Social Navigation and Migrant Agency' (2018) 57 *International Migration* 5.
Truchet, D, *Les Fonctions de La Notion d'intérêt Général Dans La Jurisprudence Du Conseil d'état* (Pichon et Durand-Auzias, 1977).
Tsourdi, E, 'Asylum in the EU: One of the Many Faces of Rule of Law Backsliding?' (2021) 17 *European Constitutional Law Review* 471.
——, 'Solidarity at Work? The Prevalence of Emergency-Driven Solidarity in the Administrative Governance of the Common European Asylum System' (2017) 24 *Maastricht Journal of European and Comparative Law* 667.
Uitz, R, 'National Constitutional Identity in the European Constitutional Project: A Recipe for Exposing Cover Ups and Masquerades' (11 November 2016), https://verfassungsblog.de/national-constitutional-identity-in-the-european-constitutional-project-a-recipe-for-exposing-cover-ups-and-masquerades/.
UNHCR, 'Resettlement Handbook: Division of International Protection' (2011).
——, 'Handbook on Procedures and Criteria for Determining Refugee Status and Guidelines on International Protection: Under The 1951 Convention and the 1967 Protocol Relating to the Status of Refugees' (2019).
van Berckel Smit, J, 'Taking Onboard the Issue of Disembarkation: The Mediterranean Need for Responsibility-Sharing after the Malta Declaration' (2020) 22 *European Journal of Migration and Law* 492.
van den Brink, T, 'Refining the Division of Competences in the EU: National Discretion in EU Legislation' in S Garben and I Govaere (eds), *The Division of Competences between the EU and the Member States: Reflections on the Past, the Present and the Future* (Hart, 2017) 251–75.
van Reenen, P, 'Impartiality in the EU Asylum Procedure' (2018) 20 *European Journal of Migration and Law* 338.
van Roermund, B, 'Law at Cross-Purposes: Conceptual Confusion and Political Divergence' in S Prechal and B van Roermund (eds), *The Coherence of EU Law: The Search for Unity in Divergent Concepts* (Oxford University Press, 2008) 315–42.
Verhoeven, M and Widdershoven, R, 'National Legality and European Obligations' in L Besselink, F Pennings and S Prechal (eds), *The Eclipse of the Legality Principle in the European Union* (Wolters Kluwer, 2011) 55–72.
Vincze, A, *Unionsrecht Und Verwaltungsrecht: Eine Rechtsvergleichende Untersuchung Zur Rezeption Des Unionsrechts* (Nomos, 2016).
——, 'Talking Past Each Other: On Common Misperceptions in the Rule of Law Debate' in A Lorenz and L Anders (eds), *Illiberal Trends and Anti-EU Politics in East Central Europe* (Palgrave Macmillan, 2021) 209–34.
von Danwitz, T, *Europäisches Verwaltungsrecht* (Springer, 2008).
Waal, T, *Integration Requirements for Immigrants in Europe: A Legal-Philosophical Inquiry* (Hart, 2021).
Wagenaar, H, 'Discretion and Street-Level Practice' in T Evans and PL Hupe (eds), *Discretion and the quest for controlled freedom* (Palgrave Macmillan, 2020) 259–78.
Warin, C, 'Individual Rights in EU Migration and Asylum Law' (*EU Immigration and Asylum Law and Policy*, 6 January 2020).
Weiß, W, *Der Europäische Verwaltungsverbund: Grundfragen, Kennzeichen, Herausforderungen* (Duncker & Humblot, 2010).
Wendel, M, 'The Refugee Crisis and the Executive: On the Limits of Administrative Discretion in the Common European Asylum System' (2016) 17 *German Law Journal* 1005.

——, *Verwaltungsermessen Als Mehrebenenproblem: Zur Verbundstruktur Administrativer Entscheidungsspielräume Am Beispiel Des Migrations- Und Regulierungsrechts* (Mohr Siebeck, 2019).

Widdershoven, R, 'Developing Administrative Law in Europe: Natural Convergence or Imposed Uniformity?' (2014) 7 *Review of European Administrative Law* 5.

——, 'National Procedural Autonomy and General EU Law Limits' (2019) 12 *Review of European Administrative Law*5.

——, 'The European Court of Justice and the Standard of Judicial Review' in J Poorter, E Hirsch Ballin and S Lavrijssen (eds), *Judicial Review of Administrative Discretion in the Administrative State* (Asser; Springer, 2019) 39–62.

Zhelyazkova, A, 'Do EU Policies Constrain Government Autonomy? Insights from the Implementation of EU Migration Policies' (2024) 47 *West European Politics* 595.

Ziebritzki, C, 'The Objective of Resettlement in an EU Constitutional Perspective' in M-C Foblets and L Leboeuf (eds), *Humanitarian Admission to Europe: The Law between Promises and Constraints* (Nomos, 2020) 285–340.

Zimmermann, A and Mahler, C, 'Article 1A, Para. 2 1951 Convention' in A Zimmermann, J Dörschner and F Machts (eds), *The 1951 Convention Relating to the Status of Refugees and its 1967 Protocol: A Commentary* (Oxford University Press, 2011) 281–466.

INDEX

www.ingramcontent.com/pod-product-compliance
Ingram Content Group UK Ltd.
Pitfield, Milton Keynes, MK11 3LW, UK
UKHW020819290926
15470UKWH00003B/1259

9 781509 984176